Adapted From
R.H. CHARLES
Original Translation From The Ethiopic Text

From 1917 Reprint by
Society for Promoting Christian Knowledge, London
Editcd by W. O. E. Oesterley and G. H. Box

WITH THE RESTORED NAME OF YAHUAH

Edited, Compiled, Commentary, Maps and Research By
Timothy Schwab, Anna Zamoranos
and The God Culture Team

CONTENTS

THE Levite BIBLE
LeviteBible.com

FOREWARD

By Timothy Schwab
Author, Publisher, Researcher, Singer/Songwriter, Founder of The God Culture
Non-Pharisee and proudly so...

Over five years ago, our team of researchers, The God Culture, began to embark upon the journey of a lifetime. We had reviewed a claim that the Philippines was the ancient land of gold in which King Solomon acquired resources for the Temple. At first we thought it would lead to perhaps a trail but such ancient geography would be very difficult to prove. As we ripped through every scripture and assessed the Hebrew especially, we were greatly intrigued to learn there appeared to be a Biblical connection but certainly that would only be a case of Bible we thought. For us, that is good enough but we all know most demand more because they don't believe the Bible.

So, we expanded our search into the realm of history, etc. which was incredibly abundant and overwhelming and pretty much all this information was new to us as it is not taught largely. However, one merely needs to read what the Spanish chroniclers wrote when they came and it is rather difficult to conclude any other land could even possibly fit Ophir. We continued this to the point that we finally created a YouTube Channel and launched Solomon's Gold Series which has been a hit internationally for millions. However, as we were proving Ophir, we kept receiving comments from many Filipinos who were telling us that land is also the location of the Garden of Eden.

Of course, being researchers, we were skeptical we would ever be able to prove that but Ophir led to so many things we did not expect. After some months, we did not release any Garden of Eden videos and we moved onto our Flood Series. When we did, we decided to take another look at this Book of Jubilees which we had all read but knew little about as seminaries and churches are willingly ignorant of the book because they are told to be by the Pharisees (Rabbis). As we reached Chapter 8, we thought it beneficial to cover what is Noah's division of the Earth among his three sons – Shem, Ham and Japheth. He had no other sons and those three inherited the entire Earth yet we are told Noah only mapped the Middle East. That makes no logical sense but it is something we are told and most have accepted as we had previously. However, we began to follow the directions on a map proving out each point. Oh my!

This mapping unveiled the location of the Garden of Eden, it defined Shem, Ham and Japheth's territories worldwide and certainly not just the Middle East, it locates the seat of Gog of Magog's power and so much more. We were flabbergasted that this book from at least 2000 years ago somehow had all this information that we are told was not known until modern times. What was more amazing is how far modern scholarship has strayed from these once known facts and they support such geography typically with etymologies of words that sound similar from languages not even associated. Frankly, it is almost as if they do not wish to know these things and perhaps some do not.

You will notice in our commentary, we will remove the modern scholarly paradigm from it's pedestal many times. We do so with evidence that proves it is operating in Pharisee leaven and certainly not in the Word at times. When we can take the Word and obliterate their positions, it is sad but we are done with placating poor scholarship. Pharisees interpret Torah through the Talmud and we find this prevalent in the church and we call it out and if that offends anyone, you're welcome. We are not affiliated with any control system nor will we ever be. In fact, we find **R.H.** Charles in his original release of this translation which remains very good as a translation, also infused the Talmud in his footnotes over a hundred times attempting to make it appear Jubilees was written by a Pharisee and that was before the Dead Sea Scrolls find. He then concludes a Pharisee must have written it which we will test and in 150 **B.C.** which we will test and would you know, the miraculous dating of the Dead Sea Scroll fragments is also 150 **B.C.** forty years later. It is truly a miracle as that is not a scientific dating, it remains a guess based on the same logic as Charles and the other Pharisees of the time. Perhaps the Rockefellers who funded that museum oddly, could not afford a scientific dating. The extremely incredible things about these Talmudic footnotes, is they prove that Jubilees was not written by the Pharisees and it's concepts were and remain extremely foreign to them as does Torah. In fact, if one truly reads it, the book condemns Pharisee doctrines and their calendar even. They were shocked by the Dead Sea Scrolls because the Levite Priests they exiled from the Temple lived there and kept scripture, commentary, hymns, etc. in which they are unfamiliar. This is because they are not Hebrews and have never represented such system except through their Samaritan/Persian worship in which they infused it. If you do not know this, even the Jewish Encyclopedia tells us Pharisees changed their names and the name of their religion after the Temple was destroyed to Judaism and they are now called Rabbis. We all know what the Bible says to call no man Rabbi nor Father of course. Yet oddly the Pharisees and Catholic Church chose those exact abominations as titles. It is almost as if Messiah knew they would.

In curating this publishing of the R.H. Charles translation from 1903 of the Book of Jubilees, we have removed practically all the Talmud references as they are impertinent. Messiah rejected the Talmud calling the traditions of the Pharisees "against His commandments" in Mark 7 and their changes render the Word of none effect. It serves no useful purpose in interpreting the Bible and it is lined with leaven as we are warned. Today, scholarship relies heavily on those first century Rabbis who are Pharisees even by name then, thoroughly rebuked and laid out by Messiah. When they do so, they are in danger of applying leaven and many times they do whether knowingly or not. None of us are perfect however but regardless, let's just get to the truth.

We are in the days Daniel predicted when knowledge will increase and we believe we are already seeing this around the world. Are you aware of a YouTube channel for instance that has been hidden or even shutdown because it's content is a threat? I recently viewed a congressional hearing in which they were chastising Facebook for acting like they are the government. Good for them if they actually do something about it of course. We know several and they were merely teaching the Bible. Imagine how evil YouTube and Facebook would have to be to act as judge and jury and replace even governments censoring content in which they do not agree and that content is the Bible? Hmmm… Well, they have and they continue to behave irresponsibly and frankly, they are applying the dumbest business practice imaginable when they do.

On our channel, we have covered many portions of Jubilees and we decided to dig even deeper. In the beginning of this book, we offer our research proving whom lived in Qumran and conduct a Torah Test. This is a right we have earned with detailed research and most scholars have not on this. The Book of Jubilees is then published in full beginning on Page 53. You can even download that book free from many sources and there would be no good reason to publish this if that was the only reason. The difference in this publishing is we explain many things you may not have considered which Jubilees clarifies that Genesis does not which we follow with a large section in the back of the book. Our maps explaining Noah's Division of the Earth, the Ark Landing, the Rivers from Eden, and the path to the Garden of Eden especially are profound and will assist in your understanding these directions in which Noah was brilliant. We also lay out the Torah Calendar of Jubilees from Creation to the Exodus by date in Anno Mundi as Jubilees documents. This is a record in which every believer should be aware.

We speak plain English. We do not sugarcoat and do not ask us to because we will not. We are not scholars and we have left mainstream churchianity in pursuit of The God Culture of Adam, Noah, Abraham and Enoch. We have never been happier. We are tired of the church not looking like the Biblical ekklesia and we are seeking His true ways in every way we can. Jubilees is very useful in defining His ways.

The real question remains is Jubilees scripture, inspired and canon? We will thoroughly vet that. Does it conflict with Genesis as it covers the same era? We will prove that out as well. Was it canon at one time? Oh, this answer will surprise many. Why was it removed from the canon? The bigger question though is when and by whom and when you understand this, much will come into focus especially satisfying why.

If that portion does not interest you, well, go download a copy of Jubilees which you can get for free and try reading it not with blinders which is a waste of time. Read what it says and what it does not say. Study it in parallel with Genesis whether our version or others. This book has over 1000 cross-references we have checked, edited and curated – many to Genesis and the rest of Torah. When you uncover that Jubilees is quoted by Messiah, James, Peter, John, Paul and Luke, it will likely astound you.

We will draw conclusions based on our investigation and offer in-depth research in the back for those who wish to go deeper. Remember, those are our conclusions and a right we have earned but do not accept any conclusion from anyone without testing it for yourself especially if they have lots of initials after their names. Just about every false prophet has hailed from a great resume in the scholarly community. Here, you will get a view from a group of researchers who wish to prove things and share our findings. Let's just get to the truth. May you find truth and grow in relationship with Yahusha.

2 Thessalonians 2:3-17 (King James Version)

Let no man deceive you by any means: for that day shall not come, except there come a falling away first, and that man of sin be revealed, the son of perdition; Who opposeth and exalteth himself above all that is called God, or that is worshipped; so that he as God sitteth in the temple of God, shewing himself that he is God. Remember ye not, that, when I was yet with you, I told you these things? And now ye know what withholdeth that he might be revealed in his time. For the mystery of iniquity doth already work: only he who now letteth will let, until he be taken out of the way. And then shall that Wicked be revealed, whom the Lord shall consume with the spirit of his mouth, and shall destroy with the brightness of his coming: Even him, whose coming is after the working of Satan with all power and signs and lying wonders, And with all deceivableness of unrighteousness in them that **perish; because they received not the love of the truth, that they might be saved.** And for this cause God shall send them **strong delusion, that they should believe a lie**: That they all might be damned who **believed not the truth**, but had pleasure in unrighteousness. But we are bound to give thanks alway to God for you, brethren beloved of the Lord, because **God hath from the beginning chosen you to salvation through sanctification of the Spirit and belief of the truth**: Whereunto he called you by our gospel, to the obtaining of the glory of our Lord Jesus Christ. Therefore, brethren, **stand fast**, and **hold the traditions which ye have been taught**, whether by word, or our epistle. Now our Lord Jesus Christ himself, and God, even our Father, which hath loved us, and hath given us everlasting consolation and good hope through grace, Comfort your hearts, and **stablish you in every good word and work**.

Do we know the truth?
Or is the strong delusion already at work?

INTRODUCTION Who Lived in Qumran?

In 1947, the voice in the wilderness cried out yet again. Did you hear it? The entire modern Old Testament canon was found in Qumran with the exception of the Book of Esther in what is inappropriately labeled and expanded in scope as the Dead Sea Scrolls as the find was specific to the Qumran area and truly remains so. This included the Book of Jubilees. For many of these books, these are the oldest copies found and some were complete such as the 24-foot long Isaiah Scroll. After over 70 years, we still know little about this community yet the archaeology, writings of the community and the large compound found there confirm these were the Aaronic Levite Priests, the sons of Zadok, who had been exiled to the Wilderness of Judaea by the Hasmoneans and Pharisees. They were the Temple High Priests replaced by a new unbiblical order. However, today, the world allows the Pharisees who defiled the Temple to teach us about this community. No wonder we know so little about them or at least we are taught so. This was the base of operations for John the Baptist and his disciples where he baptized Jesus*(Yahusha)* and was visited by Him later privately. It is among the most well-documented New Testament communities on record and the church does not even know because it is too busy defending a control narrative that the other books found with the Old Testament are somehow cursed when Jesus(Yahusha) and John the Baptist set this library as a time capsule to preserve His Word.

Photo: Stone Sundial from Qumran site. The Qumran community were the keepers of the Biblical calendar based on the sun and the canon of scripture according to the decrees from Jacob and Moses. It's called the Book of Jubilees.

In the same scroll jar alone with Genesis in one instance, the Book of Jubilees was found ranking as the #6 most abundant scrolls in Qumran. Clearly important among that community of Levite priests, this tells us much as the Temple Levites were the keepers of scripture. Jacob entrusted Levi with this role in Jubilees 45:16 and Moses authorized these same Aaronic Levites in Deuteronomy 31:24-26 to do the same. If one truly wanted to know what books were and were not included in the Bible canon at the time of Messiah, they need not look far as this preserved the Old Testament canon of scripture up until His time. There were no books yet, just scroll libraries like the one found in Qumran.

Some attempt to force the books in the Septuagint which can be a useful publishing indeed in comparison but never as a standalone text as inerrant scripture. In fact, it too was a scroll library created in Egypt and the Aaronic Levites were not in Egypt at that time. They were in the Temple where they should be soon to be driven out into the Wilderness of Judaea. They would take their Bible, scroll library in that time, with them. This was rediscovered in 1947 and immediately the Catholic Church and Pharisees moved to redefine the Bible that was found to protect the fraud they perpetrated in those days and since. The sect that created the Septuagint Greek translation in Egypt were not Aaronic Levite priests. These were Essenes in their attempt to hijack scripture which they would later write what they would call scripture in the Gnostic Gospels also found in Egypt. Not one Gnostic Gospel was found in Qumran nor do they coalesce with the New nor Old Testaments.

Essene is a name not found in the Bible even in the Greek Septuagint version demonstrating that cult has nothing to do with the Bible. The Qumran community never uses it nor anything similar. It is derived from the writings of Pliny, Josephus and others as ESSENOI, or ESSAIOI. As this is not a Bible word, we must go to an occult source to learn this originates in Egypt. In 2007, the Rosicrucian Digest weighs in on this.

Origins of the Word "Essene"

The word truly comes from the Egyptian word kashai, which means "secret." And there is a Jewish word of similar sound, chsahi, meaning "secret" or "silent"; and this word would naturally be translated into essaios or "Essene," denoting "secret" or "mystic." Even Josephus found that the Egyptian symbols of light and truth are represented by the word choshen, which transliterates into the Greek as essen. Historical references have been found also wherein the priests of the ancient temples of Ephesus bore the name of Essene. A branch of the organization established by the Greeks translated the word Essene as being derived from the Syrian word asaya, meaning "physician," into the Greek word therapeutes, having the same meaning. [9]

Again, this is an occult source and they take credit for the Essenes as a secret cult of sorcerers. To them, that is a good thing where those of us believers know better. However, what they do not connect is the "chsahi" *(kashaph: כָּשַׁף: H3784)* were the sorcerers and magicians in which Moses and Aaron faced in Egypt*(Ex. 7:11)*. Some of them exited Egypt in the Exodus and settled in Ein Gedi in ancient times and not Qumran. Pliny notes they are a very ancient cult. This same sorcery and witchcraft is recorded in Canaan*(Dt. 18:10)*, in Israel*(2 Chr. 33:6)* and even in Babylon*(Dan. 2:2)*. It is the enemy of the Bible.

Some even further connect this Aramaic word "asaya" as the origin of the word Hasmonean. These are the conquerors of the Temple in 165 B.C. who exiled the Levite Temple priest system who are rebuked by their Qumran community as the "sons of darkness." What a world in which we live. This word is the origin of the Hasidim or Hasidic Jews of today. They are Essenes. The breakdown of the factions still exists as Rabbinic Judaism generally are Pharisees essentially with a sect of Hasidim, Essenes. Sure, they call themselves pious but they do not even remotely know the relationship of Torah. This is why we find them referring to their god as Hashem. This name is a variant of Ashima, the god of the Samaritans from whom they originate. Who would replace the name of Yahuah 6,800+ times with Lord or Ba'al in Hebrew? These Samaritans would. Any attempt to associate them with Messiah and John the Baptist is ridiculous. We were warned in the end times evil would be called good and good, evil.

One of the main reasons employed by many is this assumption that Essenes lived in Qumran which they never did. Attempts are even exercised claiming Jesus(Yahusha) and John believed in resurrection and somehow that is supposed to be equated to the reincarnation doctrine of the Essenes which is among the most illiterate of positions. The two doctrines are opposites as are the Essenes from the Qumran community. In fact, human spirits cannot reincarnate. The only spirits who do are demons or spirits of Nephilim when they die. They wander the dry places and when invited, they can enter a human and possess it or even an animal as Messiah cast demons into swine. Reincarnation is literally a doctrine of demons as only they reincarnate possessing the body of another.

Essenes originated from Egypt, though perhaps truly Mesopotamian origins ultimately thus the Aramaic, where they were known as physicians or alchemists of sort. There, they were called the Therapeutae in Greek. In Biblical terms they were sorcerers such as the false prophet identified as from Judaea, Barjesus, an Essene*(Acts 13:6)*, the "child of the devil" according to Paul, Elymus*(Acts 13:8)* and the bewitching Simon the sorcerer*(Acts 8:9)*. In Greek, Paul calls this pharmakeía(φαρμακεία: *G5331)* meaning medication *("pharmacy")*, i.e. *(by extension)* magic *(literally or figuratively):*—sorcery, witchcraft."

Revelation tells us this is the end times deception in fact playing out as "by thy sorceries were all nations deceived"*(Rv. 18:23)*. This same sorcery is exactly what has happened with this entire narrative. Only a fool would claim Essenes lived in Qumran with no evidence, writings identifying themselves as Levites and incredibly significant Essene finds 25 miles South in Ein Gedi matching Pliny's directions to their headquarters. No scholar could logically draw such conclusion yet the mantra is vast. This false story permeates Judaism(Pharisaism according to the Jewish Encyclopedia) and those who manage the Rockefeller-funded museum doling out the idiotic control line. The church has bought this especially in seminaries. It is a lie.

The other list of Bible canon immediately thrown out there is that of Josephus who propagated a closed canon according to him of course. Josephus was an admitted Pharisee, Hasmonean and he was Essene trained by Banus in the wilderness*(Ein Gedi) [11: The Life of Flavius Josephus]*. Realize his "closed canon" which some Christians actually cite would mean the entire New Testament is not scripture and was already rebuked as ignoring part of the law or Torah according to Messiah*(Jn. 5:46-47)* and what they did use, they turned against scripture according to Him*(Mark 7:9)*. That is an oxymoron many do not even think through. His listing of what the Pharisees considered scripture educate us all on the paradigm at the time of Messiah and shortly after when the New Testament was just written as it already censored Jubilees especially. That is no canon.

However, whom did Jacob and Moses entrust with the keeping of scripture, Torah and what we would call Bible? The Temple Levite Priests of Aaron and Josephus was not nor were the Rabbis/Pharisees or Hasidim/Essenes. We have now found this scroll library which is the only which qualifies as the Bible canon for the entire history up until the time the Temple was destroyed. The question is, whom was ever given authority to overrule these Levites? Who was given their responsibility to keep scripture? Who was given authority to overturn Messiah's endorsement of this canon as well? Certainly not Pharisees who already threw out the Book of Jubilees in the days of Messiah. Most certainly not the cowardly general, Josephus, who ordered all of his troops to commit suicide while he failed to do so himself. Josephus is useful for history and geography to a point. However, he was no authority on scripture and his list is a spouting of Pharisee doctrine rebuked by Messiah many times. Only the Levite library records canon. Any Catholic council changing that was usurping Biblical authority it never had.

This community left history and scripture behind so that we would all know just what was and was not considered canon. They even include commentaries on different books, additional prophecy especially of the war of the "sons of darkness" versus the "sons of light," hymns, calendars, etc. The Hasmoneans*(Essenes)* and their priests *(Pharisees and Sadducees)* who exiled the true Aaronic Priests from the Temple are called the "sons of darkness" as they conquered the Temple and Judaea in 165 B.C. This battle will last until the very end times in their writings. The Temple was the center of worship in Jerusalem. Though the Second Temple no longer housed the ark of the covenant with Yahuah's presence, it still received His blessing until that time. Priestly courses continued such as that of Zacharias, father of John the Baptist, in the course of Abijah *(Abia)* but the leadership in the Temple, in all of Judaea and essentially the world in a spiritual sense had been usurped by these "sons of darkness." This was a fulfillment of the Psalm 83 war in which David predicted the Temple, not even built at the time of his prophecy, would be defiled by neighboring enemies in this exact sense.

For the Hasmoneans did not attack just the Greeks nor did they originate in Judaea. They inhabited an area called Modi'in which is across the border into Dan controlled by Samaria and the Philistines. They were not Hebrews nor Israelites. They were Samaritans who were the replacements of the Northern Tribes of Israel when they were taken captive into Assyria since around 700 B.C. This is why even in Messiah's parable of the Good Samaritan *(Lk. 10:25-37)*, what was unthinkable in the paradigm of that day, was that a Samaritan could be good.

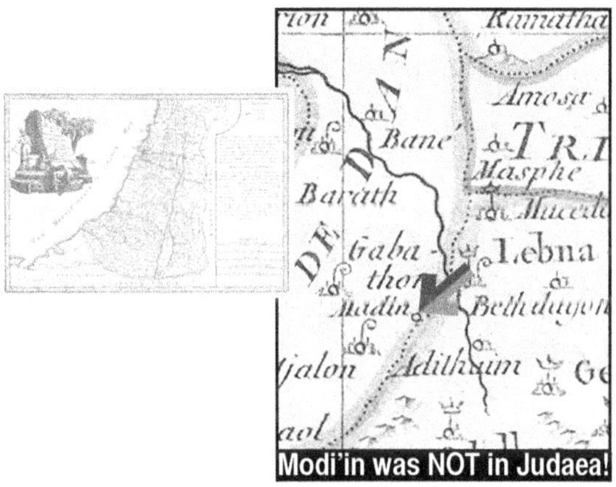

1770, Bonne Map of Israel. Rigobert Bonne 1727 – 1794. [12]

These replacements were brought into the Northern Kingdom of Samaria and kept the name. They then attempted to infuse the worship of Yahuah into pagan religions of their gods Ashima *(Hashem)*, Adrammelech *(Melech/Molech/Ba'al)* and others. However, this was never a sincere gesture. It was a response to the land which had been rejecting them as they were being attacked by wolves. They brought in a Levite Priest to teach them the rituals of the Bible. Yahuah rejected this infusion as He always has *(2 Chr. 17)*.

The Pharisees and Sadducees did not exist in Jerusalem until the so-called Hasmonean Revolt in 165 B.C. You will find the Books of Maccabees as well as Esther were not found among the Qumran scrolls because neither are scripture. Both are the stories of what would become Zionism today. This was predicted not only by David but identified in Revelation as Messiah discusses the Synagogue of Satan who say they are Jews and are not but do lie *(Rev. 2:9, 3:9)*. Even the term Jew is fraud and it never should be used in scripture as it is not of Ancient

Hebrew, Aramaic, Greek, Latin, Old French, Old German nor Old English origin. The name of Yahuah's people includes His own and such tribes would never remove His name from theirs. His people in the Old and New Testament are the Yahudim in Hebrew and Greek really. The shortened form of this word is Yah's never Jews as there is no "J" in any of the languages in which the Bible has been interpreted through. The first two letters are YH*(יה)* and that is Yah not Jew or Yah's not Jews. This fraud wraps into the rest of this false narrative coming from the modern Pharisees and the Catholic Church who changed scripture and attempt to cover it up.

Many do not realize that Qumran is identified in the Bible. However, Qumran is it's Muslim name oddly continued by Pharisees and modern Israel. Why would they do so when the Bible identifies this area by the name as Bethabara*(Greek)* or Betharabah*(Hebrew)*. Joshua identifies the Western coastline of the Dead Sea geographically when he outlines a list in North to South progression of the cities of the Dead Sea wilderness.

Joshua 15:61-62 KJV: In the wilderness, Betharabah, Middin, and Secacah, And Nibshan, and the city of Salt, and Engedi; six cities with their villages.

He begins in the North with Betharabah on the Northwestern tip. That is called Qumran today. Joshua continues as he heads South to Middin which is due South of Qumran, then further South all the way to Ein Gedi. He defined a 25 miles distance from North to South. Notice there are several cities between Betharabah*(Qumran)* and Ein Gedi so even if somehow Pliny meant just North instead of just above in the mountains, which is obvious, he still would not be identifying Qumran as the headquarters of the Essenes. Of course, Ein Gedi has the archaeology called "The Essene Find."

The Madaba Mosaic Map*(left)*, c. 6th century A.D., contains the oldest surviving original map of especially the Dead Sea and right on the intersection where the Jordon meets the Dead Sea, is labeled in Greek as Βηθαβαρά or Bethabara. This is right where Joshua placed it and it is modern Qumran.

The reason this is important as well is John the Baptist baptized Messiah at Bethabara. This was not some random journey into the wilderness but a visit to the very compound and library designed similar to the Temple

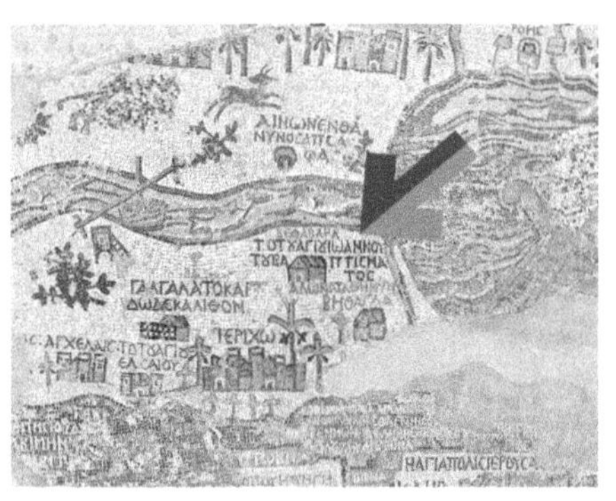

Above: Jordan. Madaba (biblical Medeba) - St. George's Church. Fragment of the oldest floor mosaic map of the Holy Land - the Jordan River and the Dead Sea. [13]

where scripture was now kept outside of the Temple. Messiah Himself visited it more than once. Jesus*(Yahusha)* grew up and initially operated in Galilee*(Mt. 2:22)*. He came from there, headed South to beyond Jordan. The Jordan is not simply the Jordan River in scripture but the entire Jordan Plain or Jordan Valley *(Gn. 13:10)*. This does not indicate crossing the river but into the Wilderness of Judaea at Qumran right on the border.

Luke 3:2-4 KJV: ...the word of God came unto John the son of Zacharias in the wilderness. And he came into all the country about Jordan, preaching the baptism of repentance for the remission of sins; As it is written in the book of the words of Esaias the prophet, saying, The voice of one crying in the wilderness, Prepare ye the way of the Lord, make his paths straight.

Matthew 3 KJV   1: In those days came John the Baptist, preaching in the wilderness of Judaea...
5-6: Then went out to him Jerusalem, and all Judaea, and all the region round about Jordan, And were baptized of him in Jordan, confessing their sins.

The Wilderness of Judaea *(Chambers Map, right)* is very specifically the area along the West coast of the Dead Sea. It is not nor ever has referred to the Jordan Plain or Valley nor River other than before there was a Dead Sea perhaps which was likely

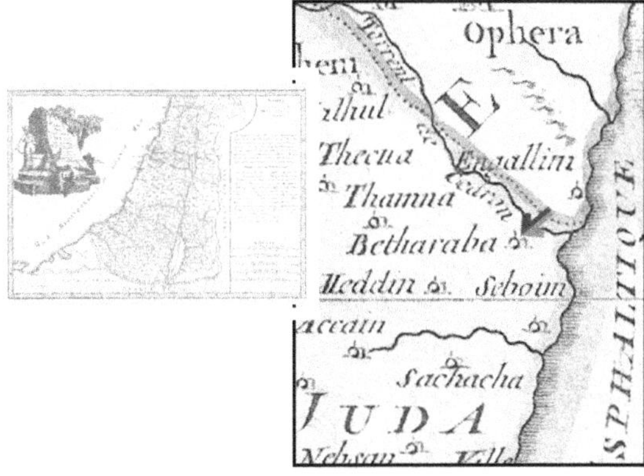

1770, Bonne Map of Israel. Rigobert Bonne 1727 – 1794 [12].

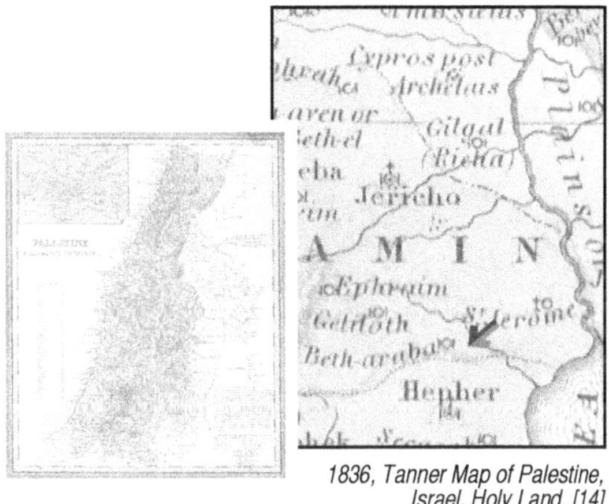

1836, Tanner Map of Palestine, Israel, Holy Land. [14]

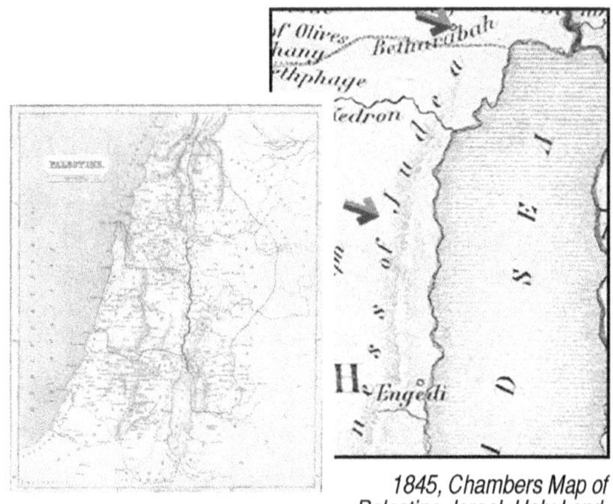

1845, Chambers Map of Palestine, Israel, Holy Land. [16]

Inset of 1852, Philip Map of Palestine, Israel, Holy Land. [17]

created by the destruction of Sodom. This has been known all along even on many maps until the 20th century *[previous page]*.

> *Matthew 3:13 KJV: Then cometh Jesus from Galilee to Jordan unto John, to be baptized of him.*

Where did Jesus *(Yahusha)* come from? Galilee. He travels South to Jordan. Where in Jordan? This verse is not specific.

> *John 1:28 KJV: These things were done in Bethabara beyond Jordan, where John was baptizing.*

Now, we have details rather than a general area. Jesus *(Yahusha)* came from Galilee heading South. He enters the Jordan Valley region and he travels "beyond" the Jordan Valley to a place called Bethabara. Where is this? The Jordan ends to the South at the Dead Sea and on the Northwest corner of the Dead Sea is Bethabara where John operated and baptized Messiah. It does not say he crossed the Jordan changing directions to the go to the East. It says he travels South beyond Jordan to Bethabara. This is very clear and maps agree. This is Qumran.

The word beyond in Greek here is peran *(πέραν)* meaning "other side, beyond, over, farther side." This is where many scholars go wrong by forgetting the orientation of the region from Galilee South which does not enter the East side of the Jordan which is still the Jordan Valley. It progresses beyond the Jordan Valley to the Wilderness of Judaea where John is said to be based. There is a reason.

John was an Aaronic bloodline Levite Priest qualified to be of High Priestly caste. He was not some hermit living under a tree eating locusts and honey. He was a righteous Aaronic Levite Priest operating in the place where his people had been exiled in the Wilderness of Judaea in Bethabara which today is called Qumran. This forerunner to Messiah, the Elijah come again, wore camel's hair clothing *(Mt. 3:4, Mk. 1:6)* akin to sackcloth as in mourning. John ate locust and honey which are both in the Biblical, covenant diet. He was essentially living the oath of a Rechabite but he was not poor and he did not live under a tree. He also is in no way the same as Banaah from the Talmud though attempts are made as Banaah lived 2-3 centuries later. John the Baptist was no Essene nor Pharisee nor was anyone in the Qumran community. John baptized mostly in fresh springs in clean water not the muddy waters of the Jordan River which few would desire to participate. Bethabara *(Qumran)* had fresh water. There is no disputing Qumran is Bethabara where Messiah was baptized and John and the Levites operated. This is the new location of the Temple practice where scripture was kept thus Bible.

THE ESSENES OF EIN GEDI

"On the west side of the Dead Sea, but out of range of the noxious exhalations of the coast, is the solitary tribe of the Essenes..."
"Lying below the Essenes was formerly the town of Engedi..." "Next comes Masada..." [10]
– Pliny the Elder, Natural History (Book V)

Pliny, a geographer, indisputably located the Essenes in the mountains overlooking Ein Gedi, 25 miles South of Qumran. He even anchors it to Masada just to the South and that is the Southern tip not near Qumran.

This is affirmed in mass scale archaeology called "The Essene Find" in Ein Gedi. This included a very ancient temple identified as a Chalcolithic Temple, c. 4th millennium B.C., which was not built by the Essenes but likely part of their compound in the mountains.

Also, archaeologists discovered a synagogue with many symbols identifying these Essenes as the secret cult throughout history fitting to everything we know about the Essenes who never lived in Qumran.

They were obsessed with peacocks as they worship the Peacock Angel*(Persian)* identified by many as the Nephilim deity known as Asmodeus. They etched swastika on the wall, very prominently display an 8-pointed star of Ishtar on the floor in tile, etc. They even offer what appears a very freemasonic warning on the wall.

There is no actual coherent data placing Essenes in Qumran.

Remnants of a Chalcolithic Temple (4th millennium BCE). [18]

Essene synagogue in Ein Gedi. [18]

Tile mosaic on synagogue floor in Ein Gedi. [18]

Peacock symbols in Ein Gedi synagogue. [18]

MESSIAH
IN JUBILEES

Regardless of whether one attempts to place the Book of Jubilees as written around 150 B.C., that was still before Messiah was born and this book offers prophecy of His coming.

> *Jubilees 16:26 (Abraham Knew of the Coming Messiah) And he blessed his Creator who had created him in his generation, for He had created him according to His good pleasure; for He knew and perceived that from him would arise the plant of righteousness for the eternal generations, and from him a holy seed, so that it should become like Him who had made all things.*

The "Plant of Righteousness for the eternal generations" can only be Messiah. It is also mentioned in 7:34. It is certainly not Israel but one man according to 1 Enoch *(1 En. 10:16, 93:5, 10)* which specifies it is Messiah. He is the "holy seed" and He is the one "who had made all things" *(Jn. 1)*. Along with Genesis, you are looking at the first major prophecy of Messiah from Moses and the origin of John 1 in doctrine. We will vet this in the Torah Test next. The Book of Jubilees is the origin of one of the most significant doctrines in the entire New Testament. The Messiah is the Creator along with Yahuah. John is quoting Jubilees here and we discover Messiah, Peter, Paul, James and Luke doing the same *(see The Torah Test)*.

> *John 1:1-3 KJV*
> *In the beginning was the Word, and the Word was with God, and the Word was God. The same was in the beginning with God. All things were made by him; and without him was not any thing made that was made.*

Messiah is among the "Us" who created (Gn. 1:26). His generations are eternal as He has no beginning and no end (Hb. 7:3) – the Alpha and Omega (Rv. 1:8).

> *Jubilees 21:24 (Abraham to Isaac)*
> *And He will bless thee in all thy deeds, And will raise up from thee the plant of righteousness through all the earth, throughout all generations of the earth, And my name and thy name will not be forgotten under heaven for ever.*

How can this plant of righteousness be raised up throughout all the earth for all generations which would include those past? Messiah existed before since Creation and became flesh within Abraham's seed. We believe this is the direct reference in which Messiah refers when He told the Pharisees they did not believe the words of Moses "for he wrote of me" *(Jn. 5:45-46)*. It is not vague. Let us begin with The Torah Test of the Book of Jubilees.

ARE THERE OTHER BOOKS THAT BELONG IN THE BIBLE CANON?

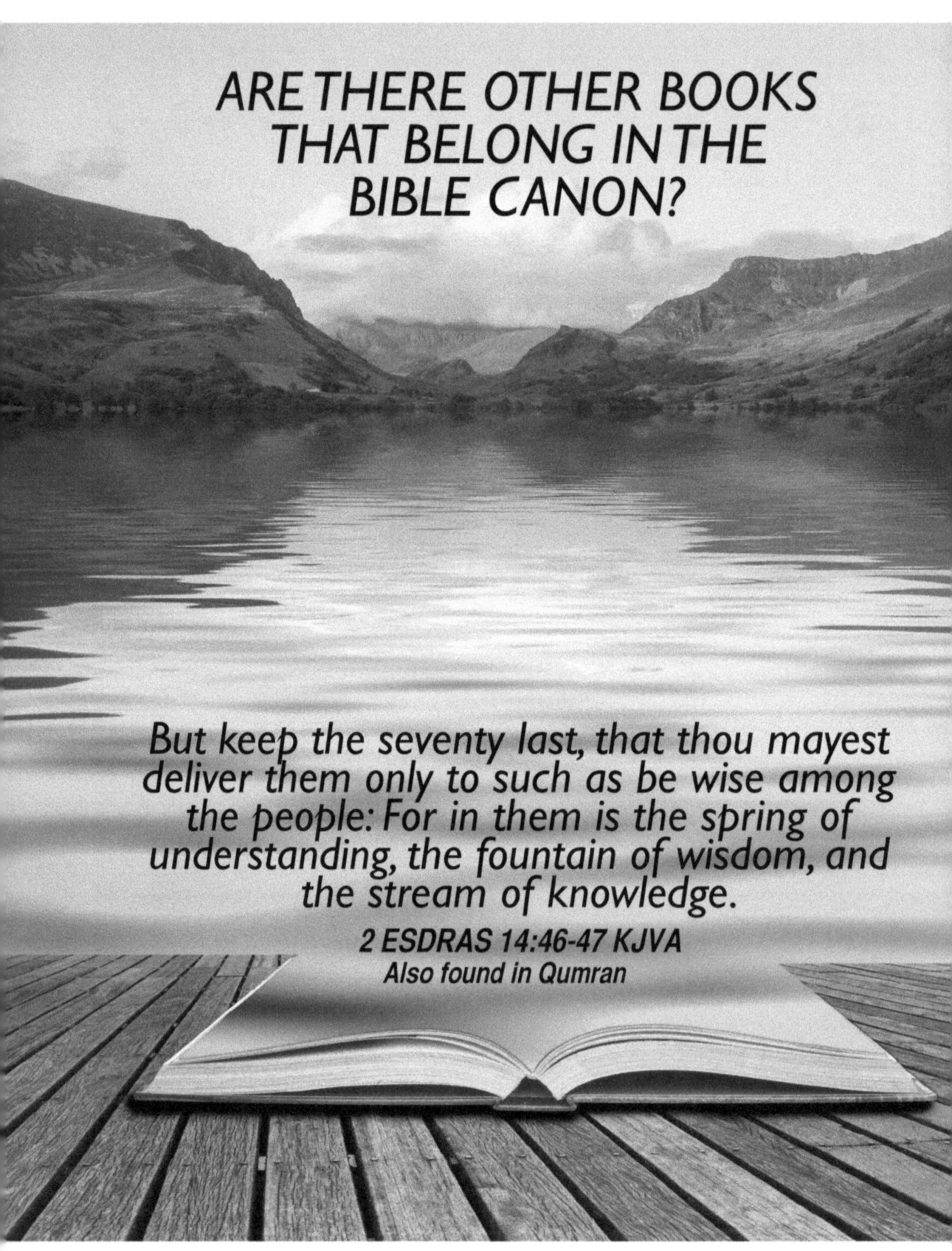

1. Prophetic Authorship

"For a book to be considered canonical, it must have been written by a prophet or apostle or by one who had a special relationship to such (Mark to Peter, Luke to Paul). Only those who had witnessed the events or had recorded eyewitness testimony could have their writings considered as Holy Scripture." (Note, Luke and Paul especially record the eyewitness accounts of others).

2. Witness of the Spirit

"The appeal to the inner witness of the Holy Spirit was also made to aid the people in understanding which books belonged in the canon and which did not." BLB quotes Pinnock who claims the canon is a matter of "historical process" (Clark Pinnock, Biblical Revelation, Grand Rapids: Baker Book House, 1973, p. 104). [2] We would agree but Pinnock ignores the most obvious such history. The Levite Library or Bible canon found in Qumran serves as a time capsule for the Old Testament canon long before the Catholic Church nor councils. Every book in the modern Old Testament canon was found there except Esther. It is Levite Priests who were the keepers of scripture and the Qumran community identifies as such over 100 times.

3. Acceptance

"The final test is the acceptance of the people of God." BLB notes this is to accept Jesus and the Apostles which we agree for New Testament but this would also be to accept His people in the time of Jubilees which is the same as Genesis and Exodus – Israel. It still prophesies of Messiah though.

4. Quoted As Doctrine In Scripture (Our Addition)

Our added test in which we will apply to Jubilees will assess whether or not this book is quoted in scripture for doctrine. This is not some arbitrary word or phrase but does doctrine derive from Jubilees which one does not find specifically in other Old Testament writings? This is the ultimate exam.

5. In Agreement With the Whole of Scripture (Our Addition)

Does it agree with scripture in whole? Even the Gospels have minor details to iron out in understanding, but how does Jubilees compare to Torah especially? The conclusion may surprise many.

1. Prophetic Authorship: Who Wrote Jubilees?

According to the Book of Jubilees, Moses is the human author of the book with the assistance of the Angel of the Presence on Mount Sinai same as Genesis. It is intended to be the second witness to Genesis as the book of times, chronology and division of territory establishing the Biblical calendar, Noah's record of the entire Earth partitioned to his three sons, more detailed lineages with the wives of the patriarchs and birthdates, a comprehensive dating since the beginning to the Exodus, etc. This is why it is called Jubilees *(a time period)* though it's full title is "The Book of the Divisions of the Times into their Jubilees and Weeks." The Qumran community applied it as Torah and established it as such. Now that we know these were the exiled Levite Temple priests, we know this was the Biblical community who kept Torah and the calendar. They are the authority set by scripture to keep the canon and Jubilees was and is canon.

To say otherwise, we demand every such scholar produce their credentials that outrank the great prophet – John the Baptist and the Levites who kept scripture as this was their library thus Bible. We demand they produce another such library from the Temple priests that disagrees with this one. They have not and they have not conducted adequate research on this. We do not overturn scripture but continue what the only ones qualified to catalogue the Bible in history curated. They guarded scripture with their lives. We have had enough of scholars sitting in the seat of the scornful in councils and boardrooms and other vacuums in willing ignorance on this topic. Imagine the amount of arrogance it takes for any church leader including Pope to dare change what the Biblical keepers of scripture kept for all of us. Once you review this book in full, you will likely begin to realize as we did and you will pronounce blessings for the level of revelation found here. You will then begin to assess the many doctrines, which men have filled in the gaps left by this censorship and this will expose just how far much of modern scholarship has deviated from the Word as well as agendas pushing Babylonian Mystery Religion down the throats of the modern church.

In the absence of Jubilees, there has been much uninformed speculation to answer questions Genesis does not and whole doctrines are sometimes surmised in blunder due, as you will observe, to this book being censored. Some immediately respond that an angel assisting Moses is somehow adding to Torah. The first challenge to that is that Moses wrote Jubilees thus it is Torah. Torah cannot add to Torah. Secondly, it is oblivious to scripture making it an unbiblical position yet it hails from many uneducated scholars on the topic.

Acts 7:53 KJV: Who have received the law by the disposition of angels, and have not kept it. (Gal. 3:19 ...it [the law] was ordained by angels in the hand of a mediator)

Luke and Paul tell us the law or Torah was in fact received by the disposition of angels. Frankly, this is really the same for the first chapters of Genesis as well. Moses was not present at Creation nor for the Flood. There are actual scholars who then question Moses' authorship of Genesis because he could not have witnessed those events first-hand. That is a false paradigm setting a trap to keep us ignorant whether said scholar even realizes. Moses did not have to witness events that Yahuah and the Angel of the Presence helped him write. In fact, let us not forget the other author of origin of Exodus especially is Yahuah who wrote the Ten Commandments and a portion of the law with His very finger. The Angel of the Presence is a witness to the events of Creation from the first day when he was created. Moses did not author that though he copied it.

Jubilees tells us those happenings from Creation have been recorded on the Heavenly Tablets by the Angel of the Presence. Thus, the angel who keeps scripture in Heaven assisted Moses with that portion of both Jubilees and Genesis which both originate from the Sinai encounter together. How many times do we have to see that scripture talks about Heavenly Tablets such as the Book of Life, etc. until we believe the concept?

Jubilees somehow gets mixed into what is called Pseudepigrapha—Greek for "false writings" or "false subscriptions." The word false more so refers to the claim in authorship as this claims to be penned by Moses. Do they prove it was not authored by Moses? Not even remotely. However, many scholars will create enough doubt to cause one to step away in many cases. We will vet much of that in this Torah Test.

It is erroneously claimed that Jubilees was written in about 150 B.C. which is the likely accurate dating of the fragment copies found in Qumran perhaps. This dating does not appear based as much on scientific assessment of the fragment as much as a guess that fits a paradigm. That paradigm is false not Moses' writings.

For instance, some will mention Jubilees quotes other portions of the Old Testament such as Psalm, etc. Then, they'll say 1 Enoch is dated to 165 B.C. which is just another ludicrous guess. Along with Jubilees was found all of the modern Old Testament canon except Esther. The dating of all such copies is between the third century B.C. and first century A.D. essentially. However, what scholar would then conclude or even suggest that Genesis was written in about 200 A.D. or so? That would be ludicrous. How about Psalm? Of course not. However, they apply one set of reasoning to the modern Bible canon scrolls found and a different one for all other books found with them which is fraudulent in nature. That is not logical and forms another false paradigm by which to set up failure in any further discussion. This is not scholarship, it's called propaganda regardless their aim. The tradition of the scribe is well established in copying over texts over time. Other than the local writings which are likely originals, it is perplexing that any scholar would not recognize Jubilees is a copy just as Genesis is a copy. Peter called that willing ignorance *(2 Pt. 3)* and oddly, Jubilees represents all three of his warnings that scoffers in the last days would deny Creation, the Flood and the deity of Messiah. That was a copy of Jubilees not the original and no one can say otherwise.

A CONCURRENT HISTORY:

However, we do not need to leave this to speculation. The Qumran community used the Book of Jubilees as authoritative.

> *"With 14 or 15 attested copies, the book of Jubilees is undoubtedly one of the best-documented texts of the Qumran library. Moreover, it is cited as an authoritative source in a sectarian work, the Damascus Document (CD 16:2-4), and seems to have been equally important to the Qumran community."*
> *– Gabriele Boccaccini, 2005 [20]*

Not only was Jubilees equally important to the Qumran community, it is quoted for law as Torah which makes sense since Moses wrote it.

> *"The Damascus Document, 4Q266, fr. 8 i, 6-9, 50 B.C.–100 A.D.:*
> *(For God made) a Covenant with you and all Israel; therefore a man shall bind himself by oath to return to the Law of Moses, for in it all things are strictly defined.* ***As for the exact determination of their times to which Israel turns a blind eye, behold it is strictly defined in the Book of the Divisions of the Times into their Jubilees and Weeks.*** *And on the day that a man swears to return to the Law of Moses, the Angel of Persecution shall cease to follow him provided he fulfills his word: for this reason Abraham circumcised himself on the day that he knew."* *[21]*

They continue as they quote right out of the Book of Jubilees chapter 23 verse 2. Where does the Qumran community derive the exact determination of the times and their definitions of how to keep Torah or the law? These are strictly defined in Jubilees which conveys alternative titles in history such as the Book of Division as it records Noah's division of the earth in territories between his three sons which we fully map at the end of Chapter 8. They believed the Law of Moses included the Book of Jubilees thus, Torah. It was written by Moses and not a Pharisee according to those who kept scripture and modern opinion fails. Do we believe the Levites who were responsible for caring for the Bible over thousands of years or the modern scholar who has not even read the book other than seeking to scoff? The Levites credit Moses as the author. Note this also tells us the Pharisees rejected Jubilees as they ran the Synagogues and the Temple in Israel at that time and they "turned a blind eye" to the Book of Jubilees. This is exactly what Messiah was referring to when He rebuked the Pharisees.

John 5:46-47 KJV
For had ye believed Moses, ye would have believed me; for he wrote of me. But if ye believe not his writings, how shall ye believe my words?

The most direct prophesies of Messiah originate in Jubilees. The Pharisees have always followed Torah with their own interpretation which transforms it against His commandments but never-the-less, they are champions of the so-called Pentateuch, a term meaning five books which is already missing one. No scripture ever defines Torah by such number. However, if the Pharisees are known to believe the rest of Torah, then Messiah is referring to another book here. We believe He is talking about Jubilees specifically.

They used a different calendar which a true assessment of the death and resurrection of Messiah reveals they followed the lunar calendar even then but Messiah and the community of John the Baptist did not. The Biblical calendar is a solar calendar not a lunar one. If a Pharisee wrote Jubilees, then why does it condemn the Pharisees several ways?

WHEN WRITTEN?

Is it possible that Jubilees is simply a paraphrase of Genesis, Exodus, etc.? Or was it written before and during the Exodus at the same time as Genesis as it says? Joseph's bones tell us it was written prior to Joshua as that is too large of an oversight for the author to have missed otherwise as the author does not record the reburial of Joseph as Moses does not in Torah and they would have known this in 150 B.C. If one would say that disqualifies Jubilees as scripture let us not pretend they represent the Biblical view nor that of those selecting what we call canon today as they included 1-2 Chronicles and Samuel-Kings which overlap in the same manner but also offer different details along the way. We could then go to the Gospels and say 3 of the 4 must be abolished with such reasoning. Of course, that would be insane just as it would be to discount Jubilees for the same reason. The point is inconsistent and unworthy of acknowledgement.

The place names in Chapter 8 are a very large red flag to anyone claiming this was written in 150 B.C. or so. There are many that are dead to history by that point and a writer during that period would have used known names more easily identifiable. Examples of this are Karaso or Khirasara, India which is a very ancient Indus Valley civilization known in Noah's time which had long disappeared by 150 B.C. and restored in recent years. It is likely Japheth who built it initially. We then have the Sea of Mâ'ûk as the South Atlantic named for Ham's wife known in Noah's time and lost to history, sea of 'Atêl as the Indian Ocean which is Bengali in origin thus the Indian Ocean and definitively by the directions, Fara for Alaska completely unknown in that age but not in Noah's, Pharnak for Saudi Arabia which specified in the directions with no real affirming history, etc. The author uses the Gihon, Hiddekel and really Pison Rivers from Eden of Genesis 2 as markers along the way which is definitively an example of a very ancient writing from the perspective of one such as Noah not in 150 B.C. nor any Pharisee as they have always been ignorant of such. Even the use of the Garden of Eden in the directions preserves it's location but demonstrates that was known in that time and we do not find that in 150 B.C. among the Pharisees as their writings in the near period are no where near the Far East for such. Pharisees do not and never knew these things. Moses and Noah did. Whomever wrote this knew much more than Pharisees then and now which is why they have formed many false doctrines regarding such locations. They do not know where these are nor were they ever privy to such information as they did not believe Jubilees nor were they ever true Tribes of Israel whose name they do not bear but remove – whose God they do not serve but hide. The mention of five great islands in the North is something that was unknown in 150 B.C. but not by Noah who had directions from around the Earth from Enoch. No one in 150 B.C would have known that Japheth's North has 5 of the 10 largest islands on Earth and four are in Canada. Also, how did a Pharisee in 150 B.C. know about the "Mountains of Fire" in Indonesia as a border when no map in that age portrays such nor much of the Far East. Islands were known such as Ophir/Chryse and Tarshish/ Argyre because they were ancient routes but otherwise there was no knowledge of these generally. However, they are firmly in these directions *[See Chapter 8 Maps]*.

If the calendar in Jubilees is a new creation in 150 B.C., why does it match the whole of scripture while the lunar calendar we are told is Hebrew fails every test? Why does it also not match the Pharisee calendar if a Pharisee wrote this? If it is "rewritten Bible" as classified by some scholars of willing ignorance, how would it ascertain a division of the entire earth including not only names dead to history at that point but areas unknown for more than 1,000 more years still as knowledge was lost. If Jubilees never would have been censored, this knowledge would have been known by much of the world all along. That is what the Dark Age approach does and it is time for the Dark Ages to end in the church beginning with the restoration of the Torah in Jubilees. This book is far more ancient.

WRITTEN BY A PHARISEE?

Jubilees claims to be written by Moses, a prophet. It either was or it is a lie. We will vet this in detail. Evidence proves it was authored long before 150 B.C. and that was a copy just as Isaiah, Psalm and other Bible books found with it were copies not originals. The Pharisee party did not exist long enough yet. Anyone claiming Jubilees was written by a Pharisee is ignoring Pharisee tradition at the time as they were forbidden to write such books relying only on Oral Traditions and they remain oblivious to Pharisee doctrine which the Book of Jubilees rebukes. No scholar could truly make such claims without ignoring most of the facts in order to propagate a false paradigm whether they realize it or not.

Not only do the Pharisees reject the Book of Jubilees, in doctrine, they were forbidden to write books in 150 B.C. Rachel Elior is Professor of Jewish Philosophy and Jewish Mystical Thought at the Hebrew University of Jerusalem and Israel Studies Professor in 2013 at the University of Chicago Divinity School. She has worked hands on with the Dead Sea Scrolls. In January 2014, Elior lectured at a Jewish Federation event in Chicago where she clarified that Essenes never lived in Qumran but the scrolls tell us these were Aaronic Levite priests relocated there after exile from the Temple. [3] Of course, she does not understand they are the keepers of scripture according to the Bible and not Pharisees. She expresses she does not understand how they were able to take scrolls with them out of the temple yet these were the Temple priests who were the curators of scripture – the ones who selected scripture long before there were Catholic Councils and with thousands of years of history doing so and appointed by Jacob *(Israel)* and Moses with such responsibility. That is a perfect example as to how a scholar simply cannot think beyond their programmed paradigm. However, she also tells us Pharisees were not permitted to write books in 150 B.C. as a matter of doctrine.

The Pharisees rejected Jubilees in the time of Messiah as they were already rejecting the Levite calendar, etc. at that point according to Mark 7 and the Qumran Damascus Document. They had exiled the priestly order from leadership in the Temple and replaced them fulfilling Psalm 83. They follow a lunar calendar which Jubilees rebukes as disruptive to the Biblical calendar which is solar-based instead. This is a massive thing for any scholar to overlook in claiming a Pharisee wrote this book. The notion is ludicrous and even Elior says so. We have even found tour guides in Israel who will honesty express there is no support for Essenes ever living in Qumran. They know better.

The Book of Jubilees agrees with Torah for law and it does not agree with Pharisee interpretation. The Pharisees expand the law, Jubilees does not. The main thing quoted as a supposed discrepancy in terms of law is no pleasure on the Sabbath which is affirmed by Isaiah and not an expansion at all. Even if that were a conflict, and it is not, it would certainly not be of the level of censoring this entire writing as a result. Talk about hair-splitting, gnat-straining and it is not even an accurate criticism. Otherwise, there are no real conflicts of note in the law. If this were written by a Pharisee who had already expanded the Torah to the point in their Oral Traditions that they earned scathing rebukes from Messiah especially in Mark 7, a reading would make that obvious and it does not. Messiah quoted Jubilees thus those accusing this book as written by such, are claiming Jesus (Yahusha) was quoting Pharisee doctrine which is certainly unthinkable. Add an angel in Heaven, Peter, John, Paul, James and Luke to that list as they all quote Jubilees for doctrine thus Pharisee doctrine? No way. There are prophesies in this book that don't fit Pharisees, a large amount of doctrine and truly a flat out rebuke of Pharisees though not by name as they did not exist as a party until 165 B.C. This further proves the book was not written in that era. Jubilees does not agree with the Talmud and that is very glaring. Frankly, reading this book makes one realize just how uneducated Pharisees truly are in scripture as they follow a different religion not that of the Bible nor have they ever. They have made up their own doctrines in many cases to replace Jubilees and they do not represent the Bible, were never curators of it and always have been illegitimate.

For instance, it is completely incoherent to actually attempt to connect the fact that Noah and Abraham were dealing with sinful people as having to refer to the era of the Greeks. It is foolhardy and very demeaning of a scholar such as Charles and others to claim that because Abraham rebukes sin and idols he must only refer to a 100-year period in history almost 2,000 years after him. That logic would cause one to assume a Pharisee wrote the Torah as well which is ridiculous. One could not attempt a more daft, counterproductive approach yet somehow, scholarship as a whole has accepted this vain rubbish. Abraham lived in the evil land of Nephilim and Canaan's remaining cursed lineage. Noah survived the most evil time in ALL of history to date and neither have to refer to a 100-year period of Hellenism every time they rebuke sin. Idols are not new in the Greek period. The practice is very ancient from Babylon and really originates before the Flood. They were dealing with far worse. Jubilees is also not invoking the Talmud but it rebukes it many times on many levels. This is as inverse as confusing Kabbalistic, Gnostic Essenes with holy Levite, Temple priests. Both are equally incongruous and unscholarly and should be rejected.

Furthermore, the writer of Jubilees was also not a Sadducee either as even Josephus as well as other early church fathers record Sadducees only followed the Pentateuch similar to the Samaritans. That is because they originate there as well.

[They] admit no observance at all apart from the laws.
- Flavius Josephus, Antiquities of the Jews, 18:16 [23]

Sadducee doctrine is not found in Jubilees as they believed "no resurrection, nor angel, nor spirit" (Acts 23:7-8; Matt. 22:23). The Book of Jubilees 2 identifies numerous angels by class and says they were created on the first day and one even wrote part of the book and communicates throughout. This was not written by a Sadducee who, same as a Pharisee nor Essene, would never have been welcomed into the Qumran community. Jubilees even alludes to resurrection.

Jubilees 16:26 KJV
And he blessed his Creator who had created him in his generation, for He had created him according to His good pleasure; for He knew and perceived that from him would arise the plant of righteousness for the eternal generations, and from him a holy seed, so that it should become like Him who had made all things.

Of course, R. H. Charles and other scholars will say this does not refer to resurrection yet they have no authority to render such definitively. They are guessing. However, the angels are a large part of Jubilees as well as the spirit and there is no placing Sadducees in Qumran.

If written in Qumran, Jubilees would not have been written by a Pharisee, Sadducee, Hasmonean nor Essene. The community is on record identifying themselves as neither party whatsoever. They were the Aaronic Levite Priesthood from the Temple who were exiled to the wilderness of Judaea which is why John the Baptist lived and operated there in Bethabara *(Qumran)*. Pharisees and Sadduccees are new parties to Judaea formed only in 165 B.C which is why we see no mention of them prior. The Essenes were a secret Kabbalistic cult originating in Egypt as the word Essene is Egyptian for secret. Pliny the Elder, and geographer, especially locates Essenses just above Ein Gedi in the mountains which is 25 miles South of Qumran. Not a shred of Essense archaeology is found in Qumran but tons in Ein Gedi and not a single mention of them in all the local Qumran community writings has been found yet we are told erroneously they lived in Qumran. Nonsense. This is a blatant fabrication of leaven and it originates in the Catholic Church who first had control of the scrolls and the Pharisees *(modern Judaism)* who have controlled it since all funded by Rockefeller.

2. *Witness of the Spirit in Historical Process*

Blue Letter Bible quotes Pinnock who claims the canon is a matter of "historical process." (Clark Pinnock, Biblical Revelation, Grand Rapids: Baker Book House, 1973, p. 104) We would agree but Pinnock ignores the most obvious such history and one must wonder how any scholar could do so. The Levite Library or Bible canon found in Qumran serves as a time capsule for the canon of scripture for the Old Testament long before there was a Catholic Church nor councils. It is the most authentic historic process imaginable including massive archaeology even. It supersedes all Catholic Councils and all Pharisee writings including Josephus and the Septuagint in authority and significance. The Aaronic Temple Levites maintain jurisdiction in that era on scripture not Pharisees ever. It was transferred from the Temple with them because they are the Biblical stewards of the Bible installed by Jacob and Moses with such administration. Pharisees, Hasomoneans and the like never had Biblical authority to replace them in any sense. John the Baptist was among them and Messiah Himself was baptized and visited that library. How is it that we even have to have this conversation? Every book in the modern Old Testament canon was found there except Esther proving the Catholic Councils compiled nothing but added Esther and other books and mislabeled some scripture as Apocrypha and Pseudepigrapha without authority to do so. It is Levite Priests who were the keepers of scripture and the Qumran community identifies as such over 100 times. This Temple Priest order kept what we would call the Bible canon today in a scroll library. There was no printing press yet so a scroll library was their compilation and they were not Catholics.

Nothing found there was arbitrary as these were the Temple Levite priests keeping the same writings they kept in the Temple thus Jubilees was used in the Temple. Prior to the Qumran find, it is understandable that one would ask the question as to what the Old Testament canon included. However, today, there is truly little logical doubt. One cannot identify a better history of canon than the very Levite library from the Temple with Jubilees included. This is it.

3. *Acceptance of Yahuah's People*

Jubilees aligns with Torah in the significance of Israel. Though it's time period is the same as Genesis, it has the first direct and most powerful prophesies of Messiah and appears the origin of portions of Revelation and End Times prophecy as being quoted by Messiah, John, James, Peter, Paul, Luke and even an angel in Heaven. A listing of such support would be pages long as there are many such occurrences throughout this book but we will cover some next. Consistent with Torah, Jubilees identifies the stranger among Israel also keeping the covenant as gentiles have always been included in the plan of salvation. That is not new in the New Testament. In 15:24, the strangers in Abraham's household were also circumcised. 16:25, tells us there was no one including gentiles among Abraham's household that were not circumcised. They were keeping the covenant. This is consistent with Torah which even during the Exodus documents the stranger among you or Gentile had the same blessings and curses under the covenant *(Ex. 12:49, Num. 9:14, 15:26-29, Lev. 16:29, 18:26, 19:34, 17:12)*.

4. Quoted As Doctrine In Scripture (Our Addition)

MESSIAH & APOSTLES QUOTED JUBILEES:

Also, the Book of Jubilees is the source of quotes in the New Testament by Jesus(Yahusha), John, Peter, Paul, James and Luke and not arbitrarily so but for doctrine not found anywhere else in the Old Testament. Everyone should know.

> *John 1:1-3 KJV*
> *In the beginning was the Word, and the Word was with God, and the Word was God. The same was in the beginning with God. All things were made by him; and without him was not any thing made that was made.*

The margin notes from the KJV anchor this passage in origin to Psalm 33:6 which is not it's source for Him who created all things.

> *Psalm 33:6 KJV*
> *By the word of the Lord were the heavens made; and all the host of them by the breath of his mouth.*

What is John doing here? Nowhere in the Old Testament does it ever define the Messiah to come as the Creator of all things along with Yahuah. Certainly this anchor in Psalm is not a direct link to that. This should be a challenge to many scholars as this has no root in the modern Old Testament. Is John manufacturing new doctrine however? No, he is quoting the prophecy of Messiah from the Book of Jubilees. Proverbs 8:22-23 and 30 are also cited in the margin note but they all pertain to wisdom not identifying Jesus *(Yahusha)* as co-creating all things.

Jubilees 16:26
And he (Abraham) blessed his Creator who had created him in his generation, for He
had created him according to His good pleasure; for He knew and perceived that from
him would arise the plant of righteousness for the eternal generations, and from him a
holy seed, so that it should become like Him who had made all things.

Who is the plant of righteousness for eternal generations who descends from Abraham? Only Messiah. All things were made by Him and that originates not in any of the Old Testament but firmly from the Book of Jubilees. Psalm certainly does not directly say such and this should haunt scholars. There is so much in this one passage that we could spend a chapter on what are the first direct prophesies of Messiah as they really originate in the Book of Jubilees. Moses did not always repeat himself in Genesis and Jubilees fills in blanks. Messiah then quotes it.

John 14:26 KJV (Words of Messiah)
But the Comforter, which is the Holy Ghost, whom the Father will send in my name,
he shall teach you all things, and bring all things to your remembrance, whatsoever I
have said unto you.

Jubilees 32:25
And Jacob said: 'Lord, how can I remember all that I have read and seen?' And he
said unto him: 'I will bring all things to thy remembrance.'

That's an exact quote word for word and though not as monumental in doctrine and ramifications as the first verse, significant none-the-less.

The writer of Acts whom many attribute as Luke quotes a timeline for the burning bush which appeared to Moses forty years after Moses entered Midian. Read the Exodus account and you will not find any indication of a dating on this but only the 40 years they wandered in the wilderness. Where did Luke get this?

Acts 7:30 KJV
And when forty years were expired, there appeared to him in the wilderness of mount
Sina(i) an angel of the Lord in a flame of fire in a bush.

Jubilees 48:1-2a
And in the sixth year of the third week of the forty-ninth jubilee thou didst depart and
dwell <in [2372 A.M.] the land of Midian>, five weeks and one year. And thou
didst return into Egypt in the second week in the second year in the fiftieth jubilee.
And thou thyself knowest what He spake unto thee on [2410 A.M.] Mount Sinai.

The author is quoting the timeline from the Book of Jubilees which does not derive in the modern Old Testament. We deduce if the writer of Acts and John can quote the Book of Jubilees, we can certainly use it.

This next scripture is actually one of the things that Jubilees is criticized as this claim that Moses received assistance from angels on Mt. Sinai in writing is not found in Torah yet no one seems to realize, the writer of Acts says the same thing. Thus to reject Jubilees over this obscure point is to also condemn Acts and we are confident those critics would not apply this consistently on that topic.

We disagree with that and so does Luke who says the Torah was received by Moses by the "disposition of angels." This is a major issue for scholars as they would have to condemn Luke for this as he is quoting a doctrine not found in the entire Old Testament. How dare he say Moses received some of the law from angels which is not found in Torah. Some will argue Yahuah wrote the law with his finger but they fail to read that was specific to the 10 commandments and their 2 tablets not all of the law nor is He an angel. Nothing in scripture disagrees with this and here we have the New Testament affirming Jubilees in a manner that is not against the Old Testament. How could Luke add to the Word, to the Torah even? He did not as he is quoting the sixth book of the Torah – the Book of Jubilees which was well-noted as such.

> *Acts 7:53 KJV*
> *Who have received the law by the disposition of angels, and have not kept it.*

> *Jubilees 1:26 (R.H. Charles, 1903)*
> *And He said to the angel of the presence: Write for Moses from the beginning of creation till My sanctuary has been built among them for all eternity.*

> *Jubilees 1:13 (R.H. Charles, 1903)*
> *And they will forget all My law and all My commandments and all My judgments, and will go astray as to new moons, and sabbaths, and festivals, and jubilees, and ordinances.*

In fact, Jubilees had already prophesied that Israel would break Yahuah's law just as Luke mentions. He was reading Jubilees and quoting it because it was scripture. No one can criticize Jubilees for it's position of the angel of the presence writing down the first portion of Genesis. Moses was not alive in that era and scholars even criticize him for that portion without cause. He had assistance which is rather obvious logically.

2 Corinthians 5:17 KJV
Therefore if any man be in Christ, he is a new creature: old things are passed away;
behold, all things are become new.

Jubilees 5:12
And he made for all his works a new and righteous nature, so that they should not
sin in their whole nature for ever, but should be all righteous each in his kind alway.

In the margin in the KJV, it anchors Paul's New Creature to Isaiah 43:18-19. However, once again not only is that not a direct quote, it has nothing to do with the nature of man. It simply says Yahuah will "do a new thing." A new thing is not a new creature nor a new and righteous nature which are precise in context. Paul is quoting the Book of Jubilees on one of the most important doctrines of the entire New Testament and scholars are rejecting the origin of that doctrine because they fail to conduct even a little research. Paul uses a second time a term he is quoting directly from Jubilees which also does not appear in the entire Old Testament.

Galatians 2:15 KJV
We who are Jews by nature, and not sinners of the Gentiles...

Jubilees 23:23a
And He will wake up against them the sinners of the Gentiles…

Paul does it again and Jesus(Yahusha) joins him when both use a term "son of perdition." We cannot find this term in the entire Old Testament even once. However, it seems to be quoting the Book of Jubilees and though it may appear to be a simple term, this has powerful implications in determining whom the beast will be. Did Jesus(Yahusha) quote Jubilees?

2 Thessalonians 2:3 KJV
Let no man deceive you by any means: for that day shall not come, except there come a
falling away first, and that man of sin be revealed, the son of perdition;

John 17:12 KJV (Words of Messiah)
While I was with them in the world, I kept them in thy name: those that thou gavest
me I have kept, and none of them is lost, but the son of perdition; that the scripture
might be fulfilled.

Jubilees 10:3a
...And hast saved me and my sons from the waters of the flood, And hast not caused
me to perish as Thou didst the sons of perdition...

This becomes extremely important as the sons of perdition in Jubilees prior to the Flood are Nephilim – the offspring of the Watcher Fallen Angels not men. They are not redeemable according to Enoch and that is why Jesus(Yahusha) says they are the lost he could not save. Paul links that the Beast will be part Nephilim. MESSIAH QUOTED JUBILEES!!! WOW!!!

Messiah quotes Jubilees again and even the Angel in Heaven joins Him in citing it in Revelation, John and Paul all mention the Book of Life. You will not find these words in the entire Old Testament but you will find them originating from the Book of Jubilees.

Revelation 17:7-8 KJV (The Angel in Heaven to John)
And the angel said unto me, Wherefore didst thou marvel? I will tell thee the mystery
of the woman, and of the beast that carrieth her, which hath the seven heads and
ten horns. The beast that thou sawest was, and is not; and shall ascend out of the
bottomless pit, and go into perdition: and they that dwell on the earth shall wonder,
whose names were not written in the book of life from the foundation of the world,
when they behold the beast that was, and is not, and yet is.

Revelation 3:1 and 5 (Messiah speaking to John)
And unto the angel of the church in Sardis write; These things saith he that hath the
seven Spirits of God, and the seven stars...
He that overcometh, the same shall be clothed in white raiment; and I will not blot
out his name out of the book of life, but I will confess his name before my Father, and
before his angels.

Philippians 4:3 KJV (Paul)
And I intreat thee also, true yokefellow, help those women which laboured with me in
the gospel, with Clement also, and with other my fellowlabourers, whose names are
in the book of life.

Revelation 13:8 KJV (John)
And all that dwell upon the earth shall worship him, whose names are not written in
the book of life of the Lamb slain from the foundation of the world.
(John also writes of the "Book of Life" in Rev. 13:8, 20:12, 20:15, 21:27 and
22:19 in his own words).

Jubilees 30:22
...they will be recorded on the heavenly tables as adversaries, and they will be destroyed out of the book of life, and they will be recorded in the book of those who will be destroyed and with those who will be rooted out of the earth.

Jubilees 36:10
But on the day of turbulence and execration and indignation and anger, with flaming devouring fire as He burnt Sodom, so likewise will He burn his land and his city and all that is his, and he will be blotted out of the book of the discipline of the children of men, and not be recorded in the book of life...

Daniel 12:1 mentions a book in which the deliverance of those written in "the book" which is definitely a reference to the Book of Life but he does not mention it by name. The name originates in Jubilees. Psalm 69:28 is closer as it calls it "the book of the living" and again it is the concept indeed. However, Jubilees was written before Psalm and Daniel and is the likely origin of both of those as well. The reference is direct from Jubilees word for word multiple times and not the modern canon.

The next one as a quote actually originates in the very heavenly tablets that are the source for the first chapters of Genesis written by an angel. We even sing about this one as it comes from James but where did James learn Abraham was called "the friend of God." Once again, we do not find an exact reference in the Old Testament. Genesis is not quite the same.

James 2:23 KJV (Brother of Messiah)
And the scripture was fulfilled which saith, Abraham believed God, and it was imputed unto him for righteousness: and he was called the Friend of God.

Jubilees 19:9
...for he was found faithful, and was recorded on the heavenly tablets as the friend of God.

Finally, Peter quotes Jubilees as well in concept. The KJV anchors this to Psalm which could fit but not as directly as the Book of Jubilees does.

2 Peter 3:8 KJV
But, beloved, be not ignorant of this one thing, that one day is with the Lord as a thousand years, and a thousand years as one day.

Psalm 90:4 KJV MARGIN
For a thousand years in thy sight are but as yesterday when it is past, and as a watch
in the night.

Jubilees 4:30
And he lacked seventy years of one thousand years; for one thousand years are as one
day in the testimony of the heavens and therefore was it written concerning the tree
of knowledge: 'On the day that ye eat thereof ye shall die.' For this reason he did not
complete the years of this day; for he died during it.

Jubilees becomes a far better match than Psalm. These are direct references and not veiled ones nor stretches. The only origin of these scriptures in the New Testament from Jesus(Yahusha), John, Paul, Luke and Peter is the Book of Jubilees which was written long before but at least documented copies were found in Qumran dating to about 150 B.C. which is 200 years or more before these New Testament quotes. Therefore, we have no issue using the Book of Jubilees as we have and we encourage all to begin reading this book and testing it thoroughly as scripture, Torah, inspired and canon. The Apostles believed it was, deriving monumental and significant doctrine from the sixth book of Torah.

EARLY CHURCH CITED JUBILEES, ETHIOPIA CONTINUED AS INSPIRED CANON:

Jubilees has always been scripture, inspired and canon all along.

THE BOOK OF JUBILEES
"...an ancient Jewish religious work of 50 chapters, considered canonical by the
Ethiopian Orthodox Church as well as Beta Israel (Ethiopian Jews), where it is
known as the Book of Division."
"It was well known to Early Christians, as evidenced by the writings of Epiphanius,
Justin Martyr, Origen, Diodorus of Tarsus, Isidore of Alexandria, Isidore of Seville,
Eutychius of Alexandria, John Malalas, George Syncellus, and George Kedrenos.
The text was also utilized by the community that originally collected the Dead Sea
Scrolls." [22]

The Qumran Community documented and preserved the Book of Jubilees as scripture and Torah even. The Apostles continue to even derive significant doctrine from the Book of Jubilees including Messiah solidifying it as scripture and Torah. The early church fathers quoted and used the Book of Jubilees in sermons through history until about the 14th century. Then, though the Catholic Church usurped the throne of Jesus (Yahusha) censoring scripture and adding to it, the Ethiopian Church continued Jubilees as canon all the way until today. These copies were rediscovered by the Western world in Ethiopia but remained in consistent circulation as scripture which does not require the West nor do they have an opinion on the matter unless they can prove it not scripture which they never have or produce their Aaronic Levite credentials from Messiah's era.

The Abyssinian Church, which has continued Jubilees as canon, names it the *"Book of the Division of Days,"* from the first words at the beginning. This also proves this book was not only in circulation but considered scripture at least by some at that time. Through history, because of it's broad importance, The Book of Jubilees has been attributed by many titles. In fact, if one searched hard enough, they would find it quoted without a title many times as well. We have already produced such examples from the New Testament. It has been known as *"Little Genesis"* due to it's scale of detail beyond that of Genesis as it is larger not smaller, *Book of Division, Apocalypse of Moses, Assumption of Moses, Testament of Moses, The Life of Adam, Book of Adam's Daughters, etc.*

Although not inducted into canon in the Roman Catholic Church, the Book of Jubilees was cited in the early church according to R.H Charles, Bible Hub and even Wikipedia as this is widely reported. In order of approximate chronology, here are such references: *(*All dates are estimates only. Reference list in which Charles offers exhaustive details.)*

> ***150*** *Justin Martyr (Apol., ii, 5: "first-born princes of the angels" quoting Jub. 2:2, 15:27)*
> ***200*** *Origen, 32:21, 40:10, 45:14.*
> ***200*** *Hippolytus, Jub. 8-10.*
> ***200*** *Ps.-Clemens Romanus, several quotes from Jubilees.*
> ***350*** *Didymus of Alexandria (cites 4:31)*
> ***350*** *Pseudo-Athanasius: (Assumption of Moses)*
> ***382*** *Jerome, Epist. 78 ad Fab. (10:21, 11:11-13 and others)*
> ***392*** *Diodorus of Antioch, 10:35.*
> ***404*** *Epiphanius, Haer. xxxix. 6*
> ***5th Century*** *Isidore Pelusiota of Alexandria, Jub. 32:2-3, 31:18-20, 41:23-28.*
> ***492*** *Decree of Pope Gelasius, Decretum Gelasii, (Book of Adam's Daughters)*
> ***542*** *Severus of Antioch discusses the death of Moses and an argument over his remains between satan and the Archangel Michael. This originates in Jubilees and no where in the Old Testament.*
> ***550*** *John Malalas*
> ***636*** *Isidore of Seville, 16:26, 2:2, 2:22.*

__802__ Catalogues of Nicephorus (Assumption of Moses)
__800__ Syncellus i. 7, 183, 192; i. 5, 185, 203; i. 7; i. 13; Apocalypse of Moses:
i. 5, i. 49. i. 48 (says Gal. 6:15 was derived from Jubilees). The Life of Adam: i.
7-9 (quotes Jub. 2:1-29)
__9th Century__ Catena of Nicephorus (Testament of Moses) i. 175 (10:21 quote)
__935__ Eutychius of Alexandria, Jub. 4:1, 8, 9, 11, 31; 11:4; 12:9.
__1000__ Suidas, 12:16, 12:2.
__1100__ Zonaras, i.18 (2:2)
__1150__ Glycas, pp. 198, 206, 392 (32:2-3 and others)
__1184__ Cedrenus i. 6, 9, 16, 48, 53, 85, 87; Apocalypse of Moses: i. 7. i. 16
__1206__ Joel, Chronographia, 37:23
__1250__ Gregorius Barhebraeus, 11:11-13.
__13th Century__ LXX MS, personal names found in Jubilees used, 5:31, 6:1.
__1332__ Theodorus Metochita (BibleHub.com)

The church was aware but the Catholic Church is much more akin to the Pharisees than the Biblical ekklesia. One should not expect it would have continued a book the Pharisees had already censored in the time of Messiah and their councils admit this as they follow the Pharisee suggestions. Certainly the church quoted Jubilees, even a Pope. However, there is not a single church father who had the authority to remove a book quoted and used by Messiah and the Apostles as Torah. If they represented the true ekklesia, they would have continued the same books that were found in the Levite library in Qumran.

Though continued in the Ethiopian canon this entire time to today, in the Western world, Jubilees appeared lost for about 400 years until it was rediscovered in the Ethiopic. Multiple English translations from the Ethiopic were released from the mid-1800s to mid-1900s before the Dead Sea Scrolls were found. Once discovered in Qumran as the sixth most numerous scroll, Jubilees is known to have originated in Hebrew and those fragments coalesce with the Ethiopic. This really proved this was preserved in the Ethiopic Geez language and there is no scripture which ever says that is not acceptable. That is a false paradigm in scholarship as the book is preserved regardless and affirmed in Hebrew as well.

There are several more such instances in which Jubilees is engrained into the prophets, apostles and even Messiah such as the use of the title Abba by Messiah in Mark 14:16 and Paul in Romans 8:15 and Galatians 4:6. This title is not found in the Old Testament and some have noted such. However, Father as a title is found in the original Torah (1:24 and 19:29). Jubilees is quoted by Messiah again.

Please identify one modern scholar in the past 2000 years who has more authority than the patriarchs of our faith who in some cases travelled with the

Son of God Himself. There is no Pope nor Cardinal nor Bishop nor Rabbi nor modern Apostle nor any position which can overrule scripture and one has to accept their authority in order to reject the Book of Jubilees. Thus, we are not suggesting convening a council to induct this into the canon as men are unlikely to do so nor are such councils Biblical. However, we can all restore this even cautiously in our readings as we should.

5. In Agreement With the Whole of Scripture (Our Addition)

In setting forth this more stringent criteria ourselves, please allow use to be clear on our understanding. Some take such a point and apply the most ridiculous of false paradigms claiming this must mean Jubilees must render everything the exact same as the rest of Torah. In other words, it cannot add any details or information to any narrative. They would then say, that means it is adding to Torah. However, there is a massive problem with such thinking. Jubilees is Torah thus cannot add to itself. The purpose for Moses to write a second account of what is covered in Genesis would be to offer a different angle and level of detail on some things. Otherwise, if it is exactly the same as Genesis, would it not just be called Genesis? This is another one of those oxymorons in scholarship which is planted to handcuff any consideration. However, the Book of Jubilees tracks extremely well with Genesis, the rest of Torah and the whole of scripture. We have already addressed much on this. However, let us review some of the information which is added and assess whether it violates Torah or enhances understanding of Torah.

As you read through this entire edition, notice the staggering number of cross-references to Torah especially but also other scripture even the New Testament. We observe Jubilees explaining things we should have understood all this time. Several doctrines of men have been formed in this information vacuum. Unfortunately, for those holding such doctrines, Jubilees shines light on them but let us remember, we should have had this book at our disposal in the canon of scripture all along. If we did, occult doctrines like the Serpent Seed Doctrine for instance, never could have found their way into Bible interpretation even in the fringes. Cain was not even born until 7 years after the Garden thus was not the product of an intimate encounter with Eve and the Serpent in the Garden. Of course, let us not forget most of the versions of that doctrine require Adam to commit the first homosexual act and we know from whom that agenda originates.

The first thing we encounter often in scholarship is skepticism based on minutiae really. Many times, such scholars have not even read the book or seemingly forget what the Bible says. It is sometimes difficult to believe we live in such era. We are supposed to be advanced yet the Dark Ages regarding Bible knowledge continue. Jubilees will shine a light on this and expose these logical fallacies.

No Pleasure on the Sabbath *(Jub. 2:2)*

Jubilees records there is to be no pleasure on the Sabbath including relations with one's spouse. This sends some especially Rabbinic Judaism and Messianics into an uproar because they do not wish to hear this. Some Rabbi once said one receives a double blessing for such actions yet that does not originate in the Bible. There lies the rub. When a doctrine does not originate in the Bible, it will be exposed. If one claims we should abolish Jubilees for this reason, then they must be consistent and throw out Isaiah with it and that would be insane.

> *Isaiah 58:13 KJV*
> *If thou turn away thy foot from the sabbath, from doing thy pleasure on my holy day; and call the sabbath a delight, the holy of the LORD, honourable; and shalt honour him, not doing thine own ways, nor finding thine own pleasure, nor speaking thine own words:*

Of course, search hard enough and one will find a blog, video or article that will tell us Isaiah didn't mean that kind of pleasure yet he certainly did. The point is to make the Sabbath the delight for one day a week and not your own person in ANY sense. That's crystal and no one gets to change Isaiah just because it does not suit their doctrine of men. This is the state of modern scholarship however. We are spending far too much time in the doctrines of men and far too little reading the Word for what it really says. Jubilees not only clarifies the Torah view on this but you can see Isaiah's view originates specifically in the Book of Jubilees. This is not an addition or we must all abolish Isaiah with it and that would be nonsense. Isaiah, the Levite priest, read and applied Jubilees as his family descendants at Qumran *(Bethabara)* did – as Torah.

Then, some of the same sources will actually say with a straight face, Sabbath is a happy day thus Isaiah could not have meant we are not allowed to have pleasure on the very day we are supposed to be happy. That is the foolish reason of a cynic really clinging to their view not one actually interested in logic. Isaiah says we are not to seek our OWN pleasure. Sabbath is about Him and His pleasure. Does that please us? Anyone keeping the Sabbath would tell you it is a delight but wait, that is exactly what Isaiah said isn't it. Therefore, they are accusing Isaiah of being confused by his own statement when this is not fuzzy at all. Yes, to delight is to pleasure but we are not to seek our OWN pleasure and only His which should be a delight to us indeed. Relations with one's spouse are not for His pleasure. It is certainly Biblical the other six days of the week but Isaiah and Jubilees agree. This truly is an enigma as the real question is why does this agree on practically all of the law of Torah and yet, somehow it is said this may be a Pharisee writing when the Pharisees changed much of Torah. Jubilees is not a Pharisee view but condemns such many times yet upholds Torah as it is written. It does not represent the things Messiah said were changed by Pharisees even and this is close to the same time frame in which the copies at Qumran are dated. Again those are copies.

Another ministry will tell you Isaiah does not actually include the word "the" in the Hebrew. He just meant an indistinct day of rest or sabbath as if there is such a thing. However, that ministry seems challenged to even read the rest of the sentence where it says on "My Holy Day" and "holy of Yahuah." Since when was Sabbath not the Sabbath and what other day of the week is set apart as holy? Only the Sabbath. They will argue back and forth on this one and let them do so but do not allow them to censor Jubilees over something Isaiah says as well. There is nothing in the Torah which states the opposite and this in no way conflicts.

Another article makes the claim that this view would make the writer a Sadducee, another says a Pharisee. However, as we established earlier both factions were considered the "sons of darkness" by the Qumran community who treated Jubilees as Torah and identifies it as a part of the Law of Moses which means it was written by Moses. They would not do so if it were just written at that time especially not by a "son of darkness." That is an irresponsible claim.

Jacob & Esau War After Jacob's Death: Jacob Kills Esau *(Jub. 37-38)*

In Genesis, Jacob and Esau reconcile at their father's death and no more is said. We have no idea how Esau died and more so, what happened that the sons of Edom (Esau) were at constant war against Israel ever since? In fact, this is a battle that has no end until the very end. If Jacob and Esau reconciled, then why are Esau's sons and Jacobs sons at war for thousands of years? Here is where Jubilees is the record of this history which brings all into focus and scholars should have been questioning this all along. In Jubilees, the two brothers also reconcile to bury their father. Esau is moved and genuine in both accounts. However, when Esau returned to Edom with his sons, they began to bicker and manipulate their father demanding their birthright be returned. They wanted war with Jacob. Esau would agree to this and they would have war in which Jacob kills Esau. Some would say censor Jubilees because it completes a story in a way that reconnects the whole of scripture. This is because scripture was never disconnected. A portion of it was censored and it is time to remedy that. We now know why Israel and Edom are arch enemies since Esau and to the end. However, if the story was left as Genesis does with the reconciliation only, we would never understand what caused this reignition of friction. This is not against Torah but completes it and it is Torah.

Bones of Joseph Not Buried in Canaan With His Brothers Initially But Were 400 Years Later *(Jub. 46)*

Some attempt the position that Jubilees and Genesis disagree on the burial of the bones of Joseph. In Jubilees, Joseph dies and was buried in Egypt. Let us remember this was 400 years before the Exodus. The sons of Jacob would take the bones of their deceased forefathers to Canaan to bury them with Abraham except the bones of Joseph which remained in Egypt at that time *(400 years before the Exodus)*. Jubilees indicates this in 46:9. Israel would begin enslavement soon after. Again, that was 400 years before Israel entered the Promised Land and no surprise the political environment in taking an Egyptian official's bones at that point may not have been possible. There is no further mention of Joseph's bones in Jubilees and this is very telling as to it's authorship because it is Joshua who buried Joseph in Israel 400 years later. This is not only consistent, it affirms Jubilees was written by Moses because a later author would have known this.

> *Joshua 24:32 KJV (AFTER ENTRY INTO THE PROMISED LAND)*
> *The bones of Joseph, which the children of Israel had brought up out of Egypt, they buried at Shechem, in the plot of ground which Jacob had bought from the sons of Hamor the father of Shechem for one hundred pieces of silver, and which had become an inheritance of the children of Joseph.*

Note this is Joshua after Israel entered the Promised Land. The account in Jubilees is not only prior to the Exodus but the time of the enslavement of Israel. Saying this is a discrepancy is inept. In fact, this is the opposite. Joseph's bones were not taken to Israel at the time of his death. If they were, that would be a discrepancy. However, almost 400 years later, Joseph's remains would be inhumed and taken in the Exodus to be finally buried in Israel fulfilling Joseph's wishes. That would have been the perfect time to take his remains with them and perhaps the only time possible. Why is this so difficult for some scholars? Again, one would claim we must censor Jubilees because they cannot read. That would be unfortunate and they have no such authority.

Feast Origins Prior to Mt. Sinai

In the Book of Jubilees, the Feast origins are known, for Shavuot hales from the time of Creation as the Day of Covenant Renewal in which Noah renewed covenant from the ark on that exact day, Abraham did the same and so did Israel. Israel was repeating an ancient cycle orchestrated by Yahuah. The Torah gives no background on this Feast at all but shows it's significance from the time of Mt. Sinai. The Pharisees claim that as the origin, Torah does not. This again is not inconsistent with Torah, it completes it yet again. This is the same for Passover, Sukkot and Yom Kippur which have earlier origins we will explore in commentary in more detail. Torah does not specify either of these originated from Mt. Sinai forward only. That is a faulty assumption which we now know to be false thanks to Jubilees. Shavuot especially is the most overlooked of all Feasts as few know what it means and it is among the most significant. They tell us that was the giving of the Torah yet that view fails to recognize that took 40 days not just one day and Moses came down, reacted to the golden calf and destroyed the first set. That was not even near Shavuot at that point. This finally makes sense.

Satan's (Mastema) Role in Egypt and as the Angel of Death (Jub. 48)

Jubilees fills in gaps such as the behind the scenes action during the final plagues. It tells us Satan (Mastema) was personally influencing Pharoah and that fits perfectly. It says he was loosed as the angel of death to kill the firstborn in Egypt that night and again, Satan's fruit *(John 10:10)* is killing thus that fits perfectly as well. It is the Archangel Michael who restrains Satan from killing men directly otherwise. If he could, he would but he cannot. He was only released that one night and those scholars who misread Torah to claim Yahuah was the angel of death are simply propagating a misunderstanding of the whole of scripture and the nature of our Elohim.

We will cover additional topics in commentaries of their own in pages forthcoming such as Sabbath and the Law, Kainam who found the occult doctrine and reinstituted it at Babel, the Watcher Fallen Angels and Nephilim, the origin of demons, etc. This is a large book of great detail which makes it an easy target for a deceptive group of so-called scholars who are truly Pharisees in their thinking to ridicule in their willing ignorance. We have exposed their thinking. You can assess from here with your own discernment.

The Book of Jubilees passes a true, authentic Torah Test. Esther, by the way, does not yet appears in the modern canon when Jubilees has always been inspired Torah. We may not receive genuine scholarship from the church generally in this age of deception and none of us should be surprised at that. This is why several times the Word tells us we are to know scripture for ourselves *(1 Thess. 5:17)*.

Conclusion: Jubilees is Torah

Criteria set forth by Blue Letter Bible with our additions. [1]

1. Prophetic Authorship

Moses wrote the Book of Jubilees. As he was a prophet and this vets as his writing consistent with his other writings, it is Torah.

2. Witness of the Spirit

Jubilees has continued as canon in Qumran which was the community of John the Baptist thus a New Testament community of Aaronic Levite priests. It prophesies of the Messiah as well. Jubilees serves as a witness to Genesis especially and this is important as scholars should be noting the absence of such in the modern canon.

3. Acceptance

The Book of Jubilees sets forth Israel as Yah's people and agrees with the Torah. It is also quoted in the New Testament and it really offers the first solid prophecies of Messiah.

4. Quoted As Doctrine In Scripture (Our Addition)

Messiah, Paul, Peter, Luke, James and John quote Jubilees for significant doctrine.

5. In Agreement With the Whole of Scripture (Our Addition)

Jubilees agrees with the Torah and the whole of scripture. It offers additional information as it should or it would just be another publishing of the same book such as Genesis and Moses would have no purpose in writing it.

The Book of Jubilees uses YHWH interpreted "the Lord" inappropriately about 300 times. It is incredibly ignorant for one to actually claim a Pharisee wrote the name of God 300 times in their writing. It proves this could not be a Pharisee document. Genesis uses YHWH 169 times also interpreted "the Lord" mostly. The modern Old Testament translations have replaced this name, YHWH, on over 6,800 occasions with generic titles such as Lord. That is a title which simply means "master" rendered back in the Hebrew as ba'al (בעל). Does בעל look like יהוה? They don't even have a single letter in common. This was a purposeful, malicious changing of scripture to hide the name of YHWH. Why would anyone censor the name of God? Well, as you have already seen, they censored part of His Torah so no surprise but this is one of the greatest hoaxes perpetrated on mankind and these are the people we have trusted to care for scripture but that is our fault because we must test.

They removed one-sixth of the Torah and they replaced the very name of YHWH. It is impossible for anyone claiming to know Hebrew even a little to render YHWH as ba'al (בעל). Now, He is our Lord just as ba'al was the lord of the Samaritans. It's a title not a name. His name was Molech, Moloch, Adrammelech and other renditions. What is worse is their doctrine is not to pronounce the name of their god and they have infused their practice into the name of YHWH fraudulently. It is time we all test that and demand that scholars behave as scholars. They must show their work and they better prove things out. New translations continue to be released and they continue the Samaritan doctrine in deliberate error. In this publishing of Jubilees, we have restored His name, YHWH, as Yahuah.

In ancient times, the Father's name was rendered

PHOENICIAN		*1100 B.C.*
PALEO-HEBREW		*1000 B.C.*
HEBREW	יהוה	*300 B.C. - TODAY*

Though the letters changed in appearance, His name has always been the same four Hebrew letters (YAD-Y, HEY-H, WAW-W, HEY-H). Some Rabbis will even claim Abraham did not know the name of God, yet using this same name of YHWH, the Creator told Abraham His name and speaks His own name at least three times in the Word. In the Book of Jubilees this is very prominent as Yahuah declares His name YHWH in Abraham, Isaac and Jacob's era in 1:18, 28; 12:26, 30; 13:4, 14:7; 18:9; 27:22, 27; and 32:18. He tells Abraham His name is YHWH at least 5 times and Jacob 3. Therefore they certainly knew His name. Here is a list of the many times the patriarchs used the name YHWH in this book:

• Enos calls upon YHWH • 4:12

• Noah speaks YHWH • 6:11 and 8:18

• Abraham calls on YHWH • 13:8,16

• Abraham speaks YHWH's name • 14:2, 8; 18:13; 19:18, 23
    (to Jacob) speaks it • 19:28-29; 22:18
    (to Ishmael and Isaac) • 20:2-3; 21:2, 7, 9, 11, 20

• Ishmael speaks YHWH • 17:14

• Isaac speaks name YHWH • 24:20, 23; 26:6, 22, 23, 24

• Rebecca • 25:12, 13, 15, 23; 26:5

• Jacob uses it • 27:25, 27
    (to Levi) • 31:13, 14, 15, 16,
    (to Judah) • 18, 32:25, 35:2, 36:3, 6, 35:3,4.

• Joseph uses YHWH • 33:21, 43:10, 18, 19, 20

Even Satan called Him YHWH (10:8) and Esau in 26:5. Moses then uses it multiple times as he does throughout the Torah. So do the prophets both major and minor for a total of over 6,800 uses of the name both writing and speaking. Therefore, there is no Biblical doctrine whatsoever to hide the name of YHWH. This practice originates in Samaria with the replacements of the Lost Tribes of the Northern Kingdom. They brought their gods and idols with them but the land was devouring them. So, they brought in a Levite to teach them the practices of Torah. However, what they did was infuse the worship of YHWH into their own worship in a mingling always rejected by YHWH in scripture. You can read of this in Chronicles especially.

Fast forward, and these same Samaritans would be among the powers in Psalm 83's prophetic war who would conquer the Temple and take it over. This happened in 165 B.C. in what is called the Hasmonean Revolt. The Qumran community of Aaronic Levite priests exiled from the Temple in that era write of this as firm history. They tell us the Temple was abducted and the Psalm 83 prophecy fulfilled by these Hasmoneans and their priests from Samaria. They would install their Samaritan priesthood of the replacements of the Northern Kingdom who would bring their infusion rejected by Yahuah into the Temple. They were called the Pharisees and Sadducees and neither party existed in Israel prior to that which is why you never see them mentioned in the Old Testament. This order is responsible for censoring Jubilees, changing the name of YHWH and they would have gotten away with it, if it were not for our dog and meddling kids (that's Scooby Doo). Seriously, in our age, they are being exposed by many as knowledge increases.

YHWH is well-documented and you can verify it easily today in sources like blueletterbible.com and similar. The question is how does one pronounce it. We realize that leads to polarize debates many times but that is for the agitators who do not really wish to know. The precedent for this is set in the names of the prophets who bear YHW and YH in their names both in definition pointing to the name of God/YHWH. For instance, Elijah in Hebrew is EliYAHU "Yahu is God/El," Jermiah is YirmiYAHU "Yahu will exalt," Isaiah is YeshaYAHU "Yahu is Salvation," Ezekiel is YAHazaqEL "Yah is a Strong God/El," Jehosophat is YAHUshapat "Yahu is Judge," Joseph is YAHUsap "May Yahu Increase." All of these names include the same first 3 letters of YHWH and Biblical precedence tells us this is pronounced YAHU. Even the Prime Minister of Israel's family changed their name to NetanYAHU meaning "Gift of Yahu." None of these is YAHW or YAHAW but YAHU. The H (HEY) on the end is AH. YAHUAH.

You will learn from Jubilees Hebrew is the language of Creation thus it must be simple and somehow for thousands of years it was written with just consonants yet spoken without ever needing vowel points. Those were added in about 1000 A.D. by the Masoretes and at times serve to offer more confusion than clarity as they clearly were not honest about the name of Yahuah since it was their practice to hide His name. Therefore, this must be a phonetic language requiring no vowels and no fancy rules. What we call Hebrew today is Yiddish-infused.

Phonetically, YH is simple. H is AH (see chart to right). That's YAH. The next combination is HW which we know by the names of the prophets is HU. Thus it's YAHU. Finally, we add the last H or AH for YAHUAH.

We recognize there is a whole church out there which stakes it's claim on the name Jehovah. Here's the largest problem with that word. It is not Ancient Hebrew, Aramaic, Greek, Latin, Old French, Old German nor Old English. In other words, every language in which the Bible has been interpreted through in origin cannot render J nor V until the Renaissance (1500s or so). The Bible was already thousands of years old and never used J nor V in any ancient text. There is a Pharisee out there deceiving many by trying to make this fit but we have the Dead Sea Scrolls dating to as early as 300 B.C. with even entire books such as the Isaiah scroll of about 25 feet in length which never renders a J nor a V even once. There is no overturning that. One may ignore it but let us not pretend they would be interested in the truth.

This leads us to the name of Messiah as the same first 3 letters YHW or YAHU as set by Yahuah. Yes, He literally meant He came in His Father's name. His name ends with SH - SHIN, A - AYIN which is SHA. He is Yahusha with Yahushua also appearing as a variant in scripture. Joshua has this same name in Hebrew. His people are the YAHUdim never Jews but YAH's.

Finally, some focus on the one time in scripture that Yahuah says His name is HYH, HAYAH as His only name ignoring the 6,800 times it is recorded as YHWH, Yahuah. However, modern Yiddish renders this as EHYEH and similar in fraud. Ancient Hebrew is HA YAH or THE YAH. It is the same name. Yahuah is being specific in saying I am The Yah not to be confused with any other. He is still invoking His name Yahuah in that passage which matches.

FATHER YAHUAH

יהוה

HEY WAW HEY YAD

HAU HAY

YAHUAH

Hebrew reads right to left.

Ancient Semitic/Hebrew

Early	Middle	Late	Name	Picture	Meaning	Sound	
		א	El	Ox head	Strong, Power, Leader	ah, eh	
		ב	Bet	Tent floorplan	Family, House, In	b, bh(v)	
		ג	Gam	Foot	Gather, Walk	g	
		ד	Dal	Door	Move, Hang, Entrance	d	
		ה	Hey	Man with arms raised	Look, Reveal, Breath	h, ah	AH
		ו	Waw	Tent peg	Add, Secure, Hook	w, o, u	U
		ז	Zan	Mattock	Food, Cut, Nourish	z	
		ח	Hhet	Tent wall	Outside, Divide, Half	hh	
		ט	Tet	Basket	Surround, Contain, Mud	t	
		י	Yad	Arm and closed hand	Work, Throw, Worship	y, ee	Y
		כ	Kaph	Open palm	Bend, Open, Allow, Tame	k, kh	
		ל	Lam	Shepherd Staff	Teach, Yoke, To, Bind	l	
		מ	Mem	Water	Chaos, Mighty, Blood	m	
		נ	Nun	Seed	Continue, Heir, Son	n	
		ס	Sin	Thorn	Grab, Hate, Protect	s	
		ע	Ghah	Eye	Watch, Know, Shade	gh(ng)	
		פ	Pey	Mouth	Blow, Scatter, Edge	p, ph(f)	
		צ	Tsad	Trail	Journey, chase, hunt	ts	
		ק	Quph	Sun on the horizon	Condense, Circle, Time	q	
		ר	Resh	Head of a man	First, Top, Beginning	r	
		ש	Shin	Two front teeth	Sharp, Press, Eat, Two	sh	
		ת	Taw	Crossed sticks	Mark, Sign, Signal, Monument	t	
			Ghah	Rope	Twist, Dark, Wicked	gh	

Ancient Hebrew Research Center 26

SON YAHUSHA

"YAHU IS SALVATION"

יהושע

AYIN SHIN WAW HEY YAD

AHS U HAY

YAHUSHA

NO "J"

NO "V"

NO VOWEL POINTS

YAHUdim יהודים
Yah's People (Never Jews, Yah's)

YAHUdah יהודה
"Yahu Be Praised" (Tribe of Judah)

Ha YAH היה
I AM or THE YAH

EliYAHU אליהו
"My God Is Yahu"

THE BOOK OF
JUBILEES

THE TORAH CALENDAR

The Book of Jubilees was written by Moses and the Qumran community of Aaronic Levite priests kept it in their library (Bible) as Torah. There is no Biblical standard for Torah being compiled into a Pentateuch or five books which is a Pharisee paradigm. That which Moses wrote is Torah and Jubilees vets as such in our opinion.

In both sides of the margins, cross-references are provided along with dates as Jubilees records them through history. These are largely from R.H. Charles with edits and additions especially since he did not have the benefit of the Dead Sea Scrolls in his time. As Jubilees passes The Torah Test generally thus far, this will serve to further fortify such conclusion. We address what are called discrepancies throughout. Regarding the many attempted infusions of the Talmud into these footnotes, we reject that as scripture nor any measure. They actually prove Jubilees does not coalesce with the Talmud in the slightest as it cannot be a Pharisee document because it condemns much Pharisee doctrine. As such we have removed them.

PROLOGUE:

The Prologue sums up the contents of the Book as at once a history and a chronological system based upon the number seven.

i. e. according to (their year-weeks): a year-week = seven years cf. Lev. 25:8 f.

Cf. Ex. 24:12

THIS is the history of the division of the days of the law and of the testimony, of the events of the years, of their (year) weeks, of their jubilees throughout all the years of the world, as Yahuah spake to Moses on Mount Sinai when he went up to receive the tables of the law and of the commandment, according to the voice of Elohim as He said unto him, "Go up to the top of the Mount."

CHAPTER 1:

Revelation at Mt. Sinai
(1:1-26: cf. Ex. 24:15-18)

1 And it came to pass in the first year of the exodus of the children of Israel out of Egypt, in the third month, on the sixteenth day of the month, that Elohim spake to Moses, saying: "Come up to Me on the Mount, and I will give thee two tables of stone of the law and of the commandment, which I have written, that thou mayst teach them." **2** And Moses went up into the mount of Elohim, and the glory of Yahuah abode on Mount Sinai, and a cloud overshadowed it six days. **3** And He called to Moses on the seventh day out of the midst of the cloud, and the appearance of the glory of Yahuah was like a flaming fire on the top of the Mount. **4** And Moses was on the Mount forty days and forty nights, and God taught him the earlier and the later history of the division of all the days of the law and of the testimony. **5** And He said: "Incline thine heart to every word which I shall speak to thee on this Mount, and write them in a book in order that their generations may see

2450 A.M. (A.M. = Anno Mundi)

Sivan/ Shavuot is on 15th Cf. Ex. 19:1

Cf. Ex. 24:12

Cf. Ex. 34:27

how I have not forsaken them for all the evil which they have wrought in transgressing the covenant which I establish between Me and thee for their generations this day on Mount Sinai. **6** And thus it will come to pass when all these things come upon them, that they will recognize that I am more righteous than they in all their judgments and in all their actions, and they will recognize that I have been truly with them. **7** And do thou write for thyself all these words which I declare unto thee this day, for I know their rebellion and their stiff neck, before I bring them into the land of which I sware to their fathers, to Abraham and to Isaac and to Jacob, saying: "Unto your seed will I give a land flowing with milk and honey. **8** And they will eat and be satisfied, and they will turn to strange gods, to (gods) which cannot deliver them from aught of their tribulation: "and this witness shall be heard for a witness against them. **9** For they will forget all My commandments, (even) all that I command them, and they will walk after the Gentiles, and after their uncleanness, and after their shame, and will serve their gods, and these will prove unto them an offence and a tribulation and an affliction and a snare. **10** And many will perish and they will be taken captive, and will fall into the hands of the enemy, because they have forsaken My ordinances and My commandments, and the festivals of My covenant, and My sabbaths, and My holy place which I have hallowed for Myself in their midst, and My tabernacle, and My sanctuary, which I have hallowed for Myself in the midst of the land, that I should set My name upon it, and that it should dwell (there). **11** And they will make to themselves high places and groves and graven images, and they will worship, each his own (graven image), so as to go astray, and they will sacrifice their children to demons, and to all the works of the error of their hearts. **12** And I will send witnesses unto them, that I may witness against them, but they will not hear, and will slay the witnesses also, and they will persecute those who seek the law, and they will abrogate and change everything so as to work evil before My eyes. **13** And I shall hide My face from them, and I shall deliver

Cf. Dt. 30:1

Cf.1:27

Cf. Dt. 31:27

Cf. Dt. 31:20

Cf. Dt. 23:13

N. Israel is referred to.

10-13 Depict the two great catastrophies which befell Israel(10) and Judah (11-13).

i. e. the Temple in Jerusalem.

The Tabernacle is apparently thought of as still in existence (in Jerusalem) during the time of the monarchy.

i. e. Judah.

Cf. 2Chr. 33:3

Cf. 2Chr. 28:3; 33:6

Cf. 2Chr. 24:19, Nh. 9:26

Cf. Mt. 23:34, Lk. 9:49

Cf. 21:22, Is. 1:15

them into the hand of the Gentiles for captivity, and *Cf. 2Ki. 21:14* for a prey, and for devouring, and I shall remove them from the midst of the land, and I *Cf. Dt. 4:27-8* *Cf. Dt. 28:36, 64* shall scatter them amongst the Gentiles. **14** And they will forget all My law and all My commandments and all My judgments, and will go astray as to new moons, and sabbaths, and festivals, and jubilees, and ordinances.

15 And after this they will *Cf. Dt. 4:30* turn to Me from amongst the Gentiles with all their heart and with all their soul and with all their strength, and I shall *Cf. Jr. 29:14* gather them from amongst all *MESSIAH cf. 16:36, likened to "Him who made all things." Cf. 21:24 cf. 1 En. 84:6 "the flesh of righteousness and uprightness establish as a seed bearing plant forever." cf. 1 En. 93:5 "Plant of Righteous Judgment" as "a man."* the Gentiles, and they will seek Me, so that I shall be found of them, when they seek Me with all their heart and with all their soul. **16** And I shall disclose to them abounding peace with righteousness, and I shall and I will plant them the plant of uprightness in the land, with all My heart and with all My soul, and they will be for a blessing *Cf. Jr. 32:41* and not for a curse, and they *Cf. Ze. 8:13* *Cf. Dt. 28:13* will be the head and not the *Not the second Temple. His ark was not there. End times. Cf. Lv. 26:12 and often. Cf. Dt. 31:6* tail. **17** And I shall build My sanctuary in their midst, and I shall dwell with them, and I shall be their Elohim and they will be My people in truth and righteousness. **18** And I

shall not forsake them nor fail them; for I am Yahuah their Elohim." **19** And Moses fell on his face and prayed and said, "O Yahuah my Elohim, do not forsake Thy people and *Cf. Dt. 9:26* Thy inheritance, so that they should wander in the error of their hearts, and do not deliver them into the hands of their enemies, the Gentiles, lest they should rule over them and cause them to sin against Thee. **20** Let Thy mercy, O Yahuah, be lifted up upon Thy people, and create in them an upright *Cf. Ps. 51:10* spirit, and let not the spirit *Beliar (Belial) is here, as in the Ascension of Isaiah (see Introduction to that work), a Satanic being, apparently "the prince of the devils."* of Beliar rule over them to accuse them before Thee, and to ensnare them from all the paths of righteousness, so that they may perish from before Thy face. **21** But they are Thy people and Thy inheritance, which Thou hast delivered *Cf. Dt. 9:29* with Thy great power from the hands of the Egyptians: create *Cf. Ps. 51:10 (and ver. 20 above).* in them a clean heart and a holy Spirit, and let them not be ensnared in their sins from henceforth until eternity." **22** And Yahuah said unto Moses: "I know their contrariness and their thoughts and their *Cf. Dt. 31:27* stiffneckedness, and they will not be obedient till they confess their own sin and the *Cf. Lv. 26:40* sin of their fathers. **23** And after this they will

Cf. Dt. 10:16
Cf. Dt. 30:6

turn to Me in all uprightness and with all (their) heart and with all (their) soul, and I shall circumcise the foreskin of their heart and the foreskin of the heart of their seed, and I shall create in them a holy spirit, and I shall cleanse them so that they shall not turn away from Me from that day unto eternity. **24** And their souls will cleave to Me and to all My commandments, and they will fulfil My commandments, and I shall be their Abba and they will be My children. **25** And they will all be called children of the living Elohim, and every angel and every spirit will know, yea, they will know that these are My children, and that I am their Abba in uprightness and righteousness, and that I love them. **26** And do thou write down for thyself all these words which I declare unto thee on this mountain, the first and the last, which shall come to pass in all the divisions of the days in the law and in the testimony and in the weeks and the jubilees unto eternity, until I descend and dwell with them throughout eternity."

Abba, Father title origin. Cf. Mk. 14:16, Rom 8:15, Gal. 4:6 Messiah uses the title of Yahuah from Jubilees. Cf. 19:29 Messiah quoted Jubilees.

Cf. Hs. 1:10

Viz. those written in the Book of the First Law (6:22 = the Law of Creation), which was written by the angel himself. The First Law was not the Law of Moses as Adam, Enoch, Noah and Abraham all had Law. Otherwise, they could never be judged righteous. Cf. 7:20-21

viz. in the perfect theocracy inaugurated by the Messianic Kingdom.

Yahuah Commands The Angel To Write *(i. 27-29)*

27 And He said to the Angel of the Presence: "Write for Moses from the beginning of creation till My sanctuary has been built among them for all eternity. **28** And Yahuah will appear to the eyes of all, and all will know that I am the Elohim of Israel and the Abba of all the children of Jacob, and King on Mount Zion for all eternity. And Zion and Jerusalem will be holy." **29** And the Angel of the Presence who went before the camp of Israel took the tables of the divisions of the years -- from the time of the creation -- of the law and of the testimony of the weeks, of the jubilees, according to the individual years, according to all the number of the jubilees [according to the individual years], from the day of the [new] creation †when† the heavens and the earth shall be renewed and all their creation according to the powers of the heaven, and according to all the creation of the earth, until the sanctuary of Yahuah shall be made in Jerusalem on Mount Zion, and all the luminaries be renewed for healing and for peace and for blessing for all the elect of Israel, and that thus it may be from that day and unto all the days of the earth.

Cf. Acts 7:53 "received the law by the disposition of angels." Cf. Gal. 3:19 "The Law... ordained through angels" Is. 63:9; Test. 12 Patr., Judah 25

Cf. Rev. 1:7 (in the final theophany).

Cf. 1:24. Jr. 31:1

Cf. Is. 24:23

Cf. Ex. 14:19

†Text corrupt. Read "from the day of creation, till the heavens."

i. e. in the Messianic Kingdom.

Cf. Rev. 22:2

CHAPTER 2:

The Angel dictates to Moses the Primæval History: the Creation of the World and Institution of the Sabbath

(2:1-33; cf. Gen. 1-2:3)

Cf. Gn. 2:2-3 The Sabbath was "hallowed," set apart as holy the seventh day of Creation. The word Sabbath in Hebrew appears in Gn. 2 also.

Jub. nor Gn. attribute darkness, the waters, the abysses as being created on the 1st day of Creation. No angels fell before they were created and no evil existed yet. Angels are not assigned a Creation role necessarily.

Cf. 2:18, 15:27, 31:14. These are the two chief orders of angels. The "angels of sanctification" sing praises to God.

The various classes of angels that follow constitute the third or lowest order. They preside over the elements and natural phenomena; cf. 1 En. 40:12-21, 75, 80; For the "angels of the winds," cf. Rev. 7:1 f.; 1 En. 18:1-5, 34-36, 76.

Cf. En. 40:17-18

Cf. Rev. 4:5, 11:19, 16:18

Cf. 1 En. 9:13-15

1 And the Angel of the Presence spake to Moses according to the word of Yahuah, saying: Write the complete history of the creation, how in six days Yahuah Elohim finished all His works and all that He created, and kept Sabbath on the seventh day and hallowed it for all ages, and appointed it as a sign for all His works. **2** For on the first day He created the heavens which are above and the earth and the waters and all the spirits which serve before Him--the Angels of the Presence, and the Angels of Sanctification, and the Angels [of the Spirit of Fire and the Angels] of the Spirit of the Winds, and the Angels of the Spirit of the clouds, and of darkness, and of snow and of hail and of hoar frost, and the Angels of the Voices and of the thunder and of the lightning, and the Angels of the Spirits of cold and of heat, and of winter and of spring and of autumn and of summer, and of all the

spirits of His creatures which are in the heavens and on the earth, (He created) the abysses and the darkness, eventide (and night), and the light, dawn and day, which He hath prepared in the knowledge of His heart. **3** And thereupon we saw His works, and praised Him, and lauded before Him on account of all His works; for seven great works did He create on the first day. **4** And on the second day He created the firmament in the midst of the waters, and the waters were divided on that day--half of them went up above and half of them went down below the firmament (that was) in the midst over the face of the whole earth. And this was the only work (Elohim) created on the second day. **5** And on the third day He commanded the waters to pass from off the face of the whole earth into one place, and the dry land to appear. **6** And the waters did so as He commanded them, and they retired from off the face of the earth into one place outside of this firmament, and the dry land appeared. **7** And on that day He created for them all the seas according to their separate gathering-places, and all the rivers, and the gatherings of the waters

Cf. 1 En. 82:13-20

Cf. Gen. 1:6-7; 2En. 26-27.

Seas with "separate gathering places" are not oceans. Yam in Hebrew is a general term for large bodies of water including the Nile River, the Dead Sea which is a lake, etc. There is no mention of an ocean prior to the Flood here nor in Gn. 2Esd. 6:42-52 notes three times that 1/7th of the world was water prior to the Flood. Cf. Gn.1:9-13

Large bodies of water, rivers and lakes compose the antediluvian construct. There was no rain but dew on the earth. Gn. 2:5.

in the mountains and on all the earth, and all the lakes, and all the dew of the earth, and the seed which is sown, and all sprouting things, and fruit-bearing trees, and trees of the wood, and the garden of Eden, in Eden, and all (plants after their kind). These four great works God created on the third day. **8** And on

Cf. Gen. 1:14-19; 2 En. 30:2-6

the fourth day He created the sun and the moon and

Note Jub. sets forth the sun as the measure for days, Sabbaths (weeks), months, feasts and years. There are feasts that begin with the moon such as Passover and the Day of Atonement but the sun is appointed as the measure. This is consistent throughout Jubilees. The moon is not omitted as suggested by Charles, it is the previous sentence and established as disrupting the calendar, Jub. 6:36-38. This matches the Gn. Creation account which on Day 1 sets forth the Day first and then night. This also proves a Pharisee did not write this book.

the stars, and set them in the firmament of the heaven, to give light upon all the earth, and to rule over the day and the night, and divide the light from the darkness. **9** And God appointed the sun to be a great sign on the earth for days and for sabbaths and for months and for feasts and for years and for sabbaths of years and for jubilees and for all seasons of the years. **10** And it divideth the light from the darkness [and] for prosperity, that all things may prosper which shoot and grow on the earth. These three kinds He made on the fourth day. **11** And on the fifth day He created great sea monsters in the depths of the waters, for these were the first things of flesh that were created by His hands, the fish and everything that moves in the waters, and

everything that flies, the birds and all their kind. **12** And the sun rose above them to prosper (them), and above everything that was on the earth, everything that shoots out of the earth, and all fruit-bearing trees, and all flesh. These three kinds He created on the fifth day. **13** And on the sixth day He created all the animals of the earth, and all cattle, and everything that moves on the earth. **14** And after all this He created man, a man and a woman created He them, and gave him dominion over all that is upon the earth, and in the seas, and over everything that flies, and over beasts and over cattle, and over everything that moves on the earth, and over the whole earth, and over all this He gave him dominion. And these four kinds He created on the sixth day. **15** And there were altogether two and twenty kinds. **16** And He finished all His work on the sixth day--all that is in the heavens and on the earth, and in the seas and in the abysses, and in the light and in the darkness, and in everything. **17** And He gave us a great sign, the Sabbath day, that we should work six days, but keep Sabbath on the seventh day from all work.

Cf. Gen. 1:20-23; 2En. 30:7 2Esd. 6:47-52. Sea monsters are inclusive of Leviathan. Job 3, 40, 41; Ps. 74:14, 104:26; Is. 27:1. It certainly is not locusts as Charles quotes a Pharisee.

Cf. Gen.1:24-28; 2 En. 30:8 f.

This appears 22 different kinds of works. It is referenced again in 2:23. Expanded note there.

This is possibly the right reading of Gen. 2:2a (so Sam. text, LXX, Syr.). It implies a severer view of Sabbath observance. The Masoretic text has "seventh." Cf. Ex. 31:13

Sabbath is for the earth too from Creation. He hid the higher classes of angels but not His Sabbath. Gentiles also keep the Sabbath in the Exodus account many times: Ex. 12:49, Num. 9:14, 15:26-29, Lev. 16:29, 18:26, 19:34, 17:12.

18 And all the Angels of the Presence, and all the Angels of Sanctification, these two great classes--He hath hidden us to keep the Sabbath with Him in heaven and on earth. **19** And He said unto us: "Behold, I will separate unto Myself a people from among all the peoples, and these will keep the Sabbath day, and I will sanctify them unto Myself

Cf. 1 Ki. 8:53

as My people, and will bless them; as I have sanctified the Sabbath day and do sanctify (it) unto Myself, even so shall I bless them, and they will be My people and I shall be their Elohim. **20** And I have

Cf. Is. 41:8, 44:1-2.

chosen the seed of Jacob from amongst all that I have seen, and have written him down

Cf. Ex. 4:22; Ps. 89:27.

as My firstborn son, and have sanctified him unto Myself

For the Sabbath day as a sign between God and Israel, cf. Ex. 31:13, 17; Ez. 20:12.

for ever and ever; and I will teach them the Sabbath day, that they may keep Sabbath thereon from all work."

However, gentiles kept Sabbath with Israel even in the Torah.

21 And thus He created therein a sign in accordance with which they should keep

i. e. with God and the superior angels.

Sabbath with us on the seventh day, to eat and to drink, and to bless Him who hath created

The Sabbath is to be a delight. Cf. Is. 58:13

all things as He hath blessed and sanctified unto Himself

Cf. Dt. 7:6

a peculiar people above all peoples, and that they should keep Sabbath together with us. **22** And He caused His commands to ascend as a

Cf. 2Cor. 2:15; Eph. 5:2

sweet savour acceptable before Him all the days. . .

23 There (were) two and

It is probable that at end of 22 above there is a lacuna in the text (indicated by the dotted line). Charles restores the missing words as follows: As there were two and twenty letters, and two and twenty (sacred) books [viz. in the Old Testament], and two and twenty heads of mankind from Adam to Jacob, so there were made two and twenty kinds of work, etc.

twenty heads of mankind from Adam to Jacob, and two and twenty kinds of work were made until the seventh day; this is blessed and holy; and the former also is blessed and holy; and this one serves with that one for sanctification and blessing. **24** And to this (Jacob and his seed) it was granted that they should always be the blessed and holy ones of the first testimony and law, even as He had sanctified and blessed the Sabbath day on the seventh day. **25** He created heaven and earth and everything

viz. the Sabbath.

that He created in six days, and Elohim made the seventh

viz. Jacob.

day holy, for all His works; therefore He commanded on its behalf that, whoever doth any work thereon shall die,

Cf. Ex. 31:14, 15, 35:2; Nm. 15:32 f.

and that he who defileth it shall surely die. **26** Wherefore do thou command the children of Israel to observe this day that they may keep it holy and

Cf. Ex. 20:8

not do thereon any work, and not to defile it, as it is holier

Cf. 2:30

than all other days. **27** And whoever profaneth it shall surely die, and whoever doeth thereon any work shall surely die eternally, that the children of Israel may observe this day throughout their generations, and not be rooted out of the land; for it is a holy day and a blessed day. **28** And every one who observeth it and keepeth Sabbath thereon from all his work, will be holy and blessed throughout all days like unto us. **29** Declare and say to the children of Israel the law of this day both that they should keep Sabbath thereon, and that they should not forsake it in the error of their hearts; (and) that it is not lawful to do any work thereon which is unseemly, to do thereon their *Cf. Is. 58:13* own pleasure, and that they should not prepare thereon *†Deduced from Ex. 16:23, 25* anything to be eaten or drunk. †and (that it is not lawful) to *The obelized words should either be omitted or read after their own pleasure above. For the law about "bringing in or taking out … any burden" on the Sabbath, cf. 2:30, 1:8; Jr. 17:21 f.; Nh. 8:19; Jn 10:10.* draw water, or bring in or take out thereon through their gates any burden,† which they had not prepared for themselves on the sixth day in their dwellings. **30** And they shall not bring in nor take out *Cf. 50:12; Ex. 35:2-3* from house to house on that day; for that day is more holy and blessed than any jubilee day of the jubilees: on this we *Cf. Jr. 17:22* kept Sabbath in the heavens before it was made known to any flesh to keep Sabbath thereon on the earth. **31** And the Creator of all things blessed it, but He did *i.e. Israel.* not sanctify all peoples and nations to keep Sabbath thereon, but Israel alone: them alone He permitted to eat and drink and to keep Sabbath thereon on the earth. **32** And the Creator of all things blessed this day which He had created for a blessing and a sanctification and a glory above all days. **33** This law and testimony was given to the children of Israel *Cf. Ex. 27:21, etc., for the phrase.* as a law for ever unto their generations.

CHAPTER 3:

Paradise and the Fall

(3:1-35; cf. Gen. 2:4-3)

1 And on the six days of the second week we brought, according to the word of Elohim, unto Adam all the beasts, and all the cattle, and all the birds, and everything that moveth on the earth, and everything that moveth in the water, according to their kinds, and according to their types: the beasts on the first day; the cattle on the second day; the birds on the third day; and all that which moveth on the earth on the fourth day; and that which moveth in the water on the fifth day. 2 And Adam named them all by their respective names, and as *Cf. Gn. 2:19* he called them, so was their name. 3 And on these five days Adam saw all these, male and female, according to every kind that was on the earth, but he was alone and found *Cf. Gn. 2:20* no helpmeet for him. 4 And Yahuah said unto us: "It is not good that the man should be alone: let us make a helpmeet *Cf. Gn. 2:18; LXX and* for him." 5 And Yahuah our *Vulg. have pl.* Elohim caused a deep sleep *("let us make* to fall upon him, and he slept, *), but MT* and He took for the woman *Sam. Syr., "I* one rib from amongst his ribs, *will make."* and this rib was the origin of the woman from amongst his ribs, and He built up the flesh in its stead, and built the woman. 6 And He awaked Adam out of his sleep and on awaking he rose on the sixth day, and He brought her to him, and he knew her, and said unto her: "This is now bone of my bones and flesh of my flesh; she will be called [my] wife; because she was taken from her husband." 7 Therefore shall man and wife be one, and therefore shall a man leave his father and his mother, and cleave unto his wife, and they shall be one flesh. 8 In the first week was Adam created, and the rib--his wife: in the second week He showed her unto him: and for this reason the commandment was given to keep in their defilement, for a male seven days, and for a female twice seven days. 9 And after Adam had completed forty days in the land where he had been created, we brought him into the Garden of Eden to till and keep it, but his wife they brought in on the eightieth day, and after this she entered into the Garden of Eden. 10 And for this reason the commandment is written on the heavenly tables in regard to her that giveth birth: "if she beareth a male, she shall

Cf. Gn. 2:21-23

Cf. Gn. 2:24

For these laws cf. Lv. 12: 2-5, according to which in the one case the mother was not to enter the sanctuary till the lapse of forty days, in the other eighty days. The reason for this is given in the following section (9), according to the author of Jubilees. This peculiar idea recurs elsewhere (Philo, Book of Adam and Eve), but not in Rabbinic literature, except for some slight traces. See Charles, ad loc. Cf. 1 En. 81:1, 2, 93:2, 103:2; the expression also occurs in Test. 12 Patriarchs. In our Book the heavenly tables are conceived of as the divine statute book of which the Mosaic Law is the earthly reproduction.

remain in her uncleanness seven days according to the first week of days, and thirty and three days shall she remain in the blood of her purifying, and she shall not touch any hallowed thing, nor enter into the sanctuary, until she accomplisheth these days which (are enjoined) in the case of a male child.

11 But in the case of a female child she shall remain in her uncleanness two weeks of days, according to the first two weeks, and sixty-six days in the blood of her purification, and they will be in all eighty days." **12** And when she had completed these eighty days we brought her into the Garden of Eden, for it is holier than all the earth besides, and every tree that is planted in it is holy. **13** Therefore, there was ordained regarding her who beareth a male or a female child the statute of those days that she should touch no hallowed thing, nor enter into the sanctuary until these days for the male or female child are accomplished. **14** This is the law and testimony which was written down for Israel, in order that they should observe (it) all the days. **15** And in the first week of the first jubilee, Adam and his wife were in the Garden of Eden for seven years tilling and keeping it, and we gave him work and we instructed him to do everything that is suitable for tillage. **16** And he tilled (the garden), and was naked and knew it not, and was not ashamed, and he protected the garden from the birds and beasts and cattle, and gathered its fruit, and ate, and put aside the residue for himself and for his wife [and put aside that which was being kept].

17 And after the completion of the seven years, which he had completed there, seven years exactly, and in the second month, on the seventeenth day (of the month), the serpent came and approached the woman, and the serpent said to the woman, "Hath God commanded you, saying, Ye shall not eat of every tree of the garden?" **18** And she said to it, "Of all the fruit of the trees of the garden Elohim hath said unto us, Eat; but of the fruit of the tree which is in the midst of the garden Elohim hath said unto us, Ye shall not eat thereof, neither shall ye touch it, lest ye die." **19** And the serpent said unto the woman, "Ye shall not surely die: for Elohim doth

1-7 A.M.

Jub. carries far more weight than a Talmudic claim that Adam was in the Garden for only 6 hours. Gn. does not breach this.

Agriculture is a divine institution. Here the instruction is given by angels; contrast Is. 28:26-29. See also 2Esd. 6:42. Test. 12 Patr. Issachar 3 Cf. Gn. 2:25. The bracketed words are a dittograph

For 17-22 cf. Gn. 3:1-7

8 A.M.

Cf. 5:23 **SAME DAY THE ARK DOOR WAS CLOSED BY YAHUAH.**

know that on the day ye shall eat thereof, your eyes will be opened, and ye will be as gods, and ye will know good and evil." **20** And the woman saw the tree that it was agreeable and pleasant to the eye, and that its fruit was good for food, and she took thereof and ate. **21** And when she had first covered her shame with fig-leaves, she gave thereof to Adam and he ate, and his eyes were opened, and he saw that he was naked. **22** And he took fig-leaves and sewed (them) together, and made an apron for himself, and covered his shame. **23** And Elohim cursed the serpent, and was wroth with it for ever. . . . **24** And He was wroth with the woman, because she hearkened to the voice of the serpent, and did eat; and He said unto her: I shall greatly multiply thy sorrow and thy pains in sorrow thou shalt bring forth children, and thy return shall be unto thy husband, and he will rule over thee." **25** And to Adam also He said, "Because thou hast hearkened unto the voice of thy wife, and hast eaten of the tree of which I commanded thee that thou shouldst not eat thereof, cursed be the ground for thy sake: thorns and thistles shall

it bring forth to thee, and thou shalt eat thy bread in the sweat of thy face, till thou returnest to the earth from whence thou wast taken; for earth thou art, and unto earth shalt thou return."

26 And He made for them coats of skin, and clothed them, and sent them forth from the Garden of Eden. **27** And on that day on which Adam went forth from the garden, he offered as a sweet savour an offering, frankincense, galbanum, and stacte, and spices in the morning with the rising of the sun from the day when he covered his shame. **28** And on that day was closed the mouth of all beasts, and of cattle, and of birds, and of whatever walketh, and of whatever moveth, so that they could no longer speak: for they had all spoken one with another with one lip and with one tongue. **29** And He sent out of the Garden of Eden all flesh that was in the Garden of Eden, and all flesh was scattered according to its kinds, and according to its types unto the places which had been created for them. **30** And to Adam alone did He give (the wherewithal) to cover his shame, of all the beasts and cattle. **31** On this

Charles suspects a lacuna here. It may have contained a statement to the effect that the serpent's four feet, which it is supposed to have originally possessed, were cut off. Cf. Targ. Ps.-Jon. on Gn. 3:14, and Josephus, Ant. 1:1, 4.

Cf. Gn. 3. M

Cf. Gn. 2:10-12

הוילה: havilah: that suffers pain; that brings forth. Land of Havah/Eve named for this curse.

So LXX and Syr. (ἡ ἀποστ ραφή σου), MT, "thy desire."

Cf. Gn.2:17-19, 21, 24

i. e. the incense-offering of Ex. 30:34; Cf. Cave of Treasures specifies gold, frankincense and myrrh same as Queen of Sheba and Wise Kings brought from same land repeating Adam's.

For this belief cf. Josephus, Ant. i. 1, 4. The idea underlying the text here is that up to this time both men and animals spoke Hebrew, which was the universal language till the building of the Tower of Babel. Cf. 12:25-26, 43:15.

We strongly disagree with Charles that this uncovering is new in the Hellenistic period as this is Adam and Eve who cover their shame first just as in Gn. 3:7. Then, Yahuah covers their shame in Gn. 3:21. Egyptians and others who worship fertility goddesses practiced sex rituals.

account, it is prescribed on the heavenly tables as touching all those who know the judgment of the law, that they should cover their shame, and should not uncover themselves as the Gentiles uncover themselves. **32** And on the new moon of the fourth month, Adam and his wife went forth from the Garden of Eden, and they dwelt in the land of 'Eldâ, in the land of their creation.

33 And Adam called the name of his wife Eve. **34** And they had no son till the first jubilee, and after this he knew her. **35** Now he tilled the land as he had been instructed in the Garden of Eden.

8 A.M.

Charles suggests that 'Elda may be a corruption of the Hebrew word meaning "nativity" (land of "nativity"). Adam and Eve's land of nativity was the land of Creation NOT Israel but the Philippines according to this book. See Ch. 8 Maps.

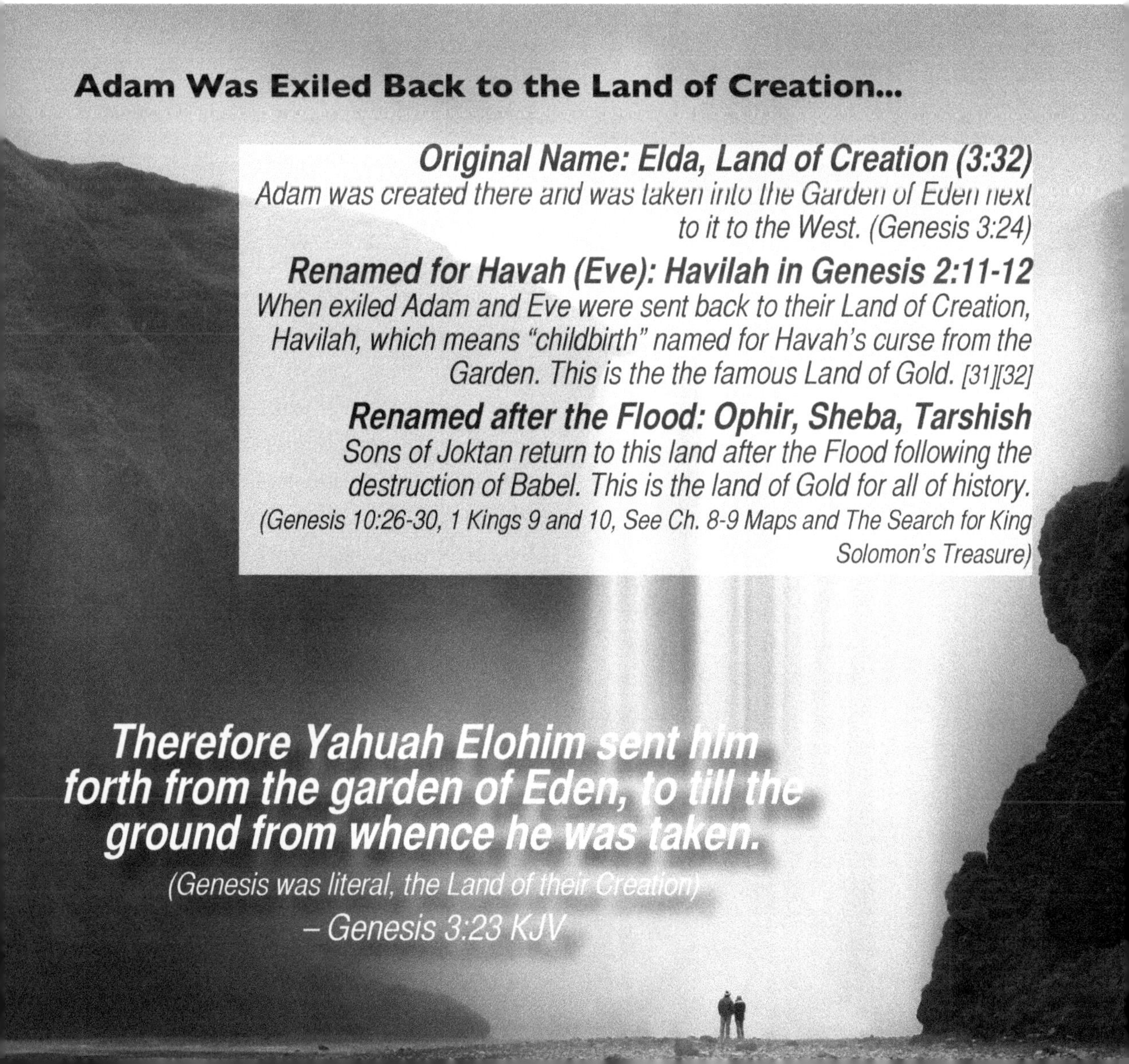

Adam Was Exiled Back to the Land of Creation...

Original Name: Elda, Land of Creation (3:32)
Adam was created there and was taken into the Garden of Eden next to it to the West. (Genesis 3:24)

Renamed for Havah (Eve): Havilah in Genesis 2:11-12
When exiled Adam and Eve were sent back to their Land of Creation, Havilah, which means "childbirth" named for Havah's curse from the Garden. This is the the famous Land of Gold. [31][32]

Renamed after the Flood: Ophir, Sheba, Tarshish
Sons of Joktan return to this land after the Flood following the destruction of Babel. This is the land of Gold for all of history.
(Genesis 10:26-30, 1 Kings 9 and 10, See Ch. 8-9 Maps and The Search for King Solomon's Treasure)

Therefore Yahuah Elohim sent him forth from the garden of Eden, to till the ground from whence he was taken.
(Genesis was literal, the Land of their Creation)
– Genesis 3:23 KJV

CHAPTER 4:

Cain and Abel
(4:1-12; cf. Gen. 4)

64-70 A.M.
71-77 A.M.
78-84 A.M.
i.e. "to eye, look at" (Heb. Awan)
99-105 A.M.

1 And in the third week in the second jubilee she gave birth to Cain, and in the fourth she gave birth to Abel, and in the fifth she gave birth to her daughter 'Âwân. **2** And in the first (year) of the third jubilee, Cain slew Abel because (Elohim) accepted the sacrifice of Abel, and did not accept the offering of Cain. **3** And he slew him in the field: and his blood cried from the ground to heaven, complaining because he had slain him.

Cf. Gn. 4:4, 5, 8, 10

4 And Yahuah reproved Cain because of Abel, because he had slain him, and he made him a fugitive on the earth because of the blood of his brother, and he cursed him upon the earth. **5** And on this account it is written on the heavenly tables, "Cursed is he who smiteth his neighbour treacherously, and let all who have seen and heard say, So be it; and the man who hath seen and not declared (it), let him be accursed as the other." **6** And for this reason we announce when we come before Yahuah our Elohim all the sin which is committed in heaven and on earth, and in light and in darkness, and

Cf. Gn. 4:11-12

Cf. Deut. 27:24

everywhere. **7** And Adam and his wife mourned for Abel four weeks of years, and in the fourth year of the fifth week they became joyful, and Adam knew his wife again, and she bare him a son, and he called his name Seth; for he said "Elohim hath raised up a second seed unto us on the earth instead of Abel; for Cain slew him."

99-127 A.M.

So Sam.; but MT "she." In our Book it is generally the father who names the child.

Cf. Gn. 4:25

8 And in the sixth week he begat his daughter 'Azûrâ. **9** And Cain took 'Âwân his sister to be his wife and she bare him Enoch at the close of the fourth jubilee. And in the first year of the first week of the fifth jubilee, houses were built on the earth, and Cain built a city, and called its name after the name of his son Enoch. **10** And Adam knew Eve his wife and she bare yet nine sons. **11** And in the fifth week of the fifth jubilee Seth took 'Azûrâ his sister to be his wife, and in the fourth (year of the sixth week) she bare him Enos. **12** He began to call on the name of the Lord on the earth.

134-140 A.M.

Cf. Gn. 4:17

190-196 A.M.

197 A.M.

Pseudo-Philo, Bibl. Antiq., gives the names of these nine sons.

225-231 A.M.

235 A.M.

Cf. Gn. 4:26

So LXX and Vulg.; but MT "then it was begun (men began)."

The Patriarchs from Adam to Noah *(cf. Gen. 5)*; Life of Enoch; Death of Adam and Cain *(4:13-33)*

13 And in the seventh jubilee in the third week Enos took

309-315 A.M.

For 13-14 cf. Gn. 5:9, 12

325 A.M.

Nôâm his sister to be his wife, and she bare him a son in the third year of the fifth week, and he called his name Kenan. **14** And at the close of the eighth jubilee Kenan took

386-392 A.M.

A fem. form = "she who praises God."

Mûalêlêth his sister to be his wife, and she bare him a son in the ninth jubilee, in the

395 A.M.

first week in the third year of this week, and he called his name Mahalalel. **15** And

449-455 A.M.

in the second week of the tenth jubilee Mahalalel took unto him to wife Dînâh, the daughter of Barâkî'êl the daughter of his father's brother, and she bare him a

461 A.M.

son in the third week in the sixth year, and he called his

Cf. Gn. 5:15

name Jared; for in his days the angels of Yahuah descended on the earth, those who are

Cf. 1 En. 6:6; Gn. 6:1-4

named the Watchers, that they

Cf. 1 En. 1:5, 10:9, 15 and often

should instruct the children

According to 1 Enoch, Enoch acquired his supernatural knowledge from the instruction of angels.

of men, and that they should do judgment and uprightness on the earth. **16** And in the eleventh jubilee Jared took to himself a wife, and her name was Bâraka, the daughter of

512-518 A.M.

Râsûjâl, a daughter of his father's brother, in the fourth

522 A.M.

week of this jubilee, and she bare him a son in the fifth week, in the fourth year of the jubilee, and he called his name

Cf. Gn. 5:18

Enoch. **17** And he was the first among men that are born on earth who learnt writing and

1 En. 6-16, 23-36, 72-110

knowledge and wisdom and who wrote down the signs of

1 En. 12:4, 15:1 "scribe of righteousness."

heaven according to the order

of their months in a book,

1 En. 72-82

that men might know the seasons of the years according to the order of their separate months. **18** And he was the first to write a testimony, and he testified to the sons of men among the generations of the earth, and recounted the weeks of the jubilees, and made known to them the days of the years, and set in order the months and recounted the Sabbaths of the years as we made (them) known to him.

19 And what was and what will be he saw in a vision of his sleep, as it will happen to the

1 En. 83-110

children of men throughout their generations until the day of judgment; he saw

1 En., Test. XII. Patriarchs

and understood everything, and wrote his testimony, and placed the testimony on earth for all the children of men and for their generations.

20 And in the twelfth jubilee, in the seventh week thereof, he

582-588 A.M.

took to himself a wife, and her name was Ednî, the daughter

Edna in 1 En. 85:33

of Dânêl, the daughter of his father's brother, and in the

587 A.M.

sixth year in this week she bare him a son and he called

Cf. Gn. 5:21

his name Methuselah. **21** And

was moreover with the angels of Elohim these six jubilees of years, and they showed him everything which is on earth and in the heavens, the rule of the sun, and he wrote down everything. **22** And he testified to the Watchers, who had sinned with the daughters of men; for these had begun to unite themselves, so as to be defiled, with the daughters of men, and Enoch testified against (them) all. **23** And he was taken from amongst the children of men, and we conducted him into the Garden of Eden in majesty and honour, and behold there he writeth down the condemnation and judgment of the world, and all the wickedness of the children of men. **24** And on account of it (God) brought the waters of the flood upon all the land of Eden; for there he was set as a sign and that he should testify against all the children of men, that he should recount all the deeds of the generations until the day of condemnation. **25** And he burnt the incense of the sanctuary, (even) sweet spices, acceptable before Yahuah on the Mount.

26 For Yahuah hath four places on the earth, the Garden of Eden, and the Mount of the East, and this mountain on which thou art this day, Mount Sinai, and Mount Zion (which) will be sanctified in the new creation for a sanctification of the earth; through it will the earth be sanctified from all (its) guilt and its uncleanness throughout the generations of the world. **27** And in the fourteenth jubilee Methuselah took unto himself a wife, Ednâ the daughter of 'Âzrîâl, the daughter of his father's brother, in the third week, in the first year of this week, and he begat a son and called his name Lamech. **28** And in the fifteenth jubilee in the third week Lamech took to himself a wife, and her name was Bêtênôs the daughter of Bârâkî'îl, the daughter of his father's brother, and in this week she bare him a son and he called his name Noah, saying, "This one will comfort me for my trouble and all my work, and for the ground which Yahuah hath cursed." **29** And at the close of the nineteenth jubilee, in the seventh week in the sixth year thereof, Adam died, and all his sons buried him in the land of his creation, and he was the first to be buried in the earth. **30** And he lacked seventy years of one thousand

Cf. En.23-36 This is why Noah knew the entire earth as you will see in the mapping in Ch. 8-9.

Cf. En.70:1-3

Cf. En.12:3 f, 14:1

Cf. 2 En.34:3

Enoch is not in Heaven but resides in the Garden of Eden until Day of Judgment. Eden is not the Garden.

Cf. 10:17

Cf. Cave of Treasures. Gold, frankincense and myrrh.

Cf. Ex.30:7

Three of these places are connected with critical events in the history of the world; Eden (with Adam), Sinai (with Moses), Zion (with David). Garden of Eden and Mt. of the East are together and one will find them located in the Chapter 8 commentary as Jub. maps these firmly.

Cf. 1:29

652 A.M.

654 A.M.

Cf. Gn. 5:25

707 A.M.

Cf. Gn. 5:29

930 A.M.

Cf. 3:32

years; for one thousand years are as one day in the testimony of the heavens and therefore was it written concerning the tree of knowledge: "On the day that ye eat thereof ye will die." For this reason he did not complete the years of this day; for he died during it. **31** At the close of this jubilee Cain was killed after him in the same year; for his house fell upon him and he died in the midst of his house, and he was killed by its stones, for with a stone he had killed Abel, and by a stone was he killed in righteous judgment. **32** For this reason it was ordained on the heavenly tables: "With the instrument with which a man killeth his neighbour with the same shall he be killed; after the manner that he wounded him, in like manner shall they deal with him." **33** And in the twenty-fifth jubilee Noah took to himself a wife, and her name was 'Ĕmzârâ, the daughter of Râkê'êl, the daughter of his father's brother, in the first year in the fifth week: and in the third year thereof she bare him Shem, in the fifth year thereof she bare him Ham, and in the first year in the sixth week she bare him Japheth.

Cf. Gn. 2:14, 3:8, 2 Pt. 3:8, Ps. 90:4 Adam died the very day he sinned before 1000 years which is one day to Yahuah. **Peter is likely quoting Jubilees.** *Ps. is not direct.*

Cf. Ex. 21:24, Lv. 24:19

1205 A.M.

Cf. Gn. 5:32, 7:13, 9:18, 10:1, 1Ch. 1:4 All place Shem first as the eldest.

1207 A.M.

1209 A.M.

1212 A.M.

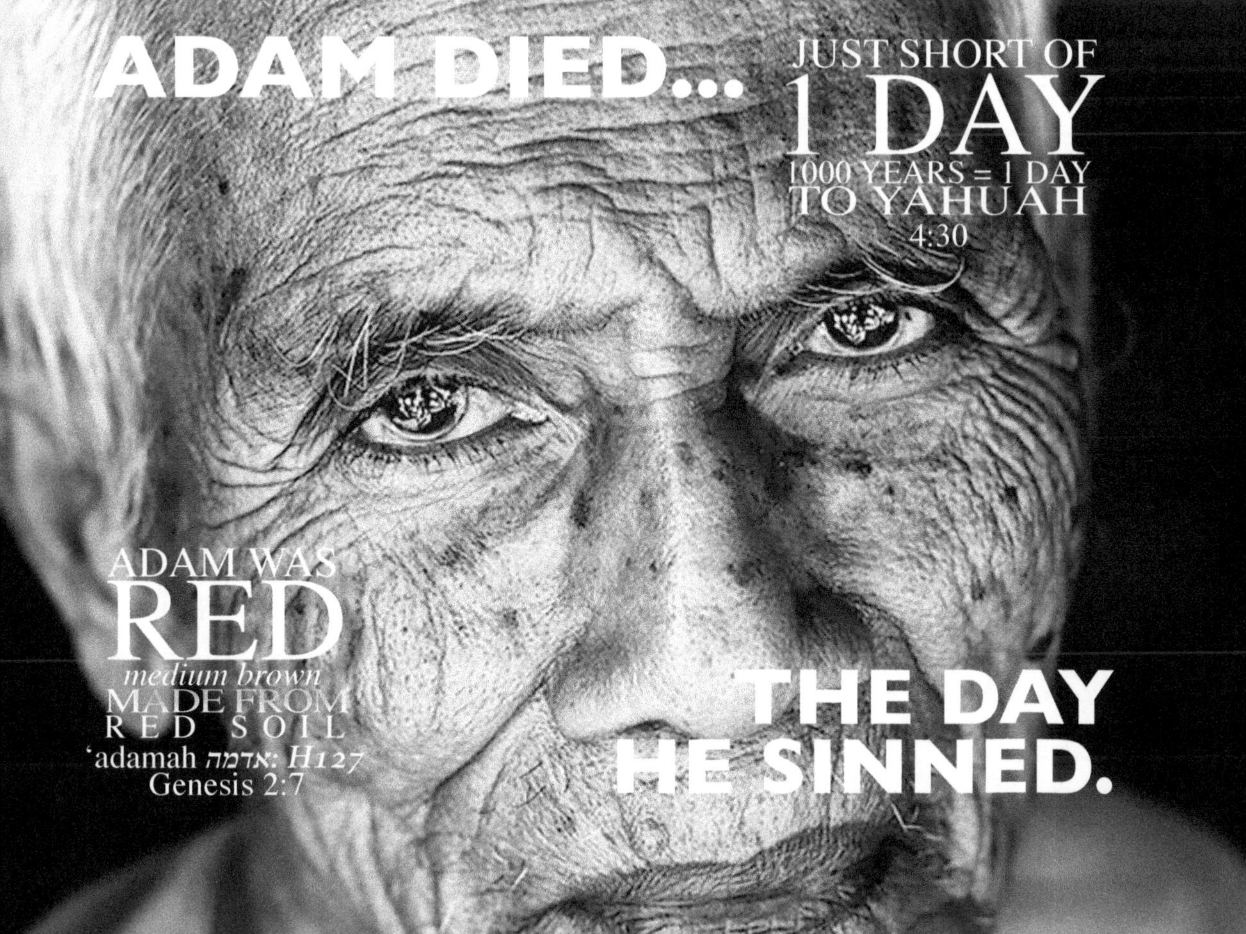

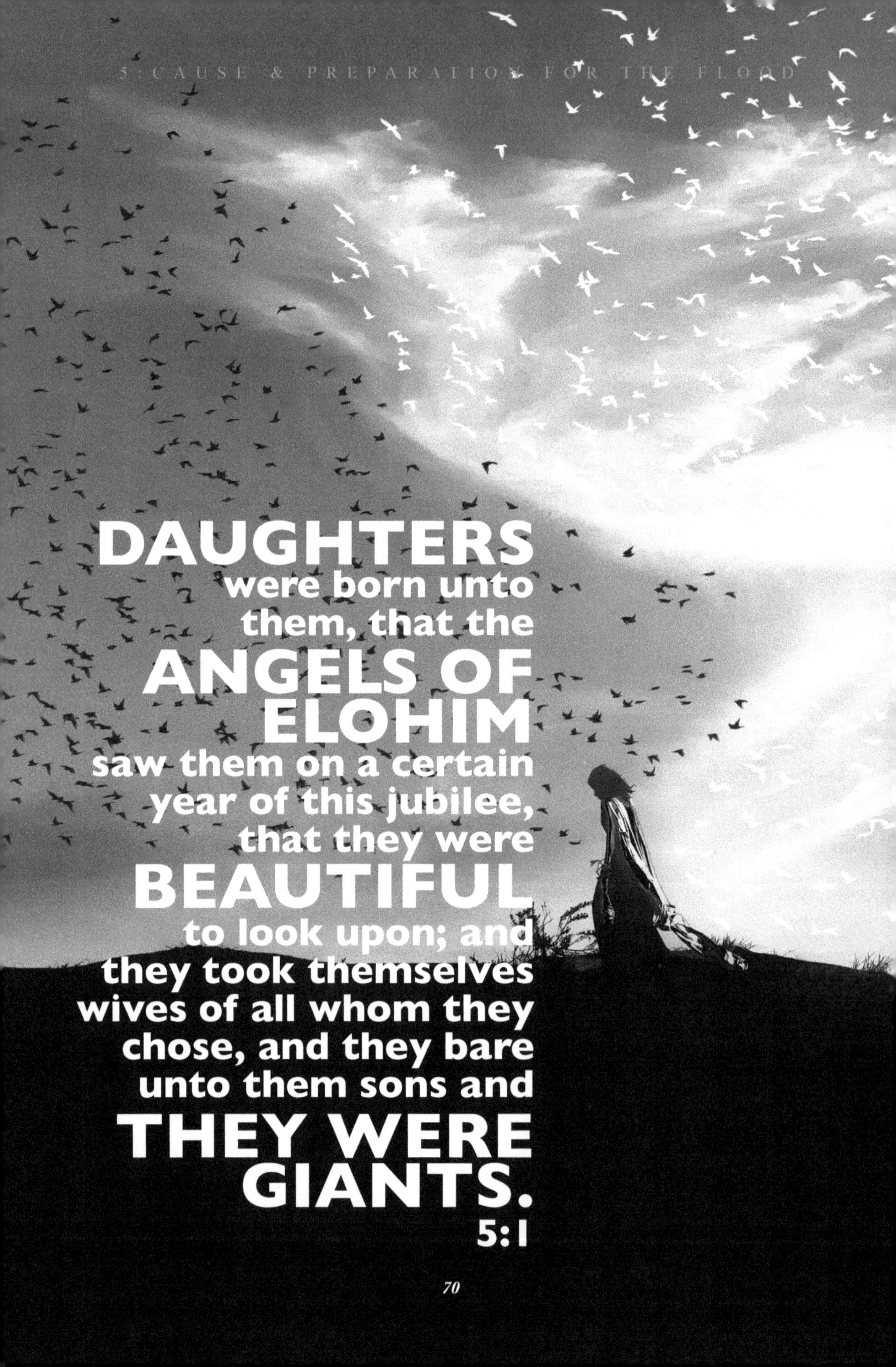

DAUGHTERS were born unto them, that the **ANGELS OF ELOHIM** saw them on a certain year of this jubilee, that they were **BEAUTIFUL** to look upon; and they took themselves wives of all whom they chose, and they bare unto them sons and **THEY WERE GIANTS.**

5:1

CHAPTER 5:

Fall of the Angels and their Punishment; the Deluge foretold
(5:1-20; cf. Gen. 6:1-12)

This is the LXX rendering of Gn. 6:2 (R.V. "sons of God"). Rabbis have no authority to change Gn., Jb., En., nor Hebrew.

1 And it came to pass when the children of men began to multiply on the face of the earth and daughters were born unto them, that the angels of Elohim saw them on a certain year of this jubilee, that they were beautiful to look upon; and they took themselves wives of all whom they chose, and they bare unto them sons and they were giants. **2** And lawlessness increased on the earth and all flesh corrupted its way, alike men and cattle and beasts and birds and everything that walketh on the earth-all of them corrupted their ways and their orders, and they began to devour each other, and lawlessness increased on the earth and every imagination of the thoughts of all men (was) thus evil continually. **3** And Elohim looked upon the earth, and behold it was corrupt, and all flesh had corrupted its orders, and all that were upon the earth had wrought all manner of evil before His eyes. **4** And He said: "I shall destroy man and all flesh upon the face of the earth which I have created." **5** But Noah found grace before the eyes of Yahuah.

Giants, i. e. "Nephilim." Humans breeding does not bring giants nor cause flesh to be corrupted.

Cf. Gn. 6:12

Cf. 1 En. 7:5

Cf. Gn. 6:5

Cf. Gn. 6:12

Cf. Gn. 6:7,8

6 And against the angels whom He had sent upon the earth, He was exceedingly wroth, and He gave commandment to root them out of all their dominion, and He bade us to bind them in the depths of the earth, and behold they are bound in the midst of them, and are (kept) separate.

7 And against their sons went forth a command from before His face that they should be smitten with the sword, and be removed from under heaven. **8** And He said "Thy spirit will not always abide on man; for they also are flesh and their days shall be one hundred and twenty years." **9** And He sent His sword into their midst that each should slay his neighbour, and they began to slay each other till they all fell by the sword and were destroyed from the earth. **10** And their fathers were witnesses (of their destruction), and after this they were bound in the depths of the earth for ever, until the day of the great condemnation when judgment is executed on all those who have corrupted their ways and their works before Yahuah.

Cf. Gn. 6:3 Genesis has always been literal on this.

Note this is Rev. language in a book in the time frame of Gn.

Cf. 1 En. 10:12

†10-12, as Charles has shown, describe the final judgment. The tenses must be altered from past to future. Render: "until the day of the great condemnation, when judgment shall be executed.. . . And He shall destroy . . . and there shall not be left one of them whom He shall not have judged. . . . And He shall make," etc.

Cf. 2 Cor. 5:17 Paul's "new creature" originates in this same renewal since the Flood as "...He made for all His works a new and righteous nature." Paul is not offering new doctrine but quoting the Book of Jubilees.

11 And He †destroyed† all from their places, and there †was† not left one of them whom He judged not according to all their wickedness. **12** And He †made† for all His works a new and righteous nature, so that they should not sin in their whole nature for ever, but should be all righteous each in his kind alway. **13** And the judgment of all is ordained and written on the heavenly tables in righteousness--even (the judgment of) all who depart from the path which is ordained for them to walk in; and if they walk not therein judgment is written down for every creature and for every kind. **14** And there is nothing in heaven or on earth, or in light or in darkness, or in Sheol or in the depth, or in the place of darkness (which is not judged); and all their judgments are ordained and written and engraved. **15** In regard to all He will judge, the great according to his greatness, and the small according to his smallness, and each according to his way. **16** And He is not one who will regard the person (of any), nor is He one who will receive gifts, if He saith that He will execute judgment on each: if one gave everything that is on the earth, He will not regard the gifts or the person (of any), nor accept anything at his hands, for He is a righteous judge. [**17** And of the children of Israel it hath been written and ordained: If they turn to Him in righteousness, He will forgive all their transgressions and pardon all their sins. **18** It is written and ordained that He will show mercy to all who turn from all their guilt once each year.] **19** And as for all those who corrupted their ways and their thoughts before the flood, no man's person was accepted save that of Noah alone; for his person was accepted in behalf of his sons, whom (Elohim) saved from the waters of the flood on his account; for his heart was righteous in all his ways, according as it was commanded regarding him, and he had not departed from aught that was ordained for him. **20** And Yahuah said that He would destroy everything which was upon the earth, both men and cattle, and beasts, and fowls of the air, and that which moveth on the earth.

Cf. 40:8; Dt. 10:17; 2 Chr. 19:7

The bracketed clauses have been either transposed here or interpolated from 34:18-19. The reference is to the Day of Atonement which takes place on the 10th of the 7th month. For "once each year," cf. Heb. 9:7.

Cf. Gn. 6:7

The Building of the Ark; the Flood
(5:21-32; cf. Gen. 6:13-8:19)

21 And He commanded Noah to make him an ark,

Cf. Gn. 6:14

1307 A.M.

that he might save himself from the waters of the flood. **22** And Noah made the ark in all respects as He commanded him, in the twenty-seventh jubilee of years, in the fifth week in the fifth year (on the new moon of the first month). **23** And he entered in the sixth (year) thereof, in the second month, on the new moon of the second month, till the sixteenth; and he entered,

1308 A.M.

Cf. 3:17. SAME DAY ADAM AND EVEN EXILED FROM THE GARDEN. 2ND MONTH, 17TH DAY.

and all that we brought to him, into the ark, and Yahuah closed it from without on the seventeenth evening. **24** And Yahuah opened seven flood-gates of heaven, And the mouths of the fountains of

Cf. Gn. 7:16

Cf. Gn. 7:11

Cf. 1 En 89:2. Note the recurrence of the number seven in these connections.

the great deep, seven mouths in number. **25** And the flood-gates began to pour down water from the heaven forty days and forty nights, And the fountains of the deep also sent up waters, until the whole world was full of water.

Cf. Gn. 7:20 We now have confirmation Gn. has always meant the Flood rose to 15 cubits aboutthe tallest mountain. The ark landed at Flood peak on the tallest mountain on day 150.

26 And the waters increased upon the earth Fifteen cubits did the waters rise above all the high mountains, And the ark was lift up above the earth, And it moved upon the face of the waters. **27** And the water prevailed on the face of the earth five months-one hundred and fifty days. **28** And the ark went and

For 24-26 cf. Gn. 7:11, 12, 18, 20

Cf. Gn. 7:24, 8:3

rested on the top of Lûbâr, one of the mountains of Ararat.

Cf. Gn.8:4. Lubar is mentioned again in vii. 1, 17.

29 And (on the new moon) in the fourth month the fountains of the great deep were closed and the flood-gates of heaven were restrained; and on the new moon of the seventh month all the mouths of the abysses of the earth were opened, and the water began to descend into the deep below.

Cf. Gn.8:2. 1 1 En. 89:7

30 And on the new moon of the tenth month the tops of the mountains were seen, and on the new moon of the first month the earth became visible. **31** And the waters disappeared from above the earth in the fifth week in the seventh year thereof, and on the seventeenth day in the second month the earth was dry. **32** And on the twenty-seventh thereof he opened the ark, and sent forth from it beasts, and cattle, and birds, and every moving thing.

1309 A.M.

Cf. Gn. 8:5, 13

Cf. Gn. 8:13, 14. This matches Gn. as the ground was dried from the 1st day of the 1st month through the 27th day of the 2nd month. The 17th of the 2nd month fits within and Noah exited the ark on the 27th in both accounts. Reading Jub. 6:25 defines the 27th day as the day the earth dried and Noah left the ark.

Cf. Gn. 8:19

CHAPTER 6:

Noah's Sacrifice; Yahuah's Covenant with him *(cf. Gen. 8:20-9:17)*. Instructions to Moses about eating of Blood, the Feast of Weeks, etc., and Division of the Year
(6:1-38)

1 And on the new moon of the third month he went forth from the ark, and built an altar on that mountain.

Cf. Gn. 8:20
The mountain is Lubar.

2 And he made atonement for the earth, and took a kid and made atonement by its blood for all the guilt of the earth; for everything that had been on it had been destroyed, save those that were in the ark with Noah. **3** And he placed the fat thereof on the altar, and he took an ox, and a goat, and a sheep and kids, and salt, and a turtle-dove, and the young of a dove, and placed a burnt sacrifice on the altar, and poured thereon an offering mingled with oil, and sprinkled wine and strewed frankincense over everything, and caused a goodly savour to arise, acceptable before Yahuah. **4** And Yahuah smelt the goodly savour, and He made a covenant with him that there should not be any more a flood to destroy the earth; that all the days of the earth seed-time and harvest should never cease; cold and heat, and summer and winter, and day and night should not change their order, nor cease for ever. **5** "And you, increase ye and multiply upon the earth, and become many upon it, and be a blessing upon it. The fear of you and the dread of you I shall inspire in everything that is on earth and in the sea. **6** And behold I have given unto you all beasts, and all winged things, and everything that moveth on the earth, and the fish in the waters, and all things for food; as the green herbs, I have given you all things to eat. **7** But flesh, with the life thereof, with the blood, ye shall not eat; for the life of all flesh is in the blood, lest your blood of your lives be required. At the hand of every man, at the hand of every (beast), shall I require the blood of man. **8** Whoso sheddeth man's blood by man shall his blood be shed; for in the image of Elohim made He man. **9** And you, increase ye, and multiply on the earth."

10 And Noah and his sons swore that they would not eat any blood that was in any flesh, and he made a covenant before Yahuah Elohim for ever

There is no atonement needed unless the law has been broken. Noah's law, similar to that of Moses is defined in Jub. 7:20. There has always been law.

Noah knew the purpose and ritual of sacrifice. Jub. 3:27 Adam and Jub. 4:25 Enoch offered sacrifices as well. This was not new. We know Abraham did as well long before the law of Moses.

Cf. 3:27, 4:25 Gn. 8:21

Cf. Gn. 9:11

Cf. Gn. 8:22

Cf. Gn. 9:7

Cf. Gn. 9:2

Cf. Gn. 9:2, 3

Cf. Gn. 9:4, 5

Cf. Gn. 9:6

throughout all the generations of the earth in this month.

11 On this account He spake to thee that thou shouldst make a covenant with the children of Israel in this month upon the mountain with an oath, and that thou shouldst sprinkle blood upon them because of all the words of the covenant, which Yahuah made with them for ever.

i. e. Moses.

The proper use of blood in the daily sacrifice is here referred to; cf. 14 below.

12 And this testimony is written concerning you that you should observe it continually, so that you should not eat on any day any blood of beasts or birds or cattle during all the days of the earth, and the man who eateth the blood of beast or of cattle or of birds during all the days of the earth, he and his seed shall be rooted out of the land. **13** And do thou command the children of Israel to eat no blood, so that their names and their seed may be before Yahuah our Elohim continually. **14** And for this law there is no limit of days, for it is for ever. They shall observe it throughout their generations, so that they may continue supplicating on your behalf with blood before the altar; every day and at the time of morning and evening they shall seek forgiveness

For 12-13 cf. Lv. 27:10, 12, 14; Dt. 12:23.

Cf. Lv. 17:2

Cf. Nm. 28:3-8.

on your behalf perpetually before Yahuah that they may keep it and not be rooted out.

15 And He gave to Noah and his sons a sign that there should not again be a flood on the earth. **16** He set His bow in the cloud for a sign of the eternal covenant that there should not again be a flood on the earth to destroy it all the days of the earth. **17** For this reason it is ordained and written on the heavenly tables, that they should celebrate the feast of weeks in this month once a year, to renew the covenant every year.

The text here returns to Noah.

Cf. Gen. 9:13-15

18 And this whole festival was celebrated in heaven from the day of creation till the days of Noah-twenty-six jubilees and five weeks of years: and Noah and his sons observed it for seven jubilees and one week of years, till the day of Noah's death, and from the day of Noah's death his sons did away with (it) until the days of Abraham, and they ate blood. **19** But Abraham observed it, and Isaac and Jacob and his children observed it up to thy days, and in thy days the children of Israel forgot it until ye celebrated it anew on this mountain. **20** And do thou command the children of Israel to observe this

The "Feast of Weeks" (cf. Ex. 34:22) is connected to Creation first. Then, Noah's covenant and in the days of Abraham before Mt. Sinai. Jub., the Torah calendar, records Shavuot on the 15th day of the 3rd month not the 6th which was chosen by a rabbi thousands of years later.

1309-1659 A.M.

festival in all their generations for a commandment unto them: one day in the year in this month they shall celebrate the festival. **21** For it is the feast of weeks and the feast of first-fruits: this feast is twofold and of a double nature: according to what is written and engraven concerning it celebrate it.

22 For I have written in the book of the first law, in that which I have written for thee, that thou shouldst celebrate it in its season, one day in the year, and I explained to thee its sacrifices that the children of Israel should remember and should celebrate it throughout their generations in this month, one day in every year.

23 And on the new moon of the first month, and on the new moon of the fourth month, and on the new moon of the seventh month, and on the new moon of the tenth month are the days of remembrance, and the days of the seasons in the four divisions of the year. These are written and ordained as a testimony for ever. **24** And Noah ordained them for himself as feasts for the generations for ever, so that they have become thereby a memorial unto him. **25** And on the new moon of the first

month he was bidden to make for himself an ark, and on that (day) the earth became dry and he opened (the ark) and saw the earth. **26** And on the new moon of thc fourth month the mouths of the depths of the abysses beneath were closed. And on the new moon of the seventh month all the mouths of the abysses of the earth were opened, and the waters began to descend into them. **27** And on the new moon of the tenth month the tops of the mountains were seen, and Noah was glad. **28** And on this account he ordained them for himself as feasts for a memorial for ever, and thus are they ordained.

29 And they placed them on the heavenly tables, each had thirteen weeks; from one to another (passed) their memorial, from the first to the second, and from the second to the third, and from the third to the fourth. **30** And all the days of the commandment will be two and fifty weeks of days, and (these will make) the entire year complete. **31** Thus it is engraven and ordained on the heavenly tables. And there is no neglecting (this commandment) for a single - year or from year to year. **32** And command thou the

The effect of a solar year reckoned at 364 days would be that the festivals would always be celebrated on the same day of the week. By the reckoning of the Qumran calendar, Nisan 14 (Passover) would always fall on a Tuesday (3rd day), Nisan 22 (First-fruits) on a Wednesday (4th day), and the Feast of Weeks, Sivan 15, on a Sunday (1st day). See intro.

The bracketed words are a dittograph.

For 33-34 cf. 1 En. 82:4-6.

children of Israel that they observe the years according to this reckoning -three hundred and sixty-four days, and (these) will constitute a complete year, and they will not disturb its time from its days and from its feasts; for everything will fall out in them according to their testimony, and they will not leave out any day nor disturb any feasts.

33 But if they do neglect and do not observe them according to His commandment, then they will disturb all their seasons, and the years will be dislodged from this (order), [and they will disturb the seasons and the years will be dislodged] and they will neglect their ordinances. **34** And all the children of Israel will forget, and will not find the path of the years, and will forget the new moons, and seasons, and sabbaths, and they will go wrong as to all the order of the years. **35** For I know and from henceforth shall I declare it unto thee, and it is not of my own devising; for the book (lieth) written before me, and on the heavenly tables the division of days is ordained, lest they forget the feasts of the covenant and walk according to the feasts of the Gentiles after their error and after their

ignorance. **36** For there will be those who will assuredly make observations of the moon-- now (it) disturbeth the seasons and cometh in from year to year ten days too soon. **37** For this reason the years will come upon them when they will disturb (the order), and make an abominable (day) the day of testimony, and an unclean day a feast day, and they will confound all the days, the holy with the unclean, and the unclean day with the holy; for they will go wrong as to the months and sabbaths and feasts and jubilees. **38** For this reason I command and testify to thee that thou mayest testify to them; for after thy death thy children will disturb (them), so that they will not make the year three hundred and sixty-four days only, and for this reason they will go wrong as to the new moons and seasons and sabbaths and festivals, and they will eat all kinds of blood with all kinds of flesh.

A lunar year is a Babylonian concept not one of the Bible. The new moon follows a 29.5 day cycle in which Jub. tests as scientifically accurate. In 12 months, following the moon throws that calendar off by 6 days + 4 days added to each quarter for exactly 10 days to soon. Nothing in the Bible disagrees with this and this is how one disturbs Yahuah's order as even the modern Hebrew calendar does. Following the moon in determining days, Sabbaths (weeks), months, years, etc. leads one to "go wrong."

*Render (for "new moons") **"beginnings of the months."** This is not "new moons."*

CHAPTER 7:

Noah offers Sacrifice; the Cursing of Canaan

(cf. Gen. 9:20-28): **Noah's Sons and Grandsons** *(cf. Gen. 10)* **and their Cities. Noah's Admonitions** *(7:1-39)*

1317 A.M. **1** And in the seventh week in the first year thereof, in this jubilee, Noah planted vines on the mountain on which the *Cf. 5:28* ark had rested, named Lûbâr, *1320 A.M.* one of the Ararat Mountains, *Cf. Lv. 19:23-25 (fruit of trees not to be touched during the first three years after planting).* *Cf. Nm. 29:.2, 5* *1321 A.M.* and they produced fruit in the fourth year, and he guarded their fruit, and gathered it in this year in the seventh month. **2** And he made wine therefrom and put it into a vessel, and kept it until the fifth year, until the first day, on the new moon of the first month. **3** And he celebrated with joy the day of this feast, and he made a burnt sacrifice unto the Lord, one young ox and one ram, and seven sheep, each a year old, and a kid of the goats, that he might make atonement thereby for himself and his sons. **4** And he prepared the kid first, and placed some of its blood on the flesh that was on the altar which he had made, and all the fat he laid on the altar where he made the burnt sacrifice, and the ox and the ram and the sheep, and he laid all their flesh upon the altar. **5** And he placed all their offerings mingled with oil upon it, and afterwards he sprinkled wine on the fire which he had previously made on the altar, and he placed incense on the altar and caused a sweet savour to ascend acceptable before Yahuah his Elohim.

6 And he rejoiced and drank of this wine, he and his children with joy. **7** And it was evening, *For 6-7 cf. Gn. 9:21* and he went into his tent, and being drunken he lay down and slept, and was uncovered in his tent as he slept. **8** And Ham saw Noah his father naked, and went forth and told his two brethren without. *For 8-9 cf. Gn. 9:22-23* **9** And Shem took his garment and arose, he and Japheth, and they placed the garment on their shoulders and went backward and covered the shame of their father, and their faces were backward. **10** And Noah awoke from his sleep and knew all that his younger son had done unto him, and he cursed his son and said: "Cursed be Canaan; *Cf. Gn. 9:24-25* an enslaved servant shall he be unto his brethren."

11 And he blessed Shem, and said: "Blessed be the Yahuah Elohim of Shem, and Canaan shall be his servant. **12** Elohim shall enlarge Japheth, and Elohim shall dwell in the dwelling of Shem, and Canaan shall be his servant." **13** And Ham knew that his father had cursed his younger son, and he was displeased that he had cursed his son, and he parted from his father, he and his sons with him, Cush and Mizraim and Put and Canaan. **14** And he built for himself a city and called its name after the name of his wife Nê'êlâtamâ'ûk.

15 And Japheth saw it, and became envious of his brother, and he too built for himself a city, and he called its name after the name of his wife 'Adâtanêsês. **16** And Shem dwelt with his father Noah, and he built a city close to his father on the mountain, and he too called its name after the name of his wife Sêdêqêtêlĕbâb. **17** And behold these three cities are near Mount Lûbâr; Sêdêqêtêlĕbâb fronting the mountain on its east; and Na'êlâtamâ'ûk on the south; 'Adatanêsês towards the west. **18** And these are the sons of Shem: Elam, and Asshur, and Arpachshad-- this (son) was born two years after the flood--and Lud, and Aram. **19** The sons of Japheth: Gomer and Magog and Madai and Javan, Tubal and Meshech and Tiras: these are the sons of Noah. **20** And in the twenty-eighth jubilee Noah began to enjoin upon his sons' sons the ordinances and commandments, and all the judgments that he knew, and he exhorted his sons to observe righteousness, and to cover the shame of their flesh, and to bless their Creator, and honour father and mother, and love their neighbour, and guard their souls from fornication and uncleanness and all iniquity. **21** For owing to these three things came the flood upon the earth, namely, owing to the fornication wherein the Watchers against the law of their ordinances went a whoring after the daughters of men, and took themselves wives of all which they chose: and they made the beginning of uncleanness. **22** And they begat sons the Nâphîdîm, and †they were all unlike†, and they devoured one another: and the Giants slew the Nâphîl, and the Nâphîl slew the Eljô, and the Eljô mankind, and one man another. **23** And every one sold himself to work iniquity and to shed much blood, and the earth was filled with

For 11-12 cf. Gn. 9:26-27
Note: Yahuah dwells in the tents of Shem NOT Japheth and Gn. says the same.

Cf. Gn. 10:6

"righteous-ness of the heart."

Cf. Gn. 10:22

Cf. Gn. 10:2

1324-1372 A.M.

From here to the end of the chapter there is incorporated a fragment of the lost Book of Noah.

Cf. 3:31

Cf. Gn. 6:2; 1 En. 7

i. e. the Nephilim.

† Text probably corrupt though Charles was not certain. It certainly could be that every Nephilim is different. Note the diverse kinds.

Cf. 1 Ki. 21:20 (phrase).

Cf. 1 En. 9:1
Cf. Gn. 6:2;
1 En. 9:9.
Cf. 1 En. 7:5
As in the days of Noah, these manipulations have returned as Messiah predicted.
Cf. Mt. 24:37, Lk. 17:26
Cf. Gn. 5:5
Cf. Gn. 6:7, 7:4

iniquity. **24** And after this they sinned against the beasts and birds, and all that moveth and walketh on the earth: and much blood was shed on the earth, and every imagination and desire of men imagined vanity and evil continually. **25** And Yahuah destroyed everything from off the face of the earth; because of the wickedness of their deeds, and because of the blood which they had shed in the midst of the earth He destroyed everything.

Noah is the speaker here and to the end of the chapter.

26 "And we were left, I and you, my sons, and everything that entered with us into the ark, and behold I see your works before me that ye do not walk in righteousness; for in the path of destruction ye have begun to walk, and ye are parting one from another, and are envious one of another, and (so it cometh) that ye are not in harmony, my sons, each with his brother. **27** For I see, and behold the demons have begun (their) seductions against you and against your children, and now I fear on your behalf, that after my death ye will shed the blood of

Cf. 10:1 (10:1-15 is another excerpt from the Noah apocalypse).

men upon the earth, and that ye, too, will be destroyed from the face of the earth. **28** For whoso sheddeth man's blood,

and whoso eateth the blood of any flesh, will all be destroyed from the earth. **29** And there will not be left any man that eateth blood. Or that sheddeth the blood of man on the earth, Nor will there be left to him any seed or descendants living under heaven; For into Sheol will they go, And into the place of condemnation will they descend. And into the darkness of the deep will they all be removed by a violent death. **30** There shall be no blood seen upon you of all the blood there shall be all the days in which ye have killed any beasts or cattle or whatever flieth upon the earth, and work ye a good work to your souls by covering that which hath been shed on the face of the earth. **31** And ye shall not be like him who eateth with blood, but guard yourselves that none may eat blood before you: cover the blood, for thus have I been commanded to testify to you and your children, together with all flesh. **32** And suffer not the soul to be eaten with the flesh, that your blood, which is your life, may not be required at the hand of any flesh that sheddeth (it) on the earth. **33** For the earth will not be clean from the blood

Cf. Gen.9:4, 6; Lev. 7:27

Cf. 22:22; 1 En. 103:7, 8.

Cf. Lv. 17:11; Ez.. 24:7 (here the precept is carried back to Noah).

One of the seven Noachic laws (binding on all men) was the prohibition of eating flesh with the blood. Cf. note on 21 above.

Cf. Gn. 9:4; Lv. 17:10, 11, 14.

Cf. 6:2

Cf. Nm. 35:33

which hath been shed upon it; for (only) through the blood of him that shed it will the earth be purified throughout all its generations. **34** And now, my children, hearken: work

MESSIAH cf. 16:36, likened to "Him who made all things." Cf. 21:24 cf. 1 En. 84:6 "the flesh of righteousness and uprightness establish as a seed bearing plant forever." cf. 1 En. 93:5 "Plant of Righteous Judgment" as "a man." Cf. 2 Pt. 2:5

judgment and righteousness that ye may be planted in righteousness over the face of the whole earth, and your glory lifted up before my Elohim, who saved me from the waters of the flood. **35** And behold, ye will go and build for yourselves cities, and plant in them all the plants that are upon the earth, and moreover all fruit-bearing trees.

36 For three years the fruit of everything that is eaten will not be gathered: and in the fourth

These words direct that in the fourth year only the first-fruits (not all the fruit) are to be offered to God. Cf. Lv. 19:23-24.

year its fruit will be accounted holy [and they will offer the first-fruits], acceptable before the Most High God, who created heaven and earth and all things. Let them offer

in abundance the first of the wine and oil (as) first-fruits on the altar of the Lord, who receiveth it, and what is left let the servants of the house of Yahuah eat before the altar which receiveth (it). **37** And in the fifth year make ye the release so that ye release it in righteousness and uprightness, and ye shall be righteous, and all that you plant will prosper. **38** For thus did Enoch, the father of your father command Methuselah, his son, and Methuselah his son Lamech, and Lamech commanded me all the things which his fathers commanded him. **39** And I also will give you commandment, my sons, as Enoch commanded his son in the first jubilees: whilst still living, the seventh in his generation, he commanded and testified to his son and to his sons' sons until the day of his death."

i. e. the priests.

Charles suspects a lacuna in the text here.

Or render "(In the seventh year) ye will let it (the land) rest and lie fallow" (Charles).

Cf. 1 En.60:8, 93:3; Jude 14

ORIGINAL
MT. ZION

Center of the
Navel of the earth.
"Whole land of Eden"
(North Pole)
Mt. Zion Israel was not
named until Abraham.
18:13

START
NORTH POLE
(Middle of Earth)
See bottom right
These directions cannot
begin in Israel

GREAT SEA
(OCEAN)

Note: River Tina located by
Riphaen Mts. and only river
that fits with mouth at the
ocean, dumping into 2 seas
and 1 connected to yet another
sea. Me'at is Azov as well. In
Scythian, the Don River was
known as Tanais River.

SHEM

ASIA

Today, Japheth expanded
into Shem's area here.

Note: The Ural/
Riphean Mts.
remain the dividing
line between
Europe and Asia
set by Noah.

The Indus Valley
is one of the oldest
civilizations in
history. Ancient
Khirasara has been
unearthed there.

ME'AT SEA TO
GREAT SEA
(Ocean)

Mouth

RIVER TINA
Modern Don (Tanais) & Volga R.
(map below) [36]

Moscow,
Russia

SHEM
(Asia)

Middle
RIPHAEN MTS.
(Mts. of Rafa)
Modern Ural Mts.

JAPHETH
(Europe = North of Tina River)

Modern
Volga R.

ME'AT SEA
(Maeotis Sea)
Modern Azov Sea

Modern Don R.
Former Tanais R.

SHEM = Asia
South and East
of Tina R.

EUROPE

BLACK SEA
ABYSS 1

CASPIAN
SEA
ABYSS 2

Mts. of
Asshur

Ararat Can
Not Be
Turkey!

Bashan,
Lebanon,
Sanir,
Amana,
Kaftur

north

Asshur,
Babel,
Maedai

east

Elam,
Susan

east

east

east

Mts. of Ararat
(Himalayas, East
of Shinar)

Mediterranean Sea

east

Israel

HAM

AFRICA
(Afra/ Aferag)

Egyptian/ Red Sea

MT. SINAI
Saudi Arabia
West side of tongue
looks toward South.
(Land mass border set)

[37]

Khirasara
Indus Valley

India
(Karaso)

HAM
(All of Africa)

Africa
Continental Shelf.
The banks of the
Gihon River
(Gn. 2 River from Eden)

Bosom

Shem does not enter Africa as
that is ALL given to Ham.

south

west

Tongue looks toward South.
Egypt and Saudi addressed later.
(Land mass border set)

GREAT SEA
Indian Ocean

SHEM

Extends East til it reaches the GARDEN OF EDEN

HAM

The Garden cannot be in Africa nor
the Middle East but Shem's very
Eastern border in the Far East!
(See Garden of Eden Map)

*All borders are approximations. This map not to scale.

©2020 Map By The Levite Bible.

RIVER TINA
Modern Don "Tanais" [36] &
Volga Rivers, Russia

Mouth
(Ocean)

Volga R.

Middle
RIPHAEN MTS.
(Mts. of Rafa)
Modern Ural Mts.

ME'AT SEA TO
GREAT SEA
(Ocean)

EUROPE

Volga R.

Moscow,
Russia

Volga R.

SHEM
ASIA

JAPHETH

ME'AT SEA
(Maeotis Sea)
Modern Azov Sea

Don R.

BLACK SEA
ABYSS 1

CASPIAN
SEA
ABYSS 2

The Only River Which Could Fit!

Note: 78% of Russia's Population is on the
European side of this border as Japheth.

NOAH'S DIVISION TO SHEM

Ancient Cosmology:

In this mindset, the navel of the earth is the North Pole not Israel which comes later. Following these directions, one would stumble over territories multiple times which cannot fit otherwise.

In ancient times, the world generally especially the writers of the Bible believed the earth a flat round disc essentially. This is the perspective from which this is written not the modern sphere. We do not enter such debate but when one follows the actual orientation of the time, they will find it revealing. Anyone claiming the ancients believed in a sphere failed to pay attention in science class and are no scholars on the topic.

Oldest surviving world map.
(c. 6th century BCE) [5]

Reconstruction of Anaximander's map.
(c. 610 – 546 BCE) [6]

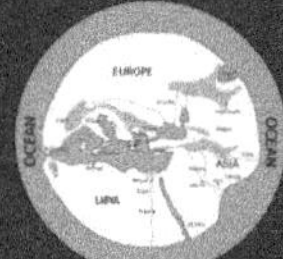

Reconstruction of Hecataeus' map.
(c. 550–476 BCE) [7]

*All borders are approximations. This map not to scale.

JAPHETH

NORTH
AMERICA

EUROPE

Gadir [39]
Spain

Mediterranean Sea

Note: Noah divided
the US into North
and South. The 37th
parallel passes thru
the Chesapeake Bay
Bridge Tunnel.

Recap:
From Gihon to the Right
of the Garden of Eden.

To be to the Right of the
Garden in Shem's East,
one must head West.
Ham cannot cross into
Shem's territory to East.

Crosses Gihon to the Right of the Garden of Eden.

west

START

AFRICA

HAM

North to Gadir

SOUTH
AMERICA

West to
Sea of Ma'uk,
named after Ham's wife.
South Atlantic. Also spelled
Ma'kaka/ Makaka is a town
in S. Africa.
(Chatsworth)
Ham named a city for his
wife as well.
(Jub. 7:13-14)
Africa has maintained
ownership of that portion
of the Atlantic until the
1800s as it was labeled the
Ethiopian Sea on maps.

west
Makaka,
South Africa

Gihon River
from Eden

Surrounds WHOLE
land of Ethiopia which
in ancient times is East
to West Coast of Africa.
Noah affirms this in this
mapping. (Gn. 2)

Ham begins in Africa where he is already
on the West side of the Gihon which
Shem has the East side. Now he heads
beyond the Gihon. He cannot enter what
is already Shem. This is because the
Gihon surrounds all of Africa on both
sides. He is headed beyond to the West
to the Garden. Shem already followed the
same to the East. He can only be Right
(East) of the Garden if he heads West.

©2020 Map By The Levite Bible.

NOAH'S
DIVISION
TO HAM

SHEM
ASIA

Indo-Iranian Continental Shelf. The banks of the Hiddekel River (Gn. 2 River from Eden).

Africa Continental Shelf. The banks of the Gihon River (Gn. 2 River from Eden).

Japan

Pacific Ocean

©2020 Map By The Levite Bible.

HAM

To the Right of the Garden of Eden. This must be the East side of Shem's Eastern border already identified.

Philippines
GARDEN OF EDEN

Sabah, Malaysia

west

Crosses Gihon to the Right of the Garden of Eden.

Indian Ocean

SHEM

All the Mountains of Fire Gunung Gunung Api. [34] Indonesia's 147 Volcanoes.

south

Turns South just as Shem's says his border is just below the Garden. The Volcanoes in Indonesia still bear Noah's name today "Mountains of Fire." Gunung Gunung Api in Javenese. The Northernmost which sets the border of Shem and Ham is on the border that splits Borneo between 2 nations to this day. Sabah, Malaysia is to the North and then, the Sulu Sea. The Garden of Eden is beneath the Sulu Sea. This also establishes Shem's Eastern border with Ham at the Philippine Trench which matches the Pison River from Eden. Noah used the Gihon and Pison and soon even the Hiddekel Rivers from Eden to establish boundaries.

west

AUSTRALIA

West to Sea of Atel Atel is a "satirical term for intellectual" in Bengali. It is the Indian Ocean linguistically and in the directions. [38]

HAM

Perhaps Antartica but it is not mentioned.

COLD LANDS

International Date Line
Did Noah set that too?

JAPHETH

We do not have a clear track on Fara in history but the directions are extremely clear it is in this region. Especially since Shem is Asia. Fara in Old Norse means "Passage." That could fit the Bering Strait. The process of elimination says so.

Extends to West of Fara.
Fairbanks, Alaska?

Fairweather Range?

Just Above 37th Parallel Even With Gadir, Spain
Farallon Islands?

San Francisco

Note: *Hawaii belongs to Ham's descendants not Japheth. Clinton even issued a formal apology but he didn't give the land back.*

HOT LANDS

Ham's lands are hot. Obviously, it becomes cold again further South. There is no indication that Japheth nor Shem would cross through Ham to get to that portion and it is not in their inheritance. It stands to reason by default that Ham received all the way to Antartica to the South.

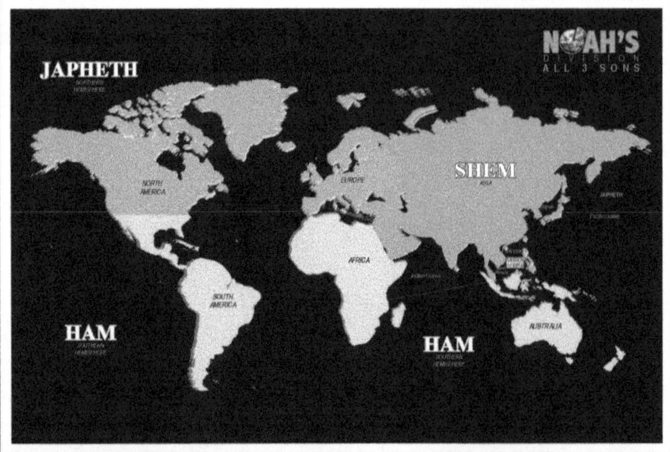

*All borders are approximations. This map not to scale.

West into the ocean beyond Gadir to Fara
west

Return towards Africa
east

east

NORTH AMERICA

Note: *No one can legally unite that which Noah divided.*

Ma'uk Sea

HAM

SOUTH AMERICA

©2020 Map By The Levite Bible.

HAM
SOUTHERN HEMISPHERE

NOAH'S
DIVISION
TO JAPHETH

Note: Shem's area of Russia was taken by Japheth long ago. Only 25% of the nation is in Europe yet it houses 78% of it's population. Modern Russia is Japheth controlled even in capital and population. In fact, Russia accounts for 39% of all of Europe's land mass and is the largest nation on Earth in geography. It is Japheth who encroahes into Shem but a Japheth nation. [33]

HOT & COLD
FIVE GREAT ISLANDS
5 OF 10 LARGEST ISLANDS IN WORLD [35]
1. GREENLAND (#1)
2. BAFFIN ISLAND, CANADA (#5)
3. GREAT BRITAIN (#8)
4. VICTORIA ISLAND, CANADA (#9)
5. ELLESMERE ISLAND, CANADA (#10)

The Celts originated in the Alps or [40] perhaps refers to British Isles, etc.

All of Europe is Japheth.

To North Border

North

All land East to Gog

NE to Gog Russia

To Riphaen Mts.

3

Alps Mts. of Qelt

EUROPE

START
North of R. Tina

Back to Me'at Sea

Mediterranean Sea

©2020 Map By The Levite Bible.

SHEM
ASIA

Japan

HAM

Philippines
GARDEN OF EDEN

Sabah, Malaysia

SHEM

Indian Ocean

AFRICA

Ma'uk Sea

Note: Noah's directions were so specific, he even divided the waters of the earth.

AUSTRALIA
HAM

HAM
SOUTHERN HEMISPHERE

Since Noah already divided the rest of the Earth, Japheth's area is pretty self-explanatory. However, Noah confirms everything yet another time firming up the borders especially the Russian boundary which still stands, the Southern border all the way across the Earth and date line and islands seal this up. Without this geography, no scholar will ever understand Biblical geography.

MADAI

Madai did not like his inheritance of Great Britain. He begged for land in Shem's territory near Babel. However, there is no record he was given such. Based on history, he may well have stolen land. This land was called Media after him. Descendants from that land would be among the first conquerers. With Brtiain vacant, it is likely Meshech absorbed it into his territory.

CANAAN

Canaan received West Africa but he chose to take land from Arphacsad instead. He stole what would become the land of Canaan thus it's name before it was Israel. He was cursed a second time by his father and brothers for doing so. This is why it was referred to as the Promised Land restored to Abraham's descendants but promised in Noah's division of the earth.

"...Noah their father, and he bound them all by an oath, imprecating a curse on every one that sought to seize the portion which had not fallen (to him) by his lot." (9:14)

*All borders are approximations. This map not to scale.

GARDEN OF EDEN
SHEM'S SOUTHEAST BORDER

MOUNTAINS OF FIRE
"Gunung Gunung Api" in Javanese
147 Volcanoes forming a natural geographic border between Shem and Ham in the Far East. [34]

GENESIS 3:24 KJV – EAST OF THE GARDEN
So he drove out the man; and he placed at the east of the garden of Eden Cherubims, and a flaming sword which turned every way, to keep the way of the tree of life.

TESTING THE RESOURCES OF HAVILAH [31][32]

GOLD

In all of history, the Philippines leads in gold mining since before 1000 B.C. and still remains #2 on earth in untapped gold reserves. There is no other land which competes. It is the ancient land of gold by historical record. [27]

PEARL

Bdellium is never a Biblical spice and all such spices are recorded in scripture. It is pearl. The Philippines has the largest pearls in all of history with no 2nd. [28]

"Puerto Princessa Pearl. 2006. 34 kg (75 lb.)

ONYX STONE

Ancient onyx especially in Egypt was known as alabaster used in ornamental construction. The Philippines has the strongest onyx and marble on earth in Romblon. [29]

MARINE LIFE

Marine life is the true measure for the Land of Creation as it was not wiped out by the Flood. The Epicenter of Marine Biodiversity on ALL of earth is the Philippines in the Sulu Sea. [30]

Tubbataha Reef in the Sulu Sea.

In resources, history, geography, science, language and the Bible, this is Ophir.
See "The Search for King Solomon's Treasure: The Lost Isles of Gold and the Garden of Eden" for Evidences.

GENESIS 2:11-12 KJV
The name of the first is Pison: that is it which compasseth the whole land of Havilah, where there is gold. And the gold of that land is good: there is bdellium and the onyx stone.

HAVILAH [31][32]
= GARDEN OF EDEN
= LAND OF CREATION
= OPHIR
= PHILIPPINES

JUBILEES 3:32
Adam and his wife went forth from the Garden of Eden, and they dwelt in the land of 'Elda, in the land of their creation.

Modern Rivers do not fit these Rivers from Eden as there was no rain before the Flood in Gen. 2:5. The Tigris, Modern Euphrates, Nile, Amazon, etc. all originate in precipitaion thus disqualified.

Genesis 2:10 KJV
And **a river went out of Eden to water the garden**; and from thence it was **parted**, and became into *four heads*.
The 60,000 km. continuous Mid-Ocean Ridge has exactly four interections with Oceanic Trench System contiguous before the Flood.

RI

SOURCE

Gihon North border 8:23

PISON

NORTH AMERICA

©2020 Map By The Levite Bible.

Gihon West 8:22

The Philippines leads the world in gold, pearl and the onyx stone in all of history.

START   1

Genesis 2:11-12 KJV
The name of the first is **Pison**: that is it which **compasseth the whole land of Havilah**, where there is **gold**; And the gold of that land is **good**: there is **bdellium** and the **onyx stone**.
The Philippines is #1 in all 3 resources to this day and is the only fit.

Why do the directions begin in the Far East?
It is the most significant and Hebrew reads East to West because all began in the East.

Genesis 2:14b KJV
And the fourth river is Euphrates.
Cannot be the modern one.

SOUTH AMERICA

RIVER FROM EDEN

PARAT.

4
START

"If you drained all the water away, it would look exactly like a river system with bends and meanders, except there are no trees along the banks..."
– Dan Parsons, PhD, Sedimentologist, University of Hull, UK to BBC News (studies undersea rivers) [41]

"...waters should be gathered in the seventh part of the earth: six parts hast thou dried up..." – 2 Esdras 6:42 KJVA (Cf. 2 Esdras 6:47, 6:49-52)

Only 15% of Pre-Flood World was Water

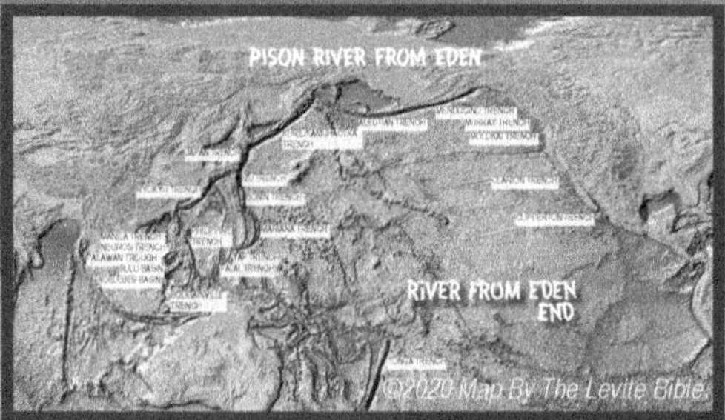

PISON RIVER FROM EDEN
RIVER FROM EDEN END
©2020 Map By The Levite Bible.

ALGERIAN BASIN
ALBORAN BASIN
MEDITERRANEAN RIDGE
ASIA
AZORES-GIBRALTOR RIDGE
LEVANTINE BASIN
CANARY BASIN
RED SEA TRENCH
CAPE VERDE BASIN
ETHIOPIA
GIHON
GULF OF ADEN
ETHIOPIA
OWEN FRACTURE
CARLSBERG RIDGE
ETHIOPIA
GUINEA BASIN
SOMALI BASIN
S. AMERICA
ANGOLA BASIN
MASCARENE BASIN
WALVIS RIDGE
MADAGASCAR BASIN
NATAL BASIN
CAPE BASIN
MOZAMBIQUE BASIN
©2020 Map By The Levite Bible.
RIVER FROM EDEN   SURROUNDS AFRICA

PRE-FLOOD WORLD

RIVERS FROM EDEN THEORY
Confirmed By Jubilees

R FROM EDEN

EUROPE

Eden is the North Pole, the "middle" and "center of navel of earth." The River begins there and flows OUT.

Jubilees places Gihon on bottom of ocean floor and surrounding Africa.

Genesis 2:14a KJV
And the name of the third river is **Hiddekel**: that is it which goeth toward the **east of Assyria.**
The Tigris is "The River" in the Bible 27 times and NEVER Hiddekel. Daniel was in Iran during the period he had a vision on the Hiddekel and that was not the Tigris but the Persian Gulf.

ON...

AFRICA

ASIA

START 2

START 3

Genesis 2:13 KJV
And the name of the second river is **Gihon**: the same is it that **compasseth the whole land of Ethiopia.**
Ancient Ethiopia is coast to coast

Gihon East border 8:15

Persian Gulf border 9:2, 9:5

"west to 'Afra...waters of Gihon, to the banks ..."
African Continental Shelf

HIDDEKEL

LAND OF GOLD — Havilah, Ophir, Sheba, Tarshish, Elda

Defines East border of Shem and Ham 9:16, 19, 22-23

PISON

See other side.

GARDEN OF EDEN — Watered at End of Rivers from Eden

AUSTRALIA

©2020 Map By The Levite Bible.

This is our theory.

RIVER FROM EDEN

All borders are approximations. This map not to scale.

NASA/Goddard Space Flight Center Map of the oceans drained. Emphasis added as we filled in the ridges and trenches with water. [15]

The flood breaketh out from the inhabitant; even the waters forgotten of the foot: they are dried up (Brought Low), they are gone away (shake) from men.." – Job 28:4 KJV
...Usually understood of (underground) streams. – Job 28:11 KJV

"...its roots (shall go down) to the Abyss [and all the rivers of Eden shall water its branches]."
– Hymn 14, (formerly 10), The Thanksgiving Hymns. Qumran Scrolls (iQH, 1Q36,4Q427-32) [42]

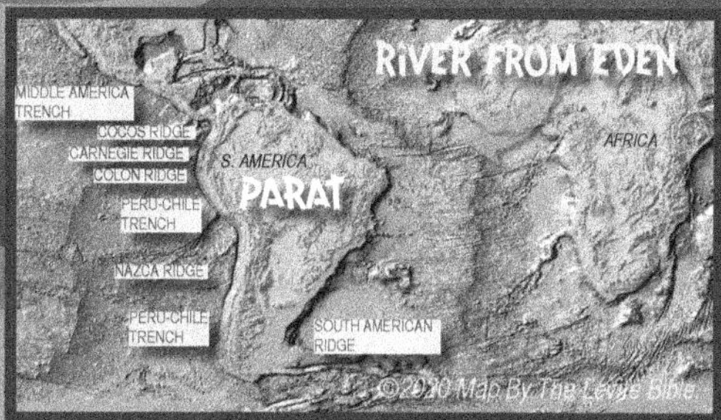

HISTORY OF THE WORLD

THE BEGINNING TO PROMISED LAND

According to Jubilees

ANNO MUNDI
All dates counted from the beginning of Creation.

Havilah Generations Before The Flood

1-7 Garden of Eden
8 Garden exile
64-70 Cain born
71-77 Abel born
78-84 Awan born
99-105 Abel killed
99-127 Seth born
134-140 Azura born
190-196 Cain's Enoch
197 Cain's city
235 Enos born
325 Kenan born
395 Mahalalel born
461 Jared born
522 Enoch born
587 Methuselah born
654 Lamech born
707 Noah born
930 Adam Died
1207 Shem born
1209 Ham born
1212 Japheth born
1307 Ark built
1308 Flood start
1309 Waters abated

After The Flood

1317 Noah Vineyard
1324 Law of Noah
1375 Occult reborn
1499 Eber born
1564 Peleg born
1569 Earth divided
1659 Noah died
1645 Babel built
1688 Babel destroyed
1687 Seroh born
1806 Terah born

Life of Abraham

1876 Abram born
1890 Abram rejects idols
1890 Ravens turned back
1891 Abram's seed planting
1904 Abram rejects idols
1925 Marries Sarai
1932 Lot born
1936 Idols burned in fire
1951 Abram relearns Hebrew
1953 Migrates to Canaan
1954 Builds altar
1956 Abram to Egypt
1963 Returns to Canaan
1964 Lot to Sodom
1964 4 Kings Attack
1681 Isaac promised
1962 Ishmael born
1980 Isaac born
2003 Abraham tested
2010 Sarah died
2046 Jacob & Esau born
2052 Law of Abraham
(to Ishmael and Isaac)
2052 Abraham died

** Not all dates from Jubilees represented.*

Isaac to Moses

2073 Isaac to Hebron
2080 Esau sells birthright
2080 Isaac to Gerar
2108 Isaac to Beersheba
2114 Jacob given birthright
2115 Yah speaks to Jacob Bethel
2122 Jacob marries Leah
2135 Jacob left Laban
2143 Dinah raped
2148 War of 7 Kings
2149 Joseph enslaved
2162 Isaac died
2162 Esau wars with Isaac
2171 Jacob's son in Egypt
2172 All Israel in Egypt
2188 Jacob dies
2330 Moses born
2372 Moses to Midian
2410 Moses returns to Egypt
2450 EXODUS TO CANAAN

SHEM
ASIA

SHINAR
ASSYRIA
BABEL

JAPHETH
NORTHERN
HEMISPHERE

MT. EVEREST
Mt. Lubar in Ararat Mts.(5:28)
Sagarmatha: "Head of Ocean"
Arkhale, Nepal

Gn. 11:2
Jb. 10:19
Jb. 8:21

to Shinar
from east

UR
Abraham born

Ark lifted
(see next page)

CANAAN
Israel

EGYPT

AFRICA

Philippines

GARDEN
OF EDEN

Sabah,
Malaysia

HAM
SOUTHERN
HEMISPHERE

Indian Ocean

©2020 Map By The Levite Bible.

HAVILAH
Land of Creation
Ancient Land of Gold
Land of Adam and Eve
Ophir, Sheba and Havilah
return there after Babel
Genesis 10:26-30

AUSTRALIA

*All borders are approximations. This map not to scale.

Tribes of Israel Born

2122 Reuben born
2124 Simeon born
2127 Levi born
2128 Judah born
2129 Dan born
2131 Naphtali born
2132 Gad born
2133 Asher born
2134 Issachar and Zebulon born
2135 Joseph born
2143 Benjamin born

THE
LEVITE
BIBLE

THE
Levite
BIBLE
LeviteBible.com

ARK LANDED AT FLOOD PEAK:
150 days = 5 months (Same day Waters Stopped)

GENESIS 7:24 KJV (Cf. 5:27)
And the waters prevailed upon the earth an hundred and fifty days

GENESIS 8:4 KJV (Cf. 5:28)
And the ark rested in the seventh month, on the seventeenth day of the month, upon the **mountains of Ararat.** (150 days, SAME)

15 CUBITS ABOVE TALLEST MOUNTAIN

GENESIS 7:19-20 KJV
And the waters prevailed exceedingly upon the earth; and **all the high hills,** that were under the whole heaven, **were covered. Fifteen cubits** upward did the waters prevail; and the mountains were covered.

JUBILEES 5:26 KJV
Fifteen cubits did the waters rise above all the high mountains

GENESIS 11:2 KJV
And it came to pass, as they **journeyed from the east,** that they found a plain in the land of **Shinar;** and they dwelt there. Cf. 10:19 "For they **departed** from the land of **Ararat eastward to Shinar"** Cf. 8:21 **Ararat East of Media**

NOAH'S ARK LANDING HIMALAYAS
TALLEST MOUNTAIN EAST OF SHINAR AFTER THE FLOOD

MOUNTAINS DON'T MOVE!
From their places. Not until the end times.

GENESIS 49:26
"everlasting hills"

DEUTERONOMY 33:15 KJV
"ancient mountains... lasting hills"

PSALM 104:5-8 KJV
Who laid the **foundations of the earth,** that it should **not be removed for ever.** Thou coveredst it with the deep as with a garment: the **waters stood above the mountains.**

ONLY THE TALLEST MOUNTAIN COULD FIT!

GENESIS 8:9 KJV (ALL MOUNTAINS STILL UNDER WATER)
But the dove found no rest for the sole of her foot, and she returned unto him into the ark, for **the waters were on the face of the whole earth.**

GENESIS 8:5 KJV (Cf. 5:30)
in the tenth month, on the first day of the month, were the tops of the mountains seen
(IF they were not seen before, they were ALL covered. Closest mountains to Mt. Ararat, Turkey = 250+ km)

©2020 Map By The Levite Bible.

THE ARK:
30 Cubits Tall (50')
18 Cubits Below
Water Level (9m/30')
IT COULD HAVE ONLY HIT
1 MOUNTAIN – THE TALLEST.
1 Cubit = 20"

All borders are approximations. This map not to scale.

REDISCOVER THE
LOST ISLES OF GOLD
OPHIR | SHEBA | TARSHISH

The Bible has always preserved the location of this ancient land of gold. Review the full case that went viral with history, geography, science, lanugage, etc. which all converge to reveal the Philippines. Almost 400 pages packed with evidence. Prove it for yourself. Follow along with our comprehensive Sourcebook with over 250 pages of sources used.

Order Your Copies Now at:
www.OphirInstitute.com

CHAPTER 8:

Genealogy Of The Descendants Of Shem: Noah And His Sons Divide The Whole Earth Before Babel

(8:1-30; cf. Gen. 10)

1373 A.M. **1** In the twenty-ninth jubilee, in the first week, in the beginning thereof Arpachshad took to himself a wife and her name was Râsû'ĕjâ, [the daughter of Sûsân,] the daughter of Elam, *1375 A.M.* and she bare him a son in the third year in this week, and he called his name Kâinâm. **2** And the son grew, and his father taught him writing, and he went to seek for himself a place where he might seize for himself a city. **3** And he found a writing which former (generations) had carved on the rock, and he read what was thereon, and he transcribed it and sinned owing to it; for it contained the teaching of the Watchers in accordance with which they used to observe the omens of the sun and moon and stars in all the signs of heaven. **4** And he wrote it down and said nothing regarding it; for he was afraid to speak to Noah about it lest he should be angry with him on account of it. **5** And in the *1429 A.M.* thirtieth jubilee, in the second

Kainam, not to be confused with Canaan from Ham, occurs in the LXX of Gn. 11:13, but not in the MT or other Versions. It also occurs in the genealogy in Luke 3:36. Note he is the origin of the occult doctrine. One must wonder why Luke and the LXX Gn. record him with Jb. but not the modern Gn. The pre-flood teachings of the Watchers crossed over the Flood.

week, in the first year thereof, he took to himself a wife, and her name was Mêlkâ, the daughter of Madai, the son of Japheth, and in the fourth year he begat a son, and called his name Shelah; for he said: "Truly I have been sent." **6** [And in the fourth year he was born], and Shelah grew up and took to himself a wife, and her name was Mû'ak, the daughter of Kêsêd, his father's brother, in the one and thirtieth jubilee, in the fifth week, in the first year thereof. **7** And she bare him a son in the fifth year thereof, and he called his name Eber: and he took unto himself a wife, and her name was 'Azûrâd the daughter of Nêbrôd, in the thirty-second jubilee, in the seventh week, in the third year thereof. **8** And in the sixth year thereof, she bare him a son, and he called his name Peleg; for in the days when he was born the children of Noah began to divide the earth amongst themselves: for this reason he called his name Peleg. **9** And they divided (it) secretly amongst themselves, and told it to Noah. **10** And it came to pass in the beginning of the thirty-third jubilee that they divided the earth into three parts, for Shem and Ham and Japheth, according

1432 A.M.

Cf. Gn. 10:24

A paronomasia is implied in the original Hebrew here.

1499 A.M.

1503 A.M.

Read 'Azûrâ.

1564 A.M.

1567 A.M.

Cf. Gn. 10:25 There is a play (in the original Hebrew) on the meaning of the name Peleg here. Peleg varies into Pulag meaning "it was divided."

1569 A.M.

This division is circumvented by Noah's upcoming division.

i. e. one of the angels.

In the perspective of the writers of the Bible, the center of the earth is the North Pole. This is not Israel and note the directions go next to Russia and then South thus they do not begin in Israel but in the North.

Cf. Ez. 38:12 KJV: "that dwell in the midst of the land" in Israel is not the "navel" of the entire earth. The North Pole is in the ancient mindset.

Rhipaean mountains (identified sometimes with the Ural mountains). Riphath, son of Gomer. Gn. 10:3

i. e. the river Tanais (Scythian god and river name-Ταναις) or Don and Volga in Moscow.

i. e. the Maeotis. ἡ Μαιῶτις λίμνη or Sea of Azov.

Khirasara, Indus Valley. Ancient Indus society found in 1976. Existed 2600-2200 B.C. Found in the bossom also.

i.e.The tongue pointing to the South of Russia is India. Others addressed later.

i.e.Saudi Arabia.

i. e. the Gulf of Akaba; cf. Isa. 11:15.

i. e. mouth where Red Sea meets Indian Ocean.

i. e. Africa in the restricted sense of the Roman province which included Egypt and the other northern parts.

i. e. Pre-Flood River from Eden Surrounds whole land of Ethiopia which on maps from 450 B.C. to 1800s was East to West Coast. Must surround all of Africa. Not Nile.

†? read "west."

Note Gn. 2:5 disqualifies all rivers originating from rain and snow as the Rivers from Eden. There was no rain as there was a mist that came up from the earth in those days. Nile, Tigris, Euphrates, Amazon, etc. all originate in rain and snow fall.

to the inheritance of each, in the first year in the first week, when one of us, who had been sent, was with them. **11** And he called his sons, and they drew nigh to him, they and their children, and he divided the earth into the lots, which his three sons were to take in possession, and they reached forth their hands, and took the writing out of the bosom of Noah, their father. **12** And there came forth on the writing as Shem's lot the middle of the earth which he should take as an inheritance for himself and for his sons for the generations of eternity, from the middle of the mountain range of Râfâ, from the mouth of the water from the river Tînâ. and his portion goeth towards the west through the midst of this river, and it extendeth till it reacheth the water of the abysses, out of which this river goeth forth and poureth its waters into the sea Mê'at, and this river floweth into the great sea. And all that is towards the north is Japheth's, and all that is towards the south belongeth to Shem. **13** And it extendeth till it reacheth Kârâsô: this is in the bosom of the tongue which looketh towards the south. **14** And his portion extendeth along the great sea, and it extendeth in a straight line till it reacheth the west of the tongue which looketh towards the south; for this sea is named the tongue of the Egyptian Sea. **15** And it turneth from here towards the south towards the mouth of the great sea on the shore of (its) waters, and it extendeth to the west to 'Afrâ and it extendeth till it reacheth the waters of the river Gihon, and to the south of the waters of Gihon, to the banks of this river. **16** And it extendeth towards the east, till it reacheth the Garden of Eden, to the south thereof, [to the south] and from the east of the whole land of Eden and of the whole east, it turneth to the †east,† and proceedeth till it reacheth the east of the mountain named Râfâ, and it descendeth to the bank of the mouth of the river Tînâ. **17** This portion came forth by lot for Shem and his sons, that they should possess it for ever unto his generations for evermore. **18** And Noah rejoiced that this portion came forth for Shem and for his sons, and he remembered all that he had spoken with his mouth in prophecy; for he had said: Blessed be Yahuah Elohim of Shem, And may

Yahuah dwell in the dwelling of Shem." **19** And he knew that the Garden of Eden is the holy of holies, and the dwelling of Yahuah, and Mount Sinai the centre of the desert, and Mount Zion--the centre of the navel of the earth: these three were created as holy places facing each other. **20** And he blessed the El of Elohim, who had put the word of Yahuah into his mouth, and Yahuah for evermore. **21** And he knew that a blessed portion and a blessing had come to Shem and his sons unto the generations for ever--the whole land of Eden and the whole land of the Red Sea, and the whole land of the east, and India, and on the Red Sea and the mountains thereof, and all the land of Bashan, and all the land of Lebanon and the islands of Kaftûr, and all the mountains of Sanîr and 'Amânâ, and the mountains of Asshur in the north, and all the land of Elam, Asshur, and Bâbêl, and Sûsân and Mâ'ĕdâi and all the mountains of Ararat, and all the region beyond the sea, which is beyond the mountains of Asshur towards the north, a blessed and spacious land, and all that is in it is very good. **22** And for Ham came forth

the second portion, beyond the Gihon towards the south to the right of the Garden, and it extendeth towards the south and it extendeth to all the mountains of fire, and it extendeth towards the west to the sea of 'Atêl and it extendeth towards the west till it reacheth the sea of Mâ'ûk -- that (sea) into which †everything which is not destroyed descendeth†. **23** And it goeth forth towards the north to the limits of Gâdîr, and it goeth forth to the coast of the waters of the sea to the waters of the great sea till it draweth near to the river Gihon, and goeth along the river Gihon till it reacheth the right of the Garden of Eden. **24** And this is the land which came forth for Ham as the portion which he was to occupy for ever for himself and his sons unto their generations for ever. **25** And for Japheth came forth the third portion beyond the river Tînâ to the north of the outflow of its waters, and it extendeth north-easterly to the whole region of Gog and to all the country east thereof. **26** And it extendeth northerly to the north, and it extendeth to the mountains of Qêlt towards the north, and towards the sea of Mâ'ûk, and it goeth forth to the east of Gâdîr as far as the region of the waters of the sea. **27** And it extendeth until it approacheth the west of Fârâ and it returneth towards 'Afêrâg, and it extendeth easterly to the waters of the sea of Mê'at. **28** And it extendeth to the region of the river Tînâ in a northeasterly direction until it approacheth the boundary of its waters towards the mountain Râfâ, and it turneth round towards the north. **29** This is the land which came forth for Japheth and his sons as the portion of his inheritance which he should possess for himself and his sons, for their generations for ever; five great islands, and a great land in the north.

30 But it is cold, and the land of Ham is hot, and the land of Shem is neither hot nor cold, but it is of blended cold and heat.

FULL COLOR MAPS
PAGES 82-94

COLONIALISM AND CONQUEST HAVE ALWAYS BEEN FORBIDDEN
ISRAEL WAS TAKING IT'S LAND BACK FROM CANAAN AND NEPHILIM WHO STOLE IT!

CHAPTER 9:

Subdivision Of The Three Portions Amongst The Grandchildren: Oath Taken By Noah's Sons

(9:1-15; cf. Gen. 10 partly)

Ethiopia. As Canaan stole Israel and did not take his land in West Africa, this was absorbed by Cush too.

i. e. Egypt.

i. e. Libya (west of Egypt).

i. e. the Atlantic. For Canaan's portion (from Libya to the Atlantic) Cf. 10: 28-29. Canaan stole Israel intead. Cf. Gn. 10:6.

Hiddekel (חידקל) is never Tigris in scripture. Daniel was in Iran not Iraq when he invokes it. He never lived on the Tigris. Tigris is "the River" in Hebrew 27 times not Hiddekel.

i.e. Saudi Arabia. Susan is South Iran. One crosses Phranak to get to the Red Sea from there.

As with the O.T. 26 times, "the river" (Ha Nahar הנהר) is the Tigris not Hiddekel.

Cf. Neh. 2:7 Nineveh, Assyria, Shinar are firmly on the Tigris.

1 And Ham divided amongst his sons, and the first portion came forth for Cush towards the east, and to the west of him for Mizraim, and to the west of him for Put, and to the west of him [and to the west thereof] on the sea for Canaan. **2** And Shem also divided amongst his sons, and the first portion came forth for Elam and his sons, to the east of the river Hiddekel till it approacheth the east, the whole land of India, and on the Red Sea on its coast, and the waters of Dêdân, and all the mountains of Mebrî and 'Êlâ, and all the land of Sûsân and all that is on the side of Pharnâk to the Red Sea and the river Tînâ. **3** And for Asshur came forth the second portion, all the land of Asshur and Nineveh and Shinar and to the border of India, and it ascendeth and skirteth the river. **4** And for Arpachshad came forth the third portion, all the land of the region of the Chaldees to the east of the Euphrates, bordering on the Red Sea, and all the waters of the desert close to the tongue of the sea which looketh towards Egypt, all the land of Lebanon and Sanîr and 'Amânâ to the border of the Euphrates.

Cf. 8:21

i. e. the Syrians.

Hiddekel (חידקל) is the Persian Gulf not the Tigris. Mesopatamia extended to the East of the Tigris as well on both sides.

Ararat is the Himalayas and a different word just mentioned as such in 8:21 just 17 verses earlier.

This is a different word essentially the origin of Armenia which is not Ararat but Arara. If it were Ararat, it would say Ararat.

i. e. Turkey. According to Josephus the descendants of Lud were the Lydians.

Including Britain and Ireland.

i.e. Greece.

i.e. Greek isles.

5 And for Aram there came forth the fourth portion, all the land of Mesopotamia between the Hiddekel and the Euphrates to the north of the Chaldees to the border of the mountains of Asshur and the land of 'Arârâ. **6** And there came forth for Lud the fifth portion, the mountains of Asshur and all appertaining to them till it reacheth the Great Sea, and till it reacheth the east of Asshur his brother. **7** And Japheth also divided the land of his inheritance amongst his sons. **8** And the first portion came forth for Gomer to the east from the north side to the river Tînâ; and in the north there came forth for Magog all the inner portions of the north until it reacheth to the sea of Mê'at. **9** And for Madai came forth as his portion that he should possess from the west of his two brothers to the islands, and to the coasts of the islands. **10** And for Javan came forth the fourth portion every island and the islands which

i. e. all of Central Europe including Italy, Germany, etc. Tubal and Meshech become the seat of power for the prince demon in the end times – Gog of Magog. Cf. Ez. 38:2-3.

i.e. the Colonial Powers of Spain, France, etc. and even British Isles by default by Madai.

Tiras is the likely origin of Tyre though that is in Shem.

i. e. Medit. Is. Sardinia, Sicily, Corsica and Crete.

Ham is Africa to the South and Shem Asia to the East.

are towards the border of Lud. **11** And for Tubal there came forth the fifth portion in the midst of the tongue which approacheth towards the border of the portion of Lud to the second tongue, to the region beyond the second tongue unto the third tongue. **12** And for Meshech came forth the sixth portion, all the region beyond the third tongue till it approacheth the east of Gâdîr. **13** And for Tiras there came forth the seventh portion, four great islands in the midst of the sea, which reach to the portion of Ham [and the islands of Kamâtûrî came out by lot for the sons of Arpachshad as his inheritance]. **14** And thus the sons of Noah divided unto their sons in the presence of Noah their father, and he bound them all by an oath, imprecating a curse on every one that sought to seize the portion which had not fallen (to him) by his lot. **15** And they all said, "So be it; so be it," for themselves and their sons for ever throughout their generations till the day of judgment, on which the Yahuah Elohim shall judge them with a sword and with fire, for all the unclean wickedness of their errors, wherewith they have filled the earth with transgression and uncleanness and fornication and sin.

FULL COLOR MAP P. 88

It is critical to understand this mapping is not arbitrary nor can it leave anything to chance as to disobey this division is to bring a curse on one's family. No brother is to take the other brother's territory. It is one thing to live there but another entirely to seize it as theirs. This is a complete rebuke of colonialism and conquest other than to restore that which was stolen such as Israel taking back the land of Canaan from Ham's descendants and Nephilim.

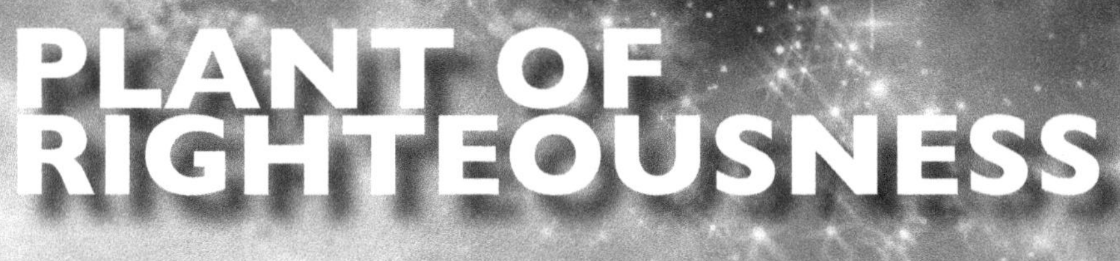

CHAPTER 10:

Noah's Sons Led Astray By Evil Spirits; Noah's Prayer; Mastêmâ; Death Of Noah

(10:1-17; cf. Gen. 9:28)

Here we have (in 10:1-15) another fragment of the lost Apocalypse of Noah (as in 7:20-39). The Hebrew original of 1-2 and 9-14 of this section is extant.

i. e. the spirits which issued from the children of the angels and the daughters of men. Nephilim.

†Omit the children of.

1 And in the third week of this jubilee the unclean demons began to lead astray †the children of† the sons of Noah; and to make to err and destroy them. **2** And the sons of Noah came to Noah their father, and they told him concerning the demons which were, leading astray and blinding and slaying his sons' sons.

Cf. Nm. 16:22, 27:16.

3 And he prayed before Yahuah his Elohim, and said: Elohim of the spirits of all flesh, who hast shown mercy unto me, And hast saved me and my sons from the waters of the flood, And hast not

Messiah Quoted Jubilees, Cf. Jn. 17:12.
"sons of perdition." Cf. 2 Th.2:3, Paul characterizes the Beast as a Nephilim quoting Jubilees. Sons of perdition = nephilim. This term is not found in the entire Old Testament.

caused me to perish as Thou didst the sons of perdition; For Thy grace hath been great towards me, And great hath been Thy mercy to my soul; Let Thy grace be lift up upon my sons, And let not wicked spirits rule over them lest they should destroy them from the earth. **4** But do Thou bless me and my sons, that we may increase and multiply and replenish the earth.

5 And Thou knowest how Thy Watchers, the fathers of these spirits, acted in my day: and as for these spirits which are living, imprison them and hold them fast in the place of condemnation, and let them not bring destruction on the sons of thy servant, my Elohim; for these are malignant, and created in order to destroy.

For 6, Cf. 1 En. 10:4, 127

6 And let them not rule over the spirits of the living; for Thou alone canst exercise dominion over them. And let them not have power over the sons of the righteous from henceforth and for evermore."

80:2 The word apparently = maṣṭîm (Hif. part of Śâṭam), "to be adverse," "inimical"; the Heb. noun maṣṭēmâ = "animosity," in Hos. ix. 7, 8. Thus the word = Satan ("adversary"). As a proper name it is practically confined to the Jubilees-literature. The evil spirits under the guidance of Mastêmâ tempt, accuse and destroy men. Mastema is satan.

7 And Yahuah our Elohim bade us to bind all.

8 And the chief of the spirits, Mastêmâ, came and said: "Yahuah, Creator, let some of them remain before me, and let them hearken to my voice, and do all that I shall say unto them; for if some of them are not left to me, I shall not be able to execute the power of my will on the sons of men; for these are for corruption and leading astray before my judgment, for great is the wickedness of the sons of men." **9** And He said: "Let

80:3 Only one-tenth are permitted to act freely against mankind till the Day of judgment.

the tenth part of them remain before him, and let nine parts descend into the place of condemnation." **10** And one

cf. Tobit 3:17, 12:14, 15

of us He commanded that we should teach Noah all their medicines; for He knew that they would not walk in uprightness, nor strive in righteousness. **11** And we did according to all His words: all the malignant evil ones we bound in the place of condemnation, and a tenth part of them we left that they might be subject before Satan on the earth. **12** And we explained to Noah all the medicines of their diseases, together with their seductions, how he might heal them with herbs of the earth. **13** And Noah wrote down all things in a book as we instructed him concerning every kind of medicine. Thus the evil spirits were precluded from (hurting) the sons of Noah. **14** And he gave all that he had written to Shem, his eldest son; for he loved him exceedingly above all his sons. **15** And Noah slept with his fathers, and was buried on Mount Lûbâr in the land of Ararat. **16** Nine hundred and fifty years he completed in his life, nineteen jubilees and two weeks and five years. **17** And in his life on earth he excelled the children of men save Enoch because of the righteousness, wherein he was perfect. For Enoch's

Thus Satan and Mastêmâ are identical.

Noah was given a book of medicines of healing herbs. This was passed to Shem. One must wonder where that is today. This is interesting as it suggests there are herbal remedies for essentially all diseases at least before some were modified in labs in modern times.

If Noah was buried on Mt. Lubar and his sons settled near that mountain, the were together in the same region where the ark landed which could not be Turkey.

1659 A.M.

office was ordained for a testimony to the generations of the world, so that he should recount all the deeds of generation unto generation, till the day of judgment.

Cf. 4:24

The Tower of Babel And The Confusion of Tongues
(10:18-27; cf. Gen. 11:1-9)

18 And in the three and thirtieth jubilee, in the first year in the second week, Peleg took to himself a wife, whose name was Lômnâ the daughter of Sînâ'ar, and she bare him a son in the fourth year of this week, and he called his name Reu; for he said: "Behold the children of men have become evil through the wicked purpose of building for themselves a city and a tower in the land of Shinar." **19** For they departed from the land of Ararat eastward to Shinar; for in his days they built the city and the tower, saying, "Go to, let us ascend thereby into heaven." **20** And they began to build, and in the fourth week they made brick with fire, and the bricks served them for stone, and the clay with which they cemented them together was asphalt which cometh out of the sea, and out of the fountains of water in the land of Shinar.

Cf. Gn. 11:18

Cf. Gn. 11:2

"they journeyed from the east" Problem: In v. 19, they migrated after Noah's death to Shinar from the East which is affirmed in Gn. Therefore, the **Mountains of Ararat must be East of Iraq not NW in Turkey.**

Cf. Gn. 11:4

Shinar was on the Tigris River in Iraq.

Cf. Gn. 11:3

Mesopotamia is famous for bitumen since ancient times documented for more than 5,000 years.

21 And they built it: forty and three years were they building it; its breadth was 203 bricks, and the height (of a brick) was the third of one; its height amounted to 5433 cubits and 2 palms, and (the extent of one wall was) thirteen stades (and of the other thirty stades). **22** And Yahuah our Elohim said unto us: "Behold, they are one people, and (this) they begin to do, and now nothing will be withholden from them. Go to, let us go down and confound their language, that they may not understand one another's speech, and they may be dispersed into cities and nations, and one purpose will no longer abide with them till the day of judgment." **23** And Yahuah descended, and we descended with Him to see the city and the tower which the children of men had built. **24** And He confounded their language, and they no longer understood one another's speech, and they ceased then to build the city and the tower. **25** For this reason the whole land of Shinar is called Babel, because Yahuah did there confound all the language of the children of men, and from thence they were dispersed into their cities, each according to his language and his nation.

26 And Yahuah sent a mighty wind against the tower and overthrew it upon the earth, and behold it was between Asshur and Babylon in the land of Shinar, and they called its name "Overthrow." **27** In the fourth week in the first year in the beginning thereof in the four and thirtieth jubilee, were they dispersed from the land of Shinar.

The Children Of Noah Enter Their Districts Canaan Seizes Palestine Wrongfully; Madai Takes Media *(10:28-36)*

28 And Ham and his sons went into the land which he was to occupy, which he acquired as his portion in the land of the south. **29** And Canaan saw the land of Lebanon to the river of Egypt that it was very good, and he went not into the land of his inheritance to the west (that is to) the sea, and he dwelt in the land of Lebanon, eastward and westward from the border of Jordan and from the border of the sea. **30** And Ham, his father, and Cush and Mizraim, his brothers, said unto him: "Thou hast settled in a land which. is not thine, and which did not fall to us by lot: do not do so; for if thou dost do so, thou and thy sons will fall in the land and (be) accursed through sedition; for by sedition ye have settled, and by sedition will thy children fall, and thou shalt be rooted out for ever. **31** Dwell not in the dwelling of Shem; for to Shem and to his sons did it come by their lot. **32** Cursed art thou, and cursed shalt thou be beyond all the sons of Noah, by the curse by which we bound ourselves by an oath in the presence of the holy judge, and in the presence of Noah our father." **33** But he did not hearken unto them, and dwelt in the land of Lebanon from Hamath to the entering of Egypt, he and his sons until this day. **34** And for this reason that land is named Canaan.

35 And Japheth and his sons went towards the sea and dwelt in the land of their portion, and Madai saw the land of the sea and it did not please him, and he begged a (portion) from Elam and Asshur and Arpachshad, his wife's brother, and he dwelt in the land of Media, near to his wife's brother until this day. **36** And he called his dwelling-place, and the dwelling-place of his sons, Media, after the name of their father Madai.

Cf. 9:14, 15

i. e. the angel who was present at the lot (8:10).

Hamath marked the northern boundary of Israel (modern Syria). the lot (8:10).

The Sinai Peninsula belonged to Egypt and serves as the Southern boundary.

Note this does not say Madai was given that which he begged. The Medes would become conquerors behind much of the world empire from the beginning. As with Canaan, Nephilim are recorded there.

CHAPTER 11:

The History Of The Patriarchs From Reu To Abraham *(cf. Gen. 11:20-30)*; The Corruption Of The Human Race *(11:1-15)*

1681 A.M.

1 And in the thirty-fifth jubilee, in the third week, in the first year thereof, Reu took to himself a wife, and her name was ʾÔrâ, the daughter of ʾÛr, the son of Kêsêd, and she bare him a son, and he called his name Sêrôḫ, in the seventh year of this week in this jubilee.

Cf. Gen. 11:20 f. (MT. has Serug for Sêrôḫ).

1687 A.M.

In 2-6 the corruption of mankind is ascribed to the period of Serug.

2 And the sons of Noah began to war on each other, to take captive and to slay each other, and to shed the blood of men on the earth, and to eat blood, and to build strong cities, and walls, and towers, and individuals (began) to exalt themselves above the nation, and to found the beginnings of kingdoms, and to go to war people against people, and nation against nation, and city against city, and all (began) to do evil, and to acquire arms, and to teach their sons war, and they began to capture cities, and to sell male and female slaves.

The place name Ur Kasdîm ("Ur of the Chaldees") is here transformed into the names of two persons, after whom the city is named.

i. e. Ur.

3 And ʾÛr, the son of Kêsêd, built the city of ʾArâ of the Chaldees, and called its name after his own name and the name of his father. **4** And they made for themselves molten images, and they worshipped each the idol, the molten image which they had made for themselves, and they began to make graven images and unclean simulacra, and malignant spirits assisted and seduced (them) into committing transgression and uncleanness.

5 And the prince Mastêmâ exerted himself to do all this, and he sent forth other spirits, those which were put under his hand, to do all manner of wrong and sin, and all manner of transgression, to corrupt and destroy, and to shed blood upon the earth.

Cf. 1 En. 16

6 For this reason he called the name of Sêrôḫ, Serug, for every one turned to do all manner of sin and transgression. **7** And he grew up, and dwelt in Ur of the Chaldees, near to the father of his wife's mother, and he worshipped idols, and he took to himself a wife in the thirty-sixth jubilee, in the fifth week, in the first year thereof, and her name was Mêlkâ, the daughter of Kâbêr, the daughter of his father's brother.

1744 A.M.

In Gn.11:29 Milcah is the name of the wife of Nahor, Abram's brother.

8 And she bare him Nahor, in the first year of this week, and he grew and dwelt in Ur of the Chaldees, and his father taught him the researches of the Chaldees to divine and augur, according to the signs of heaven. **9** And in the thirty-seventh jubilee, in the sixth week, in the first year thereof, he took to himself a wife, and her name was 'Îjâskâ, the daughter of Nêstâg of the Chaldees.

10 And she bare him Terah in the seventh year of this week. **11** And the prince Mastêmâ sent ravens and birds to devour the seed which was sown in the land, in order to destroy the land, and rob the children of men of their labours. Before they could plough in the seed, the ravens picked (it) from the surface of the ground. **12** And for this reason he called his name Terah, because the ravens and the birds reduced them to destitution and devoured their seed. **13** And the years began to be barren, owing to the birds, and they devoured all the fruit of the trees from the trees: it was only with great effort that they could save a little of all the fruit of the earth in their days. **14** And in this thirty-ninth jubilee, in the second week in the first year, Terah took to himself a wife, and her name was 'Êdnâ, the daughter of 'Abrâm the

daughter of his father's sister. **15** And in the seventh year of this week she bare him a son, and he called his name Abram, by the name of the father of his mother; for he had died before his daughter had conceived a son.

Abram's Knowledge of Yahuah and wonderful Deeds *(11:16-24)*

16 And the child began to understand the errors of the earth that all went astray after graven images and after uncleanness, and his father taught him writing, and he was two weeks of years old, and he separated himself from his father that he might not worship idols with him. **17** And he began to pray to the Creator of all things that He might save him from the errors of the children of men, and that his portion should not fall into error after uncleanness and vileness. **18** And the seed time came for the sowing of seed upon the land, and they all went forth together to protect their seed against the ravens, and Abram went forth with those that went, and the child was a lad of fourteen years. **19** And a cloud of ravens came to devour the seed, and Abram

1800 A.M.

Iscah (cf. Gn. 11:29; but there she is daughter of Haran).

1806 A.M.
Cf. Gn. 11:24

1870 A.M.

The talmud is wrong on yet another name.

i. e. the grandfather of the Biblical Abram.

1876 A.M.
It was customary to name a child after a grandfather. Here the child's name apparently perpetuates the memory of a grandfather who had died before the child was conceived.

1890 A.M.
See especially the first part of the Apocalypse of Abraham, an edition of which appears in this series. Cf. xii. 1-14 below.

ran to meet them before they settled on the ground, and cried to them, before they settled on the ground to devour the seed, and said, "Descend not: return to the place whence ye came," and they proceeded to turn back. **20** And he caused the clouds of ravens to turn back that day seventy times, and of all the ravens throughout all the land where Abram was there settled there not so much as one. **21** And all who were with him throughout all the land saw him cry out, and all the ravens turn back, and his name became great in all the land of the Chaldees. **22** And there came to him this year all those that wished to sow, and he went with them until the time of sowing ceased:

and they sowed their land, and that year they brought enough grain home and ate and were satisfied. **23** And in the first year of the fifth *1891 A.M.* week Abram taught those who made implements for oxen, the artificers in wood, and they made a vessel above the ground, facing the frame of the plough, in order to put the seed thereon, and the seed fell down therefrom upon the share of the plough, and was hidden in the earth, and they no longer feared the ravens. **24** And after this manner they made (vessels) above the ground on all the frames of the ploughs, and they sowed and tilled all the land, according as Abram commanded them, and they no longer feared the birds.

An improved method of sowing by means of a seed-scatterer attached to the plough (Arab. bûk) is here described. This marked an advance on the primitive method of scattering the seed by hand, and its invention is ascribed to Abraham.

And he caused the
CLOUDS OF
RAVENS
to turn back that day
SEVENTY
TIMES
11:20

CHAPTER 12:

Cf. 4Q225-226, fr. II. 12:12, 28 **Abram seeks to convert Terah from Idolatry; the Family of Terah** (*cf. Gen. 11:27-30*). **Abram burns the Idols. Death of Haran** (*cf. Gen. 11:28*) (12:1-14)

1904 A.M.

In 1-14 we have an early form of the legend of Abram's protest against idolatry. This section has remarkable parallels, both in thought and expression, with chaps. i.-viii. of the Apocalypse of Abraham.

1 And it came to pass in the sixth week, in the seventh year thereof, that Abram said to Terah his father, saying, "Father!" And he said, "Behold, here am I, my son." **2** And he said, "What help and profit have we from those idols which thou dost worship, And before which thou dost bow thyself? **3** For there is no spirit in them, For they are dumb forms, and a misleading of the heart. Worship them not: **4** Worship the Elohim of heaven, Who causeth the rain and the dew to descend on the earth, And doeth everything upon the earth, And hath created everything by His word, And all life is from before His face. **5** Why do ye worship things that have no spirit in them? For they are the work of (men's) hands, And on your shoulders do ye bear them, And ye have no help from them, But they are a great cause of shame to those who make them, And

Cf. Ps. 83:17

Cf. 20:9; Jr. 14:22.

Cf. Ps. 83:6; Heb. 11:3; 2 Pet. 3:5; 2 Esd. 6:3.

Cf. Jr.10:3, 9

Cf. Isa. 46:7; Jer. 10:5; Assumpt. Moses, 8:4

a misleading of the heart to those who worship them: Worship them not." **6** And his father said unto him, "I also know it, my son, but what shall I do with a people who have made me to serve before them? **7** And if I tell them the truth, they will slay me; for their soul cleaveth to them to worship them and honour them. Keep silent, my son, lest they slay thee." **8** And these words he spake to his two brothers, and they were angry with him and he kept silent.

9 And in the fortieth jubilee, in the second week, in the seventh year thereof, Abram took to himself a wife, and her name was Sarai, the daughter of his father, and she became his wife. **10** And Haran, his brother, took to himself a wife in the third year of the third week, and she bare him a son in the seventh year of this week and he called his name Lot. **11** And Nahor, his brother, took to himself a wife. **12** And in the sixtieth year of the life of Abram, that is, in the fourth week, in the fourth year thereof, Abram arose by night, and burned the house of the idols, and he burned all that was in the house, and no man knew it. **13** And they arose in the night and sought

In Ap. Abraham Terah is indignant with Abraham for deriding the idols.

1925 A.M.

Cf. Gn. 20:12, according to which Sarah was Abraham's half-sister. In Lev. xviii. 9, 11, xx. 17, marriage with a sister or half-sister is strictly forbidden.

1932 A.M.

According to Gn. 11:29, Milcah.

1936 A.M.

to save their gods from the midst of the fire.

14 And Haran hasted to save them, but the fire flamed over him, and he was burnt in the fire, and he died in Ur of the Chaldees before Terah his father, and they buried him in Ur of the Chaldees.

In Ap. Abraham, viii. the fire descends from heaven and burns the house and all in it (including Terah). Only Abraham, escapes.

The Family Of Terah In Haran; Abram's Experiences There; His Journey To Canaan
(12:15-31; cf. Gen. 11:31-12:3)

Cf. Gn. 11:31

15 And Terah went forth from Ur of the Chaldees, he and his sons, to go into the land of Lebanon and into the land of Canaan, and he dwelt in the land of Haran, and Abram, dwelt with Terah his father in Haran two weeks of years. **16** And in the sixth week, in the fifth year thereof, Abram sat up throughout the night on the new moon of the seventh month to observe the stars from the evening to the morning, in order to see what would be the character of the year with regard to the rains, and he was alone as he sat and observed. **17** And a word came into his heart and he said: "All the signs of the stars, and the signs of the moon and of the sun are all in the hand of Yahuah. Why do

I search (them) out? **18** If He desireth, He causeth it to rain, morning and evening; And if He desireth, He withholdeth it, And all things are in His hand." **19** And he prayed that night and said "My Elohim, Elohim Most High, Thou alone art my Elohim, And Thee and Thy dominion have I chosen. And Thou hast created all things, And all things that are are the work of Thy hands.

20 Deliver me from the hands of evil spirits who have sway over the thoughts of men's hearts, And let them not lead me astray from Thee, my Elohim. And stablish Thou me and my seed for ever That we go not astray from henceforth and for evermore." **21** And he said Shall I return unto Ur of the Chaldees who seek my face that I may return to them, or am I to remain here in this place? The right path before Thee prosper it in the hands of Thy servant that he may fulfil (it) and that I may not walk in the deceitfulness of my heart, O my Elohim." **22** And he made an end of speaking and praying, and behold the word of Yahuah was sent to him through me, saying: "Get thee up from thy country, and from thy kindred and from the house of thy father unto a land which I shall show thee, and I shall make thee a great and numerous nation. **23** And I shall bless thee And I shall make thy name great, And thou wilt be blessed in the earth, And in thee will all families of the earth be blessed, And I shall bless them that bless thee, And curse them that curse thee. **24** And I shall be an Elohim to thee and thy son, and to thy son's son, and to all thy seed: fear not, from henceforth and unto all generations of the earth I am thy Elohim." **25** And Yahuah Elohim said: "Open his mouth and his ears, that he may hear and speak with his mouth, with the language which hath been revealed"; for it had ceased from the mouths of all the children of men from the day of the overthrow (of Babel). **26** And I opened his mouth, and his ears and his lips, and I began to speak with him in Hebrew in the tongue of the creation. **27** And he took the books of his fathers, and these were written in Hebrew and he transcribed them, and he began from henceforth to study them, and I made known to him that which he could not (understand), and he studied them during the six rainy months. **28** And it came to pass in the seventh year of the sixth week that he spoke to his father, and informed him that he would leave Haran to go into the land of Canaan to see it and return to him.

29 And Terah his father said unto him; "Go in peace: May the eternal Elohim make thy path straight, And Yahuah [(be) with thee, and] protect thee from all evil, And grant unto thee grace, mercy and favour before those who see thee, And may none of the children of men have power over thee to harm thee; Go in peace. **30** And if thou seest a land pleasant to thy eyes to dwell in, then arise and take me to thee and take Lot with thee, the son of Haran thy brother, as thine own son: Yahuah be with thee. **31** And Nahor thy brother leave with me till thou returnest in peace, and we go with thee all together."

1951 A.M.

Cf. Gn. 12:1-3 (cf. Acts 7:3)

i. e. the sacred language, Hebrew, knowledge of which had been lost since the overthrow of Babel. According to another tradition Heber alone retained knowledge of Hebrew because he had taken no part in the building of the Tower.

The angel is the speaker.

There is no language which preceded Hebrew, the tongue of Creation.

i. e. the winter.

1953 A.M.

LeviteBible.com

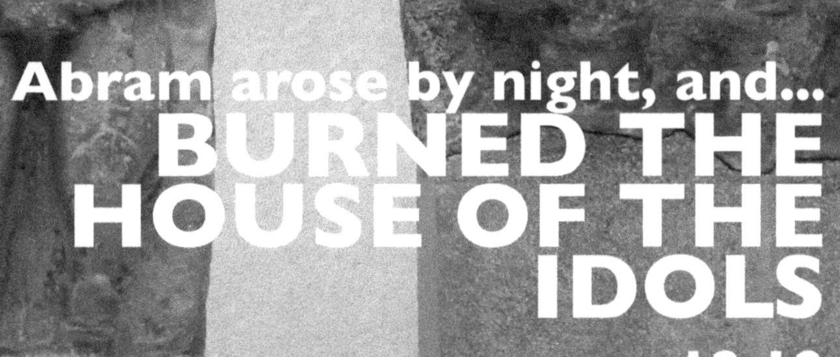

Right: BERLIN, GERMANY - 23,03,2015 : Exhibits of the Pergamon Museum, situated on the Museum Island in Berlin. It's subdivided into the antiquity, the Middle East, and the museum of Islamic art.

CHAPTER 13:

Abram With Lot In Canaan And Egypt (cf. Gen. 12:4-20). Abram Separates From Lot (cf. Gen. 13:11-18) (13:1-21)

1 And Abram journeyed from Haran, and he took Sarai, his wife, and Lot his brother Haran's son, to the land of Canaan, and he came into †Asshur†, and proceeded to Shechem, and dwelt near a lofty oak. 2 And he saw, and, behold, the land was very pleasant from the entering of Hamath to the lofty oak. 3 And Yahuah said to him: "To thee and to thy seed will I give this land." 4 And he built an altar there, and he offered thereon a burnt sacrifice to the Lord, who had appeared to him. 5 And he removed from thence unto the mountain . . . Bethel on the west and Ai on the east, and pitched his tent there. 6 And he saw and behold, the land was very wide and good, and everything grew thereon--vines and figs and pomegranates, oaks and ilexes, and terebinths and oil trees, and cedars and cypresses and date trees, and all trees of the field, and there was water on the mountains. 7 And he blessed Yahuah who had led him out of Ur of the Chaldees, and had brought him to this land. 8 And it came to pass in the first year, in the seventh week, on the new moon of the first month, that he built an altar on this mountain, and called on the name of the Yahuah: "Thou, the eternal Elohim, art my Elohim." 9 And he offered on the altar a burnt sacrifice unto Yahuah that He should be with him and not forsake him all the days of his life.

10 And he removed from thence and went towards the south, and he came to Hebron, and Hebron was built at, that time, and he dwelt there two years, and he went (thence) into the land of the south, to Bealoth and there was a famine in the land. 11 And Abram went into Egypt in the third year of the week, and he dwelt in Egypt five years before his wife was torn away from him. 12 NOW Tanais in Egypt was at that time built--seven years after Hebron. 13 And it came to pass when Pharaoh seized Sarai, the wife of Abram, that Yahuah plagued Pharaoh and his house with great plagues because of Sarai, Abram's wife. 14 And Abram was very glorious by reason of possessions in sheep, and

Marginal notes:

† Corrupt. Read probably Canaan. For 1 cf. Gn. 12:5-6. For "lofty oak" (so LXX) NIT has "oak of Moreh."

Supply (?) "to the east of Bethel with" (Charles).

For 3-5 cf. Gn. 12:7, 8

1954 A.M.

Cf. Gn. 12:8

Cf. Gn. 12:9

A town in S. Judah (Js. 15:24)

1956 A.M. Cf. Gn. 12:10

i. e. Zoan.

Cf. Nm. 8:22

cattle, and asses, and horses, and camels, and menservants,

For 13-15a cf. Gn. 12:15-20 (note that Gen. 12:18 is omitted).

and maidservants, and in silver and gold exceedingly. And Lot also, his brother's son, was wealthy. **15** And Pharaoh gave back Sarai, the wife of Abram, and he sent him out of the land of Egypt, and he journeyed to the place where he had pitched his tent at the beginning, to the place of the

Cf. Gn. 13:3-4.

altar, with Ai on the east, and Bethel on the west, and he blessed Yahuah his Elohim who had brought him back in peace. **16** And it came to pass

1963 A.M.

in the forty-first jubilee, in the third year of the first week, that he returned to this place and offered thereon a burnt sacrifice, and called on the name of Yahuah, and said: "Thou, the most high Elohim, art my Elohim for ever and

1964 A.M.

ever." **17** And in the fourth year of this week Lot parted from him, and Lot dwelt in Sodom,

Cf. 8 above

and the men of Sodom were sinners exceedingly. **18** And it grieved him in his heart

Cf. Gn. 13:11, 13.

that his brother's son had parted from him; for he had

For 19-21 cf. Gn. 13: 14-18.

no children. **19** In that year when Lot was taken captive, Yahuah said unto Abram, after that Lot had parted from him, in the fourth year of this week: "Lift up thine eyes

from the place where thou art dwelling, northward and southward, and westward and eastward. **20** For all the land which thou seest I shall give to thee and to thy seed for ever, and I shall make thy seed as the sand of the sea: though

Cf. Gn. 22:17 (Gn.13: 16 has as the dust of the earth").

a man may number the dust of the earth, yet thy seed shall not be numbered. **21** Arise, walk (through the land) in the length of it and the breadth of

"So that if a man can number then shall thy seed also be numbered" (Gn. 13:16).

it, and see it all; for to thy seed shall I give it." And Abram went to Hebron, and dwelt there.

The Campaign of Chedorlaomer

(13:22-29; cf. Gen. 14)

22 And in this year came Chedorlaomer, king of Elam, and Amraphel, king of Shinar, and Arioch, king of Sêllâsar and Têrgâl, king of

MT Ellasar.

MT Tidal (for form here cf. LXX Θαργάλ).

nations, and slew the king of Gomorrah, and the king of Sodom fled, and many fell through wounds in the vale of Siddim, by the Salt Sea.

23 And they took captive Sodom and Adam and

i. e. Admah.

Zeboim, and they took captive Lot also, the son of Abram's brother, and all his possessions,

Cf. Gn. 14:14

and they went to Dan.

24 And one who had escaped came and told Abram that his

brother's son had been taken captive and (Abram) armed his household servants.

25 . . . . for Abram, and for his seed, a tenth of the first-fruits to Yahuah, and Yahuah ordained it as an ordinance for ever that they should give it to the priests who served before Him, that they should possess it for ever. **26** And to this law there is no limit of days; for He hath ordained it for the generations for ever that they should give to Yahuah the tenth of everything, of the seed and of the wine and of the oil and of the cattle and of the sheep. **27** And He gave (it) unto His priests to eat and to drink with joy before Him.

28 And the king of Sodom came to him and bowed himself before him, and said: "Our lord Abram, give unto us the souls which thou hast rescued, but let the booty be thine." **29** And Abram said unto him: "I lift up my hands to the Most High Elohim, that from a thread to a shoe-latchet I shall not take aught that is thine, lest thou shouldst say I have made Abram rich; save only what the young men have eaten, and the portion of the men who went with me--Aner, Eschol, and Mamre. These will take their portion."

Below: Abraham tithes Melchizedek the King and Priest.
Right: Ancient Sumerian artifact.

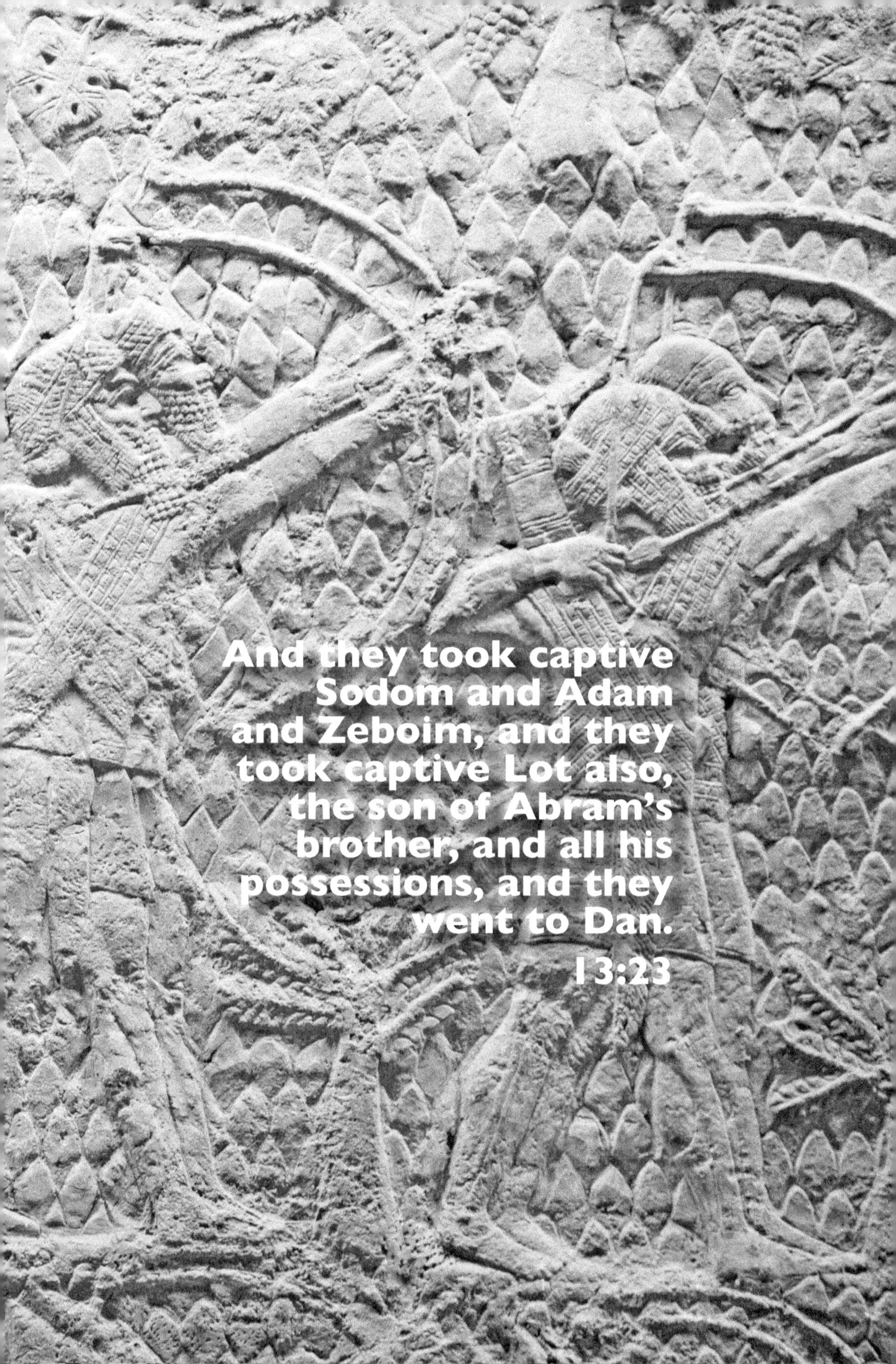
And they took captive
Sodom and Adam
and Zeboim, and they
took captive Lot also,
the son of Abram's
brother, and all his
possessions, and they
went to Dan.

I 3:23

CHAPTER 14:

Yahuah's Covenant with Abram *(14:1-20; cf. Gen. 15)*

1681 A.M.

For 1-6 cf. Gn. 15:1-6

1 After these things, in the fourth year of this week, on the new moon of the third month, the word of Yahuah came to Abram in a dream, saying: "Fear not, Abram; I am thy defender, and thy reward will be exceeding great." **2** And he said: "Yahuah, Yahuah, what wilt thou give me, seeing I go hence childless, and the son of Mâsêq, the son of my handmaid, is the Dammasek Eliezer: he will be my heir, and to me thou hast given no seed." **3** And He said unto him: "This (man) will not be thy heir, but one that will come out of thine own bowels; he will be thine heir." **4** And He brought him forth abroad, and said unto him: "Look toward heaven and number the stars, if thou art able to number them." **5** And he looked toward heaven, and beheld the stars. And He said unto him: "So shall thy seed be." **6** And he believed in Yahuah, and it was counted to him for righteousness. **7** And He said unto him: "I am Yahuah that brought thee out of Ur of the Chaldees, to give thee the land

Wrongly taken as a proper name (cf. RX.). So LXX.

of the Canaanites to possess it for ever; and I shall be Elohim unto thee and to thy seed after thee." **8** And he said: "Yahuah, Yahuah, whereby shall I know that I shall inherit (it)?" **9** And he said unto him: "Take Me an heifer of three years, and a goat of three years, and a sheep of three years, and a turtle-dove, and a pigeon." **10** And he took all these in the middle of the month; and he dwelt at the oak of Mamre, which is near Hebron.

11 And he built there an altar, and sacrificed all these; and he poured their blood upon the altar, and divided them in the midst, and laid them over against each other; but the birds divided he not. **12** And birds came down upon the pieces, and Abram drove them away, and did not suffer the birds to touch them. **13** And it came to pass, when the sun had set, that an ecstasy fell upon Abram, and lo! an horror of great darkness fell upon him, and it was said unto Abram: "Know of a surety that thy seed shall be a stranger in a land (that is) not theirs, and they will bring them into bondage, and afflict them four hundred years. **14** And the nation also to whom they will be in bondage

Cf. Gn. 15:7

For 8-9 cf. Gn. 15:8-9

Sivan 15 = Shavuot. Day of Covenant Renewal. Cf. 5:32-6:2

Cf. Gn. 14:13

For 11-12 cf. Gn.15:10-11

Cf. Gn. xv. 13, but Exod. xii. 40 gives the number 430. Tradition assumes that the number includes the sojourn of the Patriarchs in Canaan. Our text reckons the period from the birth of Isaac (when Abraham was 100 years old). St. Paul (Gal. iii. 16-17) reckons 430 years from the announcement. According to Targ. Ps.-Jon. on Exod. xii. 40 f., the odd 30 years cover the period between the announcement and Isaac's birth.

For 13-16 cf. Gn. 15:12-16

shall I judge, and after that they will come forth thence with much substance. **15** And thou wilt go to thy fathers in peace, and be buried in a good old age. **16** But in the fourth generation they will return hither; for the iniquity of the Amorites is not yet full."

A generation = 100 years. Isaac was born when Abraham was 100 years old (Gn. 21:5). The same applies to the curse for breaking the 2nd commandment to the 3rd and 4th or 3-400 yrs.

17 And he awoke from his sleep, and he arose, and the sun had set; and there was a flame, and behold! a furnace was smoking, and a flame of fire passed between the pieces. **18** And on that day

For 17-18 cf. Gn. 15:17-21

Yahuah made a covenant with Abram, saying: "To thy seed will I give this land, from the river of Egypt unto the great river, the river Euphrates, the Kenites, the

Absent from NIT (which inserts "Hittite" before "Perizite").

Kenizzites, the Kadmonites, the Perizzites, and the Rephaim, the Phakorites,

So LXX and Sam. here (Gn. 15:20); but MT, Syr. and Vulg. omit.

and the Hivites, and the Amorites, and the Canaanites, and the Girgashites, and the Jebusites." **19** And the day passed, and Abram offered the pieces, and the birds, and their fruit-offerings, and their drink-offerings, and the fire devoured them. **20** And on that day we made a covenant with Abram, according as we had covenanted with Noah in this month; and Abram renewed the festival and ordinance for himself for ever.

i. e. the 15th of Sivan. Shavuot.

Probably, according to our author, on the same day of the month.

The Birth of Ishmael
(14:21-24; cf. Gen. 16:1-4. 11)

21 And Abram rejoiced, and made all these things known to Sarai his wife; and he believed that he would have seed, but she did not bear. **22** And Sarai advised her husband Abram, and said unto him: "Go in unto Hagar, my Egyptian maid: it may be that I shall build up seed unto thee by her." **23** And Abram hearkened unto the voice of Sarai his wife, and said unto her, "Do (so)." And Sarai took Hagar, her maid, the Egyptian, and gave her to Abram, her husband, to be his wife. **24** And he went in unto her, and she conceived and bare him a son, and he called his name Ishmael, in the fifth year of this week; and this was the eighty-sixth year in the life of Abram.

1965 A.M.

CHAPTER 15:

The Feast Of First-fruits Circumcision Instituted. The Promise Of Isaac's Birth. Circumcision Ordained For All Israel

(15:1-34; cf. Gen. 17)

1979 A.M.
† Read "third."

i. e. the 15th of Sivan.

i. e. the Feast of Weeks. The Pharisees celebrated this feast not on Sivan 15th, but on Sivan 6th which is wrong.

The offerings prescribed for this festival in Lv. 23:18-20 are different though not significantly. Cf. 14:9

For 3-4 cf. Gn. 17:1 f

For 5-10 cf. Gn. 17:3-8

Yahuah is the origin of Law not Moses. He wrote such with his very finger and no man can abolish them.

1 And in the fifth year of the †fourth† week of this jubilee, in the third month, in the middle of the month, Abram celebrated the feast of the first-fruits of the grain harvest. **2** And he offered new offerings on the altar, the first-fruits of the produce, unto Yahuah, an heifer and a goat and a sheep on the altar as a burnt sacrifice unto Yahuah; their fruit-offerings and their drink-offerings he offered upon the altar with frankincense. **3** And Yahuah appeared to Abram, and said unto him: "I am Elohim Almighty; approve thyself before Me and be thou perfect. **4** And I will make My covenant between Me and thee, and I will multiply thee exceedingly." **5** And Abram fell on his face, and Elohim talked with him, and said: **6** "Behold My ordinance is with thee, And thou wilt be the father of many nations. **7** Neither will thy name any more be called Abram, But thy name from

henceforth, even for ever, shall be Abraham. For the father of many nations have I made thee. **8** And I shall make thee very great, And I shall make thee into nations, And kings will come forth from thee.

9 And I shall establish My covenant between Me and thee, and thy seed after thee, throughout their generations, for an eternal covenant, so that I may be a Elohim unto thee, and to thy seed after thee. **10** (And I shall give to thee and to thy seed after thee) the land where thou hast been a sojourner, the land of Canaan, that thou mayst possess it for ever, and I shall be their Elohim." **11** And Yahuah said unto Abraham: "And as for thee, do thou keep My Covenant, thou and thy seed after thee, and circumcise ye every male among you, and circumcise your foreskins, and it will be a token of an eternal covenant between Me and you. **12** And the child on the eighth day ye will circumcise, every male throughout your generations, him that is born in the house, or whom ye have bought with money from any stranger, whom ye have acquired who is not of thy seed. **13** He that is born in thy house will surely be

The bracketed words (lost through homo-ioteleuton) are restored from Gn. 17:8.

For 11-13 cf. Gn. 17:9-13

Cf. Lv. 12:3, Phl. 3:5. Paul was circumcised on the 8th day. This is consistent.

Ethiop. MSS. and Lat. have "till."

circumcised, and those whom thou hast bought with money will be circumcised, and My covenant will be in your flesh for an eternal ordinance.

For 14 cf. Gn. 17:14

14 And the uncircumcised male who is not circumcised in the flesh of his foreskin on the eighth day, that soul will be cut off from his people, for he hath broken My covenant."

Later Judaism changed this as they have much of Torah.

For 15-22 cf. Gn. 17:15-22

15 And Elohim said unto Abraham: "As for Sarai thy wife, her name will no more be called Sarai, but Sarah will be her name. **16** And I shall bless her, and give thee a son by her, and I shall bless him, and he will become a nation, and kings of nations will proceed from him." **17** And Abraham fell on his face, and rejoiced, and said in his heart: "Shall a son be born to him that is a hundred years old, and shall Sarah, who is ninety years old, bring forth?" **18** And Abraham said unto Elohim: "O that Ishmael might live before thee!" **19** And Elohim said: "Yea, and Sarah also will bear thee a son, and thou wilt call his name Isaac, and I shall establish My covenant with him, an everlasting covenant, and for his seed after him.

So LXX, Sam., Syr and Vulg. of Gn. 17:22. But MT makes the text refer to Sarah ("yea, I will bless her, [and she shall be a mother of nations: kings of peoples shall be of her]," R.V.).

20 And as for Ishmael also have I heard thee, and behold I shall bless him, and make him great, and multiply him exceedingly, and he will beget twelve princes, and I shall make him a great nation. **21** But My covenant shall I establish with Isaac, whom Sarah will bear to thee, in these days, in the next year." **22** And He left off speaking with him, and Elohim went up from Abraham. **23** And Abraham did according as Elohim had said unto him, and he took Ishmael his son, and all that were born in his house, and whom he had bought with his money, every male in his house, and circumcised the flesh of their foreskin.

For 23-24 cf. Gn. 17:23-27

24 And on the selfsame day was Abraham circumcised, and all the men of his house, (and those born in the house), and all those, whom he had bought with money from the children of the stranger, were circumcised with him.

i. e. the 15th of Sivan. Shavuot.

25 This law is for all the generations for ever, and there is no circumcision of the days, and no omission of one day out of the eight days; for it is an eternal ordinance, ordained and written on the heavenly tables.

i. e.? of the days preceding the eighth day.

26 And every one that is born, the flesh of whose foreskin is not circumcised on the eighth day, belongeth not to the children of the

Only on the eighth day is the rite to be performed.

covenant which Yahuah made with Abraham, but to the children of destruction; nor is there, moreover, any sign on him that he is Yahuah's, but (he is destined) to be destroyed and slain from the earth, and to be rooted out of the earth, for he hath broken the covenant of the Yahuah our Elohim. **27** For all the angels of the presence and all the angels of sanctification have been so created from the day of their creation, and before the angels of the presence and the angels of sanctification He hath sanctified Israel, that they should be with Him and with His holy angels. **28** And do thou command the children of Israel and let them observe the sign of this covenant for their generations as an eternal ordinance, and they will not be rooted out of the land. **29** For the command is ordained for a covenant, that they should observe it for ever among all the children of Israel. **30** For Ishmael and his sons and his brothers and Esau, Yahuah did not cause to approach Him, and he chose them not because they are the children of Abraham, because He knew them, but He chose Israel to be His people.

31 And He sanctified it, and gathered it from amongst all the children of men; for there are many nations and many peoples, and all are His, and over all hath He placed spirits in authority to lead them astray from Him. **32** But over Israel He did not appoint any angel or spirit, for He alone is their ruler, and He will preserve them and require them at the hand of His angels and His spirits, and at the hand of all His powers in order that He may preserve them and bless them, and that they may be His and He may be theirs from henceforth for ever. **33** And now I announce unto thee that the children of Israel will not keep true to this ordinance, and they will not circumcise their sons according to all this law; for in the flesh of their circumcision they will omit this circumcision of their sons, and all of them, sons of Beliar, will leave their sons uncircumcised as they were born. **34** And there will be great wrath from Yahuah against the children of Israel, because they have forsaken His covenant and turned aside from His word, and provoked and blasphemed, inasmuch as they do not observe the ordinance of this law; for they have treated their members

i. e. have been created circumcised.

Israel is God's portion; cf. Deut. xxxii. 8-9 in the LXX form of which "angels" is read instead of "children of Israel"; cf. also Ecclus. xvii. 17. The "seventy nations of the earth were placed under the dominion of seventy angels"; but in Dan. x. 13, 20, 21, xii. 1, Michael is referred to as Israel's angel-prince.

This describes the result, not the original purpose of their appointment.

In 1:20 (see note). Beliar is clearly a Satanic being. This meaning may possibly be present in the use of the expression here. "Sons of Belial" is common in the O.T. (cf. e.g. 1 Sa. 2:12).

like the Gentiles, so that they may be removed and rooted out of the land. And there will no more be pardon or forgiveness unto them [so that there should be forgiveness and pardon] for all the sin of this eternal error.

And he offered new offerings on the altar, the first-fruits of the produce, unto Yahuah, an heifer and a goat and a sheep on the altar as a burnt sacrifice unto Yahuah; their fruit-offerings and their drink-offerings he offered...

UPON THE ALTAR WITH FRANKINCENSE

15:2

CHAPTER 16:

Angelic Visitation Of Abraham In Hebron; Promise Of Isaac's Birth Repeated. The Destruction Of Sodom And Lot's Deliverance *(16:1-9; cf. Gen. 18-19)*

i. e. the angels.

For 1 cf. Gn. 18:1, 10 (v. 2-9 omitted).

1 And on the new moon of the fourth month we appeared unto Abraham, at the oak of Mamre, and we talked with him, and we announced to him that a son would be given to him by Sarah his wife.

Cf. Gn. 18:10, 12, 15

2 And Sarah laughed, for she heard that we had spoken these words with Abraham, and we admonished her, and she became afraid, and denied that she had laughed on account of the words. 3 And we told her the name of her son, as his name is ordained and written in the heavenly tables (i.e.) Isaac. 4 And (that) when we returned to her at a set time, she would have conceived a son. 5 And in this month Yahuah executed

Cf. Gn. 14:2, 8

his judgments on Sodom, and Gomorrah, and Zeboim, and all the region of the Jordan, and He burned them with fire and brimstone, and destroyed them until this day, even as [lo] I have declared

unto thee all their works, that they are wicked and sinners

For 5 cf. Gn. 19:24

exceedingly, and that they defile themselves and commit fornication in their flesh, and work uncleanness on the earth. 6 And, in like manner, God will execute judgment on the places where they have done according to the uncleanness of the Sodomites, like unto the judgment of Sodom. 7 But Lot we saved; for Elohim remembered Abraham, and sent him out from the midst of the overthrow.

For 7-8 cf. Gn. 19:29, 31 ff

8 And he and his daughters committed sin upon the earth, such as had not been on the earth since the days of Adam till his time; for the man lay with his daughters. 9 And, behold, it was commanded and engraven concerning all his seed, on the heavenly tables, to remove them and root them out, and to execute judgment upon them like the judgment of Sodom, and to leave no seed of the man on earth on the day of condemnation.

Abraham at Beersheba. Birth and Circumcision of Isaac *(cf. Gen. 21:1-4).* Institution of the Feast of Tabernacles *(16:10-31)*

10 And in this month

Or "territories."

Abraham moved from Hebron, and departed and dwelt between Kadesh and Shur in the mountains of Gerar. **11** And in the middle of the fifth month he moved *i. e. Beersheba; cf. Gn. 21:31* from thence, and dwelt at the Well of the Oath. **12** And in *For 12-14 cf. Gn. 21:1-4* the middle of the sixth month Yahuah visited Sarah and did *1980 A.M.* unto her as He had spoken, and she conceived. **13** And *i. e. the 15th of Sivan. Shavuot.* she bare a son in the third month, and in the middle of the month, at the time of *i. e. Shavuot/ Pentecost.* which Yahuah had spoken to Abraham, on the festival of the first-fruits of the harvest, Isaac was born. **14** And Abraham circumcised his son on the eighth day: he was the first that was circumcised according to the covenant which is ordained for ever. *†Read "third" as in 15:1 (Charles).* **15** And in the sixth year of the †fourth† week we came to Abraham, to the Well of the Oath, and we appeared unto *The bracketed words are an incorrect gloss, according to Charles, and should be omitted.* him [as we had told Sarah that we should return to her, and she would have conceived a son. **16** And we returned in the seventh month, and found Sarah with child before us] and we blessed him, and we announced to him all the things which had been decreed concerning him, that he should not die till he should beget six sons more, and *Six sons by Keturah (Gn. 25:2).* should see (them) before he died; but (that) in Isaac should his name and seed be called: *Cf. Gn. 21:12* **17** And (that) all the seed of his sons should be Gentiles, *All Abraham's descendants, except Jacob and his seed, were to be reckoned among the Gentiles.* and be reckoned with the Gentiles; but from the sons of Isaac one should become a holy seed, and should not be reckoned among the Gentiles. *Cf. 15:31 f* **18** For he should become the portion of the Most High, and all his seed had fallen into the possession of Elohim, that it should be unto Yahuah *Cf. Dt. 7:6; Ex. 19:5* a people for (His) possession above all nations and that it *Cf. Ex. 19:6 (MT has "a kingdom of priests"); cf. Rev. 5:10, 1:6, which agree with our text substantially, and this may be the original sense.* should become a kingdom and priests and a holy nation. **19** And we went our way, and we announced to Sarah all that we had told him, and they both rejoiced with exceeding great joy.

20 And he built there an altar to Yahuah who had delivered him, and who was making him rejoice in the land of his sojourning, and he celebrated a festival of joy in this month seven days, near the altar which he had built at the Well of the Oath. **21** And he built booths for himself and for his servants on this festival, and he was the first to celebrate the feast of tabernacles on the earth. **22** And during these seven days he brought each day to the altar a burnt-offering to Yahuah, two oxen, two rams, seven sheep, one he-goat, for a sin-offering, that he might atone thereby for himself and for his seed. 23 And, as a thank-offering, seven rams, seven kids, seven sheep, and seven he-goats, and their fruit-offerings and their drink-offerings; and he burnt all the fat thereof on the altar, a chosen offering unto Yahuah for a sweet smelling savour. 24 And morning and evening he burnt fragrant substances, frankincense and galbanum, and stacte, and nard, and myrrh, and spice, and costum; all these seven he offered, crushed, mixed together in equal parts (and) pure. 25 And he celebrated this feast during seven days, rejoicing with all his heart and with all his soul, he and all those who were in his house; and there was no stranger with him, nor any that was uncircumcised. 26 And he blessed his Creator who had created him in his generation, for He had created him according to His good pleasure; for He knew and perceived that from him would arise the plant of righteousness for the eternal generations, and from him

a holy seed, so that it should become like Him who had made all things. 27 And he blessed and rejoiced, and he called the name of this festival the festival of Yahuah, a joy acceptable to the Most High Elohim. 28 And we blessed him for ever, and all his seed after him throughout all the generations of the earth, because he celebrated this festival in its season, according to the testimony of the heavenly tables. 29 For this reason it is ordained on the heavenly tables concerning Israel, that they shall celebrate the feast of tabernacles seven days with joy, in the seventh month, acceptable before Yahuah -- a statute for ever throughout their generations every year. 30 And to this there is no limit of days; for it is ordained for ever regarding Israel that they should celebrate it and dwell in booths, and set wreaths upon their heads, and take leafy boughs, and willows from the brook. 31 And Abraham took branches of palm trees, and the fruit of goodly trees, and every day going round the altar with the branches seven times [a day] in the morning, he praised and gave thanks to his Elohim for all things in joy.

But Lot we saved; for
ELOHIM
REMEMBERED
ABRAHAM
and sent him out
from the midst of the
overthrow.
16:7

Right: The Dead Sea in Israel remains the lowest place on earth and, in ancient times, likely a continuation of the Jordan River which flows into it today still. As Sodom was destroyed by fire ad brimstone or salt, this is the most likely location of Sodom and Gomorrah which was utterly destroyed. There should be no archaeology to find, just salt. Voila!

Yahuah executed his judgments on SODOM, GOMORRAH, and Zeboim, and all the region of the Jordan, and He burned them with fire and brimstone, and destroyed them until this day

16:5

The likely creation
of the Dead Sea, the
lowest place on Earth
filled with traces of
fire and brimstone.

CHAPTER 17:

The Expulsion Of Hagar And Ishmael

(17:1-14; cf. Gen. 21:8-21)

1982 A.M.

† Read "fourth" (Charles).

1 And in the first year of the †fifth† week Isaac was weaned in this jubilee, and Abraham made a great banquet in the third month, on the day his son Isaac was weaned.

Cf. Gn. 21:8

2 And Ishmael, the son of Hagar, the Egyptian, was before the face of Abraham, his father, in his place, and Abraham rejoiced and blessed Elohim because he had seen his sons and had not died childless.

Cf.16:16

3 And he remembered the words which He had spoken to him on the day on which Lot had parted from him, and he rejoiced because Yahuah had given him seed upon the earth to inherit the earth, and he blessed with all his mouth the Creator of all things.

Cf. 13:19 ff

4 And Sarah saw Ishmael playing and dancing and Abraham rejoicing with great joy, and she became jealous of Ishmael and said to Abraham, "Cast out this bondwoman and her son; for the son of this bondwoman will not be heir with my son, Isaac."

Possibly and dancing is corrupt for with Isaac, which is read in LXX and Vulg.; cf. Gn. 21:9.

5 And the thing was grievous in Abraham's sight, because of his maidservant and because of his son, that he should drive them from him.

For 4-13 cf. Gn. 21:9-21

6 And Elohim said to Abraham "Let it not be grievous in thy sight, because of the child and because of the bondwoman; in all that Sarah hath said unto thee, hearken to her words and do (them); for in Isaac shall thy name and seed be called.

7 But as for the son of this bondwoman I will make him a great nation, because he is of thy seed."

LXX, Sam., Syr. and Vulg. of Gn. 21:13, have great; but MT omits.

8 And Abraham rose up early in the morning and took bread and a bottle of water, and placed them on the shoulders of Hagar and the child, and sent her away.

9 And she departed and wandered in the wilderness of Beersheba, and the water in the bottle was spent, and the child thirsted, and was not able to go on, and fell down.

10 And his mother took him and cast him under an olive tree, and went and sat her down over against him, at the distance of a bow-shot;

LXX (Gen. 21:15) "under a fir tree"; MT "under one of the shrubs."

for she said, "Let me not see the death of my child," and as she sat she wept.

11 And an angel of Elohim, one of the holy ones, said unto her, "Why weepest thou, Hagar? Arise, take the child, and hold him in thine hand; for Elohim hath heard thy voice, and hath seen the child."

12 And she opened her eyes, and she saw a well of water, and she went and filled

Read (?) "He" (God).

her bottle with water, and she gave her child to drink, and she arose and went towards the wilderness of Paran. **13** And the child grew and became an archer, and Elohim was with him; and his mother took him a wife from among the daughters of Egypt. **14** And she bare him a son, and he called his name Nebaioth; for she said, "Yahuah was nigh to me when I called upon him."

Cf. Gn. 25:13

Mastêmâ Proposes To Yahuah That Abraham Shall Be Put To The Proof
(17:15-18)

15 And it came to pass in the seventh week, in the first year thereof, in the first month in this jubilee, on the twelfth of this month, there were voices in heaven regarding Abraham, that he was faithful in all that He told him, and that he loved Yahuah, and that in every affliction he was faithful. **16** And the

2003 A.M.

According to the chronology of our Book (Cf. 16:12 with this passage) Isaac was twenty-three years old when he was offered up.

prince Mastêmâ came and said before Yahuah, "Behold, Abraham loveth Isaac his son, and he delighteth in him above all things else; bid him offer him as a burnt-offering on the altar, and Thou wilt see if he will do this command, and Thou wilt know if he is faithful in everything wherein Thou dost try him." **17** And Yahuah knew that Abraham was faithful in all his afflictions; for He had tried him through his country and with famine, and had tried him with the wealth of kings, and had tried him again through his wife, when she was torn (from him), and with circumcision, and had tried him through Ishmael and Hagar, his maid-servant, when he sent them away. **18** And in everything wherein He had tried him, he was found faithful, and his soul was not impatient, and he was not slow to act; for he was faithful and a lover of Yahuah.

Cf. Job 1:6-12. This is a Biblical testing affirmed in Job. It is no surprise to seee it with Abraham as well.

Seven of the traditional ten trials of Abraham are here mentioned: (1) Departure from his country; (2) famine; (3) the wealth of kings; (4) seizure of his wife; (5) circumcision; (6) and (7) expulsion of Hagar and Ishmael [(8) is the unfruitfulness of Sarah; (9) the sacrifice of Isaac, and (10) the burial of Sarah; Cf. 14:21 and 19:3, 8].

Abraham loved Ishmael as well and did not wish to send him away. That was a test.

CHAPTER 18:

The Sacrifice of Isaac: Abraham returns to Beersheba

(18:1-19; Cf. Gen. 22:1-19)

In Gn. 22:1 it is God Himself who directly proves Abraham.

1 And God said to him, "Abraham, Abraham"; and he said, "Behold, (here) am I." **2** And He said, "Take thy beloved son whom thou lovest, (even) Isaac, and go unto the high country, and offer him on one of the mountains which I will point out unto thee." **3** And he rose early in the morning and saddled his ass, and took his two young men with him, and Isaac his son, and clave the wood of the burnt-offering, and he went to the place on the third day, and he saw the place afar off. **4** And he came to a well of water, and he said to his young men, "Abide ye here with the ass, and I and the lad shall go (yonder), and when we have worshipped we shall come again to you." **5** And he took the wood of the burnt-offering and laid it on Isaac his son, and he took in his hand the fire and the knife, and they went both of them together to that place. **6** And Isaac said to his father, "Father"; and he said, "Here am I, my son." And he said unto him, "Behold the fire, and the knife, and the wood; but where is the sheep for the burnt-offering, father?" **7** And he said, "God will provide for himself a sheep for a burnt-offering, my son." And he drew near to the place of the mount of God. **8** And he built an altar, and he placed the wood on the altar, and bound Isaac his son, and placed him on the wood which was upon the altar, and stretched forth his hand to take the knife to slay Isaac his son. **9** And I stood before him, and before the prince of the Mastêmâ, and the Lord said, "Bid him not to lay his hand on the lad, nor to do anything to him, for I have shown that he feareth the Lord." **10** And I called to him from heaven, and said unto him: "Abraham, Abraham"; and he was terrified and said: "Behold, (here) am I." **11** And I said unto him: "Lay not thy hand upon the lad, neither do thou anything to him; for now I have shown that thou fearest the Lord, and hast not withheld thy son, thy first-born son, from me." **12** And the prince of the Mastêmâ was put to shame; and Abraham lifted up his eyes and looked, and, behold, a single ram

So LXX (Gn. 22:2): MT only (son).

So LXX; but NIT "the land of Moriah."

Instead of the words of the mount of God, MT (Gn. 22:9) reads, which God hath told him of.

Here (cf., also, 18:12, 47:9, 12, 15), Mastêmâ is the name given to the whole class of evil spirits, or Satans; elsewhere of the prince of these himself.

? add in a thicket. caught [in a thicket] by his horns, and Abraham went and took the ram and offered it for *Syr. and Vulg. render (Gn. 22:14) "will see," "seeth." MT "it shall be seen" (provided).* a burnt-offering in the stead of his son. **13** And Abraham called that place "The Lord hath seen," so that it is said "(in the mount) the Lord hath *Mt. Zion in Israel is not an ancient name before Abraham, he named it. This tells us why Jubilees seems to place the true Mt. Zion in the North Pole not Israel.* seen": that is Mount Sion. **14** And the Lord called Abraham by his name a second time from heaven, as he caused us to appear to speak to him in the name of the Lord. **15** And He said: "By Myself *MT "thine only" (Gn. 22:16).* have I sworn, saith the Lord, Because thou hast done this thing, And hast not withheld thy son, thy beloved son, from Me, That in blessing I shall bless thee And in multiplying I shall multiply thy seed As the stars of heaven, And as the sand which is on the seashore. And thy seed will inherit the cities of its enemies, **16** And *So Sam., version, LXX: MT "gate" (Gn. 22:17).* in thy seed will all nations of the earth be blessed; Because thou hast obeyed My voice, And I have shown to all that thou art faithful unto Me in all *Cf. 1 Sam. 1:17* that I have said unto thee: Go in peace." **17** And Abraham went to his young men, and they arose and went together to Beersheba, and Abraham dwelt by the Well of the Oath. **18** And he celebrated this festival every year, seven days with joy, and he called it the festival of the Lord according to the seven days during which he went and returned in peace. **19** And accordingly hath it been ordained and written on the heavenly tables regarding Israel and its seed that they should observe this festival seven days with the joy of festival.

CHAPTER 19:

The Death and Burial of Sarah

(19:1-9; cf. Gen. 23)

2010 A.M. **1** And in the first year of the first week in the forty-second jubilee, Abraham returned and dwelt opposite Hebron, that is Kirjath Arba, two weeks of years. **2** And in the first year of the †third† week of this jubilee the days of the life of Sarah were accomplished, and she died in Hebron.

†Read "second" (Charles).

3 And Abraham went to mourn over her and bury her, and we tried him [to see] if his spirit were patient and he were not indignant in the words of his mouth; and he was found patient in this, and was not disturbed. **4** For in patience of spirit he conversed with the children of Heth, to the intent that they should give him a place in which to bury his dead. **5** And Yahuah gave him grace before all who saw him, and he besought in gentleness the sons of Heth, and they gave him the land of the double cave over against Mamre, that is Hebron, for four hundred pieces of silver. **6** And they besought him, saying, "We shall give it to thee for nothing"; but he would not take it from their hands for

This is the tenth trial of Abraham; cf. 17:17 note. Cf. 19:8

i. e. the cave of Machpelah (LXX, τὸ σπήλαιον τὸ διπλοῦν).

nothing, for he gave the price of the place, the money in full, and he bowed down before them twice; and after this he buried his dead in the double cave. **7** And all the days of the life of Sarah were one hundred and twenty-seven years, that is, two jubilees and four weeks and one year: these are the days of the years of the life of Sarah. **8** This is the tenth trial wherewith Abraham was tried, and he was found faithful, patient in spirit. **9** And he said not a single word regarding the rumour in the land how that Elohim had said that He would give it to him and to his seed after him, and he begged a place there to bury his dead; for he was found faithful, and was recorded on the heavenly tables as the friend of Elohim.

Cf. 1 Sam. 1:17

This is the tenth trial of Abraham; cf. 17:17 note.

Cf. Is. 41:8 "Abraham my friend;" cf. Jas. 2:23 is an exact quote "friend of God (Elohim)." James is likely quoting Jubilees.

Marriage Of Isaac And Second Marriage Of Abraham

(cf. Gen. 24:15,25:1-4); **The Birth Of Esau And Jacob** *(cf. Gen. 25:19 ff.) (19:10-14)*

10 And in the fourth year thereof he took a wife for his son Isaac and her name was Rebecca [the daughter of Bethuel, the son of Nahor, the brother of Abraham] the sister of Laban and daughter

2020 A.M.

The bracketed words a dittograph.

of Bethuel; and Bethuel was the son of Mêlcâ, who was the wife of Nahor, the brother of Abraham. **11** And Abraham took to himself a third wife, and her name was Keturah, from among the daughters of his household servants, for Hagar had died before Sarah. **12** And she bare him six sons, Zimram, and Jokshan, and Medan, and Midian, and Ishbak, and Shuah, in the two weeks of years. **13** And in the sixth week, in the second year thereof, Rebecca bare to Isaac two sons, Jacob and Esau, and Jacob was a smooth and upright man, and Esau was fierce, a man of the field, and hairy, and Jacob dwelt in tents. **14** And the youths grew, and Jacob learned to write; but Esau did not learn, for he was a man of the field and a hunter, and he learnt war, and all his deeds were fierce.

This explains why Abraham did not take Hagar back. The later tradition (cf. e. g. Pirke de R. Eliezer xxx.) identifies Hagar with Keturah erroneously as you will find Jubilees exposes the Talmud details as wrong.

2046 A.M.

Gn. 25:27 (where "plain" = lit. "upright"), and Gn. 27:11 (combined here).

Abraham Loves Jacob And Blesses Him *(19:15-31)*

15 And Abraham loved Jacob, but Isaac loved Esau. **16** And Abraham saw the deeds of Esau, and he knew that in Jacob should his name and seed be called; and he called Rebecca and gave commandment regarding Jacob, for he knew that she

Jacob was to be the founder of the chosen nation; cf. 2:20.

(too) loved Jacob much more than Esau. **17** And he said unto her: "My daughter, watch over my son Jacob, For he shall be in my stead on the earth, And for a blessing in the midst of the children of men, And for the glory of the whole seed of Shem. **18** For I know that Yahuah will choose him to be a people for possession unto Himself, above all peoples that are upon the face of the earth. **19** And behold, Isaac my son loveth Esau more than Jacob, but I see that thou truly lovest Jacob. **20** Add still further to thy kindness to him, And let thine eyes be upon him in love; For he will be a blessing unto us on the earth from henceforth unto all generations of the earth.

21 Let thy hands be strong And let thy heart rejoice in thy son Jacob; For I have loved him far beyond all my sons. He will be blessed for ever, And his seed will fill the whole earth. **22** If a man can number the sand of the earth, His seed also will be numbered. **23** And all the blessings wherewith Yahuah hath blessed me and my seed shall belong to Jacob and his seed alway. **24** And in his seed shall my name be blessed, and the name of my fathers, Shem, and Noah, and Enoch,

Cf. Dt. 7:6

Note: Abraham's seed is not a land, it is a people. One possessing the land does not become Abraham's seed. Israel is a people not a land. As Gog takes Israel, his allies are not Israel. In Ch. 8-9 mapping, Gog is Britain and West and Central Europe. They conquered the land in 1917 giving it back to the Pharisees. That is not Israel's seed but Samaritan. Ez. 38-39.

Cf. Gn. 13:16 (cf. also 13:20 of our Book)

Notice that Methuselah is omitted, and Adam is reckoned among the saints (with Noah and Enoch). There is no evidence that Adam ever sinned again after the Garden. He taught his generations how to be holy as we see them sacrificing and they are aware of the Law even from Cain and Abel.

and Mahalalel, and Enos, and Seth, and Adam. **25** And these shall serve To lay the foundations of the heaven, And to strengthen the earth, And to renew all the luminaries which are in the firmament." **26** And he called Jacob before the eyes of Rebecca his mother, and kissed him, and blessed him, and said: **27** "Jacob, my beloved son, whom my soul loveth, may Elohim bless thee from above the firmament, and may He give thee all the blessings wherewith He blessed Adam, and Enoch, and Noah, and Shem; and all the things of which He told me, and all the things which He promised to give me, may He cause to cleave to thee and to thy seed for ever, according to the days of heaven above the earth. **28** And the spirits of Mastêmâ shall not rule over thee or over thy seed to turn thee from Yahuah, who is thy Elohim from henceforth for ever. **29** And may Yahuah Elohim be an Abba to thee and thou the first-born son, and to the people alway. Go in peace, my son." **30** And they both went forth together from Abraham. **31** And Rebecca loved Jacob, with all her heart and with all her soul, very much more than Esau; but Isaac loved Esau much more than Jacob.

Cf. 22:13

Jubilees is the likely origin of Is. 41:8 which is not exact; cf. Jas. 2:23 is exact.

Here we find the title of Father used again for Yahuah or Abba in Aramaic. This is it's origin which we do not find in the Old Testament but Messiah used as He quoted Jub. Cf. 1:24

they gave him the land of the DOUBLE CAVE

over against MAMRE, that is Hebron, for four hundred pieces of silver.

19:5

CHAPTER 20:

Abraham's Last Words To His Children And Grandchildren (20:1-11)

2052 A.M.

†Probably corrupt for "sixth" (Charles).

Cf. Gn. 25:13-15

Circumcision, according to our author, is binding upon Ishmael's and Keturah's descendants (cf. Gn. 17:9-10 f.). 'Notice the omission of Esau's descendants. According to Pirke de R. Eliezer 29, Esau, though he had been circumcised, "despised circumcision" (his birthright). The Talmud is proven false again. It does not agree with Jubilees proving this is not a Pharisee writing.

Bracketed as a dittograph.

According to the Law only the adulterous priest's daughter was to be burned with fire; others were to be stoned (cf. Lev. 21:9, 20:10).

1 And in the forty-second jubilee, in the first year of the †seventh† week, Abraham called Ishmael, and his twelve sons, and Isaac and his two sons, and the six sons of Keturah, and their sons.

2 And he commanded them that they should observe the way of Yahuah; that they should work righteousness, and love each his neighbour, and act on this manner amongst all men; that they should each so walk with regard to them as to do judgment and righteousness on the earth.

3 That they should circumcise their sons, according to the covenant which He had made with them, and not deviate to the right hand or the left of all the paths which Yahuah had commanded us; and that we should keep ourselves from all fornication and uncleanness, [and renounce from amongst us all fornication and uncleanness]. **4** And if any woman or maid commit fornication amongst you, burn her with fire, and let them not commit fornication with

Cf. 4Q220, fr. I. Jun. 21:5-10

her after their eyes and their heart; and let them not take to themselves wives from the daughters of Canaan; for the seed of Canaan will be rooted out of the land. **5** And he told them of the judgment of the giants, and the judgment of the Sodomites, how they had been judged on account of their wickedness, and had died on account of their fornication, and uncleanness, and mutual corruption through fornication. **6** "And guard yourselves from all fornication and uncleanness, And from all pollution of sin, Lest ye make our name a curse, And your whole life a hissing, And all your sons be destroyed by the sword,

Cf. Is. 65:15; Jr. 29:18

And ye become accursed like Sodom, And all your remnant as the sons of Gomorrah.

7 I implore you, my sons, love the Elohim of heaven, And cleave ye to all His commandments. And walk not after their idols, and after their uncleanness, **8** And make not for yourselves molten or graven gods; For they are

For 8 cf. 12:5, 22:18

vanity, And there is no spirit in them; For they are work of (men's) hands, And all who

Cf. Dt. 27:15

trust in them, trust in nothing. Serve them not, nor worship them, **9** But serve ye the Most

Cf. Ex. 20:5 High Elohim, and worship Him continually: And hope for His countenance always, And work uprightness and righteousness before Him, That He may have pleasure in you and grant you His mercy, And send rain upon you *Cf. 12:4, 18* morning and evening, And bless all your works which ye have wrought upon the earth, And bless thy bread and thy water, And bless the fruit of *Cf. Ex. 23:2* thy womb and the fruit of thy land, And the herds of thy cattle, and the flocks of thy sheep. **10** And ye will be for a blessing on the earth, And all *Cf. Dt. 7:13* nations of the earth will desire *Cf. Gn. 12:2* you, And bless your sons in my name, That they may be blessed as I am."

11 And he gave to Ishmael and to his sons, and to the sons of Keturah, gifts, and sent them away from Isaac his son, and he gave everything to Isaac his son. *Cf. Gn. 25:5-6*

The Dwelling-Places of the Ishmaelites and of the Sons of Keturah *(xx. 12-13)*

12 And Ishmael and his sons, and the sons of Keturah and their sons, went together and dwelt from Paran to the entering in of Babylon in all the land which is towards the East facing the desert. 13 And these mingled with each other, and their name was called Arabs, and Ishmaelites. *i.e. Saudi Arabia essentially.*

Saudi Arabia Desert Sheep Farming.

CHAPTER 21:

Abraham's Last Words To Isaac *(21:1-26)*

2052 A.M.
†Read "sixth" (Charles).

Test. 12 Patriarchs, Levi 9, Isaac offers similar instruction to Levi.

Gn. 27:2, Isaac uses the same words.

Cf. Gn. 25:7

The bracketed words are supplied from the Latin.

Cf. Dt. 10:17

4Q219, Col. II, Ln. 35-6 dates Abraham's death in the 43rd Jubilee. Fragments from 21 and 22 found.

1 And in the sixth year of the †seventh† week of this jubilee Abraham called Isaac his son, and commanded him, saying: "I am become old, and know not the day of my death, and am full of my days. 2 And behold, I am one hundred and seventy-five years old, and throughout all the days of my life I have remembered Yahuah, and sought with all my heart to do His will, and to walk uprightly in all His ways. 3 My soul hath hated idols, (and I have despised those that served them, and I have given my heart and spirit) that I might observe to do the will of Him who created me. 4 For He is the living Elohim, and He is holy and faithful, and He is righteous beyond all, and there is with Him no accepting of (men's) persons and no accepting of gifts; for Elohim is righteous, and executeth judgment on all those who transgress His commandments and despise His covenant. 5 And do thou, my son, observe His commandments and His ordinances and His judgments, and walk not after

the abominations and after the graven images and after the molten images. 6 And eat no blood at all of animals or cattle, or of any bird which flieth in the heaven. 7 And if thou dost slay a victim as an acceptable peace-offering, slay ye it, and pour out its blood upon the altar, and all the fat of the offering offer on the altar with fine flour (and the meat-offering) mingled with oil, with its drink-offering -- offer them all together on the altar of burnt-offering; it is a sweet savour before Yahuah. 8 And thou wilt offer the fat of the sacrifice of thank-offerings on the fire which is upon the altar, and the fat which is on the belly, and all the fat on the inwards and the two kidneys, and all the fat that is upon them, and upon the loins and liver thou shalt remove together with the kidneys. 9 And offer all these for a sweet savour acceptable before Yahuah, with its meat-offering and with its drink-offering, for a sweet savour, the bread of the offering unto Yahuah, 10 And eat its meat on that day and on the second day, and let not the sun on the second day go down upon it till it is eaten, and let nothing be left over for the third day;

Cf. 7:28 (note).

For 7-9 cf. the summary in Test. 12 Patr. Levi 9:7.

Cf. Lv. 2:4

For 7 cf. Lv. 3:7-10

Cf. Lev. 3: 9-10

"Or food"; cf. Lv. 3:11

Bracketed words a dittograph.

No trace of such halakic rules exists in the Books of Enoch or the fragments of the Noah apocalypse that are extant. Are there other books as well?

Cf. Lv. 2:13; Test. Levi 9:14

In Test. Levi ix. 12 "twelve" evergreen trees are mentioned; here fourteen, and this number is probably correct.

dêfrân Probably a kind of fir.

The Mishna (Tamid 2:3) allows all kinds of wood except that of the olive and vine; cf., also, Sifra on Lev. 1:8. Did Pharisees change the Bible again?

for it is not acceptable [for it is not approved] and let it no longer be eaten, and all who eat thereof will bring sin upon themselves; for thus I have found it written in the books of my forefathers, and in the words of Enoch, and in the words of Noah. **11** And on all and let not the salt of the covenant be lacking in all thy oblations before Yahuah. **12** And as regards the wood of the sacrifices, beware lest thou bring (other) wood for the altar in addition to these: cypress, dêfrân, sagâd, pine, fir, cedar, savin, palm, olive, myrrh, laurel, and citron, juniper, and balsam. **13** And of these kinds of wood lay upon the altar under the sacrifice, such as have been tested as to their appearance, and do not lay (thereon) any split or dark wood, (but) hard and clean, without fault, a sound and new growth; and do not lay (thereon) old wood, [for its fragrance is gone] for there is no longer fragrance in it as before. **14** Besides these kinds of wood there is none other that thou shalt place (on the altar), for the fragrance is dispersed, and the smell of its fragrance goeth not up to heaven. **15** Observe this commandment and do it,

my son, that thou mayst be upright in all thy deeds. **16** And at all times be clean in thy body, and wash thyself with water before thou approachest to offer on the altar, and wash thy hands and thy feet before thou drawest near to the altar; and when thou art done sacrificing, wash again thy hands and thy feet. **17** And let no blood appear upon you nor upon your clothes; be on thy guard, my son, against blood, be on thy guard exceedingly; cover it with dust. **18** And do not eat any blood, for it is the soul; eat no blood whatever. **19** And take no gifts for the blood of man, lest it be shed with impunity, without judgment; for it is the blood that is shed that causeth the earth to sin, and the earth cannot be cleansed from the blood of man save by the blood of him who shed it. **20** And take no present or gift for the blood of man: blood for blood, that thou mayest be accepted before Yahuah, the Most High Elohim; for He is the defence of the good: and that thou mayest be preserved from all evil, and that He may save thee from every kind of death. **21** I see, my son, That all the works of the children of men are sin

Cf. Ex. 30:19-21; cf. Test. Levi 9:2

Cf. Lv. 17:13. 7:28 (note).

Cf. Lv. 17:14; Dt. 12:23

Cf. 7:33; Num. 35:33

and wickedness, And all their deeds are uncleanness and an abomination and a pollution, And there is no righteousness with them. **22** Beware, lest thou shouldest walk in their ways And tread in their paths, *Cf. 33:18* And sin a sin unto death before the Most High Elohim. Else *Bracketed by Charles as an interpolation.* He will [hide His face from thee, And] give thee back into *i. e. into the power of.* the hands of thy transgression, And root thee out of the land, and thy seed likewise from under heaven, And thy name and thy seed will perish from the whole earth. **23** Turn away from all their deeds and all their uncleanness, And observe the ordinance of the Most High Elohim, And do His will and be upright in all things. **24** And He will bless thee in all thy deeds, And will *Cf. 16:26* raise up from thee the plant *Messianic Prophecy: CF. 1 En. 10:16, 93:5, 10.* of righteousness through all the earth, throughout all generations of the earth, And my name and thy name will not be forgotten under heaven for ever. **25** Go, my son, in peace. May the Most High Yahuah, my Elohim and thy Elohim, strengthen thee to do His will, And may He bless all thy seed and the residue of thy seed for the generations *Cf. 20:10* for ever, with all righteous blessings, That thou mayest be a blessing on all the earth." **26** And he went out from him rejoicing.

IN THE WORDS OF ENOCH AND... NOAH

CHAPTER 22:

Isaac, Ishmael And Jacob Join In Festival With Abraham For The Last Time. Abraham's Prayer
(22:1-9)

† Read "sixth" (Charles). †Read "forty-second" (Charles).

1 And it came to pass in the †first† week in the †forty-fourth† jubilee, in the †second† year, that is, the year in which Abraham died, that Isaac and Ishmael came from the Well of the Oath to celebrate the feast of weeks -- that is, the feast of the first-fruits of the harvest -- to Abraham, their father, and Abraham rejoiced because his two sons had come. **2** For Isaac had many possessions in Beersheba, and Isaac was wont to go and see his possessions and to return to his father. **3** And in those days Ishmael came to see his father, and they both came together, and Isaac offered a sacrifice for a burnt-offering, and presented it on the altar of his father which he had made in Hebron. **4** And he offered a thank-offering and made a feast of joy before Ishmael, his brother: and Rebecca made new cakes from the new grain, and gave them to Jacob, her son, to take them to Abraham, his father, from the first-fruits of the land, that he might eat and bless the Creator of all things before he died.

5 And Isaac, too, sent by the hand of Jacob to Abraham a best thank-offering, that he might eat and drink.

6 And he ate and drank, and blessed the Most High Elohim, Who hath created heaven and earth, Who hath made all the fat things of the earth, And given them to the children of men That they might eat and drink and bless their Creator. **7** "And now I give thanks unto Thee, my Elohim, because Thou hast caused me to see this day: behold, I am one hundred three score and fifteen years, an old man and full of days, and all my days have been unto me peace.

Cf. 21:1

8 The sword of the adversary hath not overcome me in all that Thou hast given me and my children all the days of my life until this day.

Cf. Jr. 6:25.

9 My Elohim, may Thy mercy and Thy peace be upon Thy servant, and upon the seed of his sons, that they may be to Thee a chosen nation and an inheritance from amongst all the nations of the earth from henceforth unto all the days of the generations of the earth, unto all the ages."

Israel is God's inheritance; cf. Dt. 4:20. Israel is a people not a land. This follows seed not whomever occupies the land. Gentile believers have been grafted into this seed in the days of Abraham and throughout the Exodus accounts.

Abraham's Last Words To And Blessings Of Jacob *(22:10-30)*

10 And he called Jacob and said My son Jacob, may the Elohim of all bless thee and strengthen thee to do righteousness, and His will before Him, and may He choose thee and thy seed that ye may become a people for His inheritance according to His will alway. And do thou, my son, Jacob, draw near and kiss me." **11** And he drew near and kissed him, and he said: "Blessed be my son Jacob And all the sons of Elohim Most High, unto all the ages: May Elohim give unto thee a seed of righteousness; And some of thy sons may He sanctify in the midst of the whole earth; May nations serve thee, And all the nations bow themselves before thy seed. **12** Be strong in the presence of men, And exercise authority over all the seed of Seth. Then thy ways and the ways of thy sons will be justified, So that they shall become a holy nation.

13 May the Most High Elohim give thee all the blessings Wherewith he hath blessed me And wherewith He blessed Noah and Adam; May they rest on the sacred head of thy seed from generation to generation for ever. **14** And may He cleanse thee from all unrighteousness and impurity, That thou mayest be forgiven all (thy) transgressions; (and) thy sins of ignorance. And may He strengthen thee, And bless thee. And mayest thou inherit the whole earth, **15** And may He renew His covenant with thee, That thou mayest be to Him a nation for His inheritance for all the ages, And that He may be to thee and to thy seed a Elohim in truth and righteousness throughout all the days of the earth. **16** And do thou, my son Jacob, remember my words, And observe the commandments of Abraham, thy father: Separate thyself from the nations, And eat not with them: And do not according to their works, And become not their associate; For their works are unclean, And all their ways are a pollution and an abomination and uncleanness. **17** They offer their sacrifices to the dead And they worship evil spirits, And they eat over the graves, And all their works are vanity and nothingness. **18** They have no heart to understand And their eyes do not see what their works are, And how they err in saying to

Note: Jacob's seed not the land. These prophesies are specific.

Verbally from Gn. 27:29 (Isaac's blessing of Jacob).

This does not say all mankind.

Cf. 19:27

Cf. 22:9

Abraham lived in Canaan among Nephilim even. It is ludicrous to assume this refers to the Hellenistic period and assert there was no such evil in Canaan. We find that view illiterate in attempt to attribute an erroneous dating.

Cf. Dt. 26:14; Ecclus. 30:18, 19, etc.

This is a rebuke of the ancient practice associated today with All Saints/ Souls Day in Catholicism. A pagan origin. Cf. 1 Cor. 10:20 (1 En. 19:1)

cf. Dt. 26:14 (according to one interpretation).

a piece of wood: 'Thou art my God,' And to a stone: 'Thou *Cf. Jr. 2:27* art my God and thou art my *Bracketed words a dittograph.* deliverer.' [And they have no heart.]

19 And as for thee, my son Jacob, May the Most High Elohim help thee And the Elohim of heaven bless thee And remove thee from their uncleanness and from all their error. **20** Be thou ware, my son Jacob, of taking a wife from any seed of the *Cf. Gn. 28:1; Test. Levi 1:9,10* daughters of Canaan; For all his seed is to be rooted out of the earth. **21** For, owing *Cf. 7:8* to the transgression of Ham, *Canaan wrongfully seized Palestine; cf. 10:29-34.* Canaan erred, And all his seed will be destroyed from off the earth and all the residue thereof, And none springing from him will be saved on the day of judgment. **22** And as *The four following lines have been transposed by Charles for the sake of parallelism.* for all the worshippers of idols and the profane (b) There will be no hope for them in the land of the living; (e) And there will be no remembrance of them on the earth; (c) For they will descend into Sheol, (d) And into the place of *Cf. 7:29* condemnation will they go, As the children of Sodom were taken away from the earth So will all those who worship idols be taken away. **23** Fear not, my son Jacob, And be not dismayed, O son of Abraham:

May the Most High Elohim preserve thee from destruction, And from all the paths of error may He deliver thee. **24** This house have I built for myself that I might put my name upon it in the earth: [it *Bracketed words a dittograph.* is given to thee and to thy seed for ever], and it will be named the house of Abraham; it is *"House" throughout this passage = "family."* given to thee and to thy seed for ever; for thou wilt build my house and establish my name before Elohim for ever: thy seed and thy name will stand throughout all generations *i. e. giving the last commands; cf. Gn. 44:33 and often.* of the earth." **25** And he ceased commanding him and blessing him. **26** And the two lay together on one bed, and Jacob slept in the bosom of Abraham, his father's father and he kissed him seven times, and his affection and his heart *Charles suspects 27 may be an interpolation.* rejoiced over him. **27** And he blessed him with all his heart and said: "The Most High Yahuah, the Elohim of all, and Creator of all, who brought me forth from Ur of the Chaldees, that He might give me this land to inherit *Cf. Gn. 15:7; Nh. 9:7.* it for ever, and that I might *Note: Holy seed. Unholy seed is rejected regardless of bloodline and Gentile believers have always been grafted into this seed.* establish a holy seed--blessed be the Most High for ever." **28** And he blessed Jacob and said: "My son, over whom with all my heart and my affection I rejoice, may Thy

Cf. Nm. 6:26 grace and Thy mercy be lift up upon him and upon his seed alway. **29** And do not forsake him, nor set him at nought from henceforth unto the days of eternity, and may *Cf. 1 Ki. 8:29, 52; Dan. 9:18* Thine eyes be opened upon him and upon his seed, that Thou mayest preserve him, and bless him, and mayest sanctify him as a nation for Thine inheritance;

30 And bless him with all Thy blessings from henceforth unto all the days of eternity, and renew Thy covenant and Thy grace with him and with his seed according to all Thy good pleasure unto all the generations of the earth."

CHAPTER 23:

The Death And Burial Of Abraham
(23:1-8; cf. Gen. 25:7-10)

Cf. Gn. 46:4. **1** And he placed two fingers of Jacob on his eyes, and he blessed the Elohim of elohim, *Cf. Gn. 44:33 (of the death of Jacob).* and he covered his face and stretched out his feet and slept *Cf. Jr. 51:39, 57* the sleep of eternity, and was gathered to his fathers. **2** And notwithstanding all this Jacob was lying in his bosom, and knew not that Abraham, his father's father, was dead.

3 And Jacob awoke from his sleep, and behold Abraham was cold as ice, and he said: "Father, father!"; but there was none that spake, and he knew that he was dead. **4** And he arose from his bosom and ran and told Rebecca, his mother; and Rebecca went to Isaac in the night and told him; and they went together, and Jacob with them, and a lamp was in his hand, and when they had gone in they found Abraham lying dead. **5** And Isaac fell on the face of his father, and wept and kissed him. **6** And *Cf. Gn. 50:1* the voices were heard in the house of Abraham, and Ishmael his son arose, and went to Abraham his father, and wept over Abraham his father, he and all the house of Abraham, and they wept with a great weeping. **7** And his sons Isaac and Ishmael buried him *i. e. Machpelah; cf. Gn. 25:9* in the double cave, near Sarah his wife, and they wept for him forty days, all the men of his house, and Isaac and Ishmael, and all their sons, and all the sons of Keturah in their places, and the days of weeping for Abraham were ended. **8** And he lived three jubilees and four weeks of years, one hundred and seventy-five years, and completed the days of his life, *2052 A.M.* being old and full of days.

The Decreasing Years And Increasing Corruption Of Mankind
(23:9-17)

9 For the days of the forefathers, of their life, were nineteen jubilees; and after the Flood they began to grow less than nineteen jubilees, and to decrease in jubilees, and to grow old quickly, and to be full of their days by reason of manifold tribulation and the wickedness of their ways, with the exception of Abraham. *CF. Gn. 6:3, "yet his days shall be an hundred and twenty years." 2 Esd. 5:50-55 Yahuah decreased lifespans gradually over time since the Flood as He promised. You can even note the patriarchs live shorter over time. Today, this continues to hold closely to 120 years of age. Debate settled.* **10** For Abraham was perfect in all his deeds with Yahuah, and well-pleasing in righteousness all the days of his life; and behold, he did not complete four jubilees in his life, when he had grown old by reason of the wickedness and was *Man ages quicker due to wickedness.*

100 years. Noah and the patriarchs before the Flood did not age as quickly as modern man. We also lose our faculties but the patriarchs did not.

Bracketed words a dittograph.

full of his days. **11** And all the generations which will arise from this time until the day of the great judgment will grow old quickly, before they complete two jubilees, and their knowledge will forsake them by reason of their old age [and all their knowledge will vanish away]. **12** And in those days, if a man live a jubilee and a half of years, they will say regarding him: "He hath lived long, and the greater part of his days are pain and

Cf. Ps. 90:10

sorrow and tribulation, and there is no peace: **13** For calamity followeth on calamity, and wound on wound, and tribulation on tribulation, and evil tidings on evil tidings, and illness on illness, and all evil judgments such as these, one with another, illness and overthrow, and snow and frost and ice, and fever, and

Such misfortunes are not limited to the Hellenistic era. To say so is illiterate.

chills, and torpor, and famine, and death, and sword, and captivity, and all kinds of calamities and pains."

14 And all these will come on an evil generation, which transgresseth on the earth: their works are uncleanness and fornication, and pollution

Cf. 7:21, 20:5, 22:16

and abominations. **15** Then they will say: "The days of the forefathers were many (even), unto a thousand years, and were good; but, behold, the days of our life, if a man hath lived many, are three score years and ten, and, if he is strong, four score years, and those evil and there is no peace in the days of this evil

Cf. Ps. 90:10.

Abraham, Isaac and Jacob lived in Canaan, an evil and perverse land in their era. This context is 2000 years before Hellenism and not associated.

generation." **16** And in that generation the sons will convict their fathers and their elders of sin and unrighteousness, and of the words of their mouth and the great wickednesses which they perpetrate, and concerning their forsaking the covenant which Yahuah made between them and Him, that they should observe and do all His commandments and His ordinances and all His laws, without departing either to the right hand or to the left. **17** For all have

Cf. Dt. 10:31-32, 28:14

done evil, and every mouth speaketh iniquity and all their works are an uncleanness and an abomination, and all their ways are pollution, uncleanness and destruction.

The Messianic Woes

(23:18-25). [Eschatological partly.]

18 Behold the earth will be destroyed on account of all their works, and there will be no seed of the vine, and no oil; for their works are altogether faithless, and they will all perish together, beasts and cattle and birds, *Cf. 2 Esd. 5:7 (Ez. 38:20)* and all the fish of the sea, on account of the children of *Internecine strife is a standing feature in such eschatological passages; cf. 2 Esd 6:24; Matt. 24:10; Ap. Bar. 70:3-4.* men. **19** And they will strive one with another, the young with the old, and the old with the young, the poor with the rich, and the lowly with the great, and the beggar with the prince, on account of the law and the covenant; for they have forgotten commandment, and covenant, and feasts, and months, and Sabbaths, and jubilees, and all judgments. **20** And they will stand (with *Cf. Jn. 14:6, Messiah is "the way." Is. 30:21, Acts 9:2.* bows and) swords and war to turn them back into the way; but they will not return until *This has nothing to do with 200 B.C., it's 2000 B.C.* much blood hath been shed on the earth, one by another. **21** And those who have escaped will not return from their wickedness to the way of righteousness, but they will all exalt themselves to deceit and wealth, that they may each take all that is his neighbour's, and they will name the great name, but not in truth and not in righteousness, and they will defile the holy of holies with their uncleanness and the *This has nothing to do with 200 B.C., it's 2000 B.C.* corruption of their pollution. **22** And a great punishment will befall the deeds of this generation from Yahuah, and He will give them over to the sword and to judgment and to captivity, and to be plundered and devoured. **23** And He *Cf. Gal. 2:15 "sinners of the Gentiles" **Paul quoted Jubilees.*** will wake up against them the sinners of the Gentiles, who have neither mercy nor compassion, and who will respect the person of none, neither old nor young, nor any one, for they are more wicked and strong to do evil than all the children of men. And they will use violence against Israel and transgression against *This has nothing to do with 200 B.C., it's 2000 B.C. For the last line cf. Jr. 8:2.* Jacob, And much blood will be shed upon the earth, And there will be none to gather and none to bury. **24** In those days they will cry aloud, And call and pray that they may be saved from the hand of *Cf. Gal. 2:15 is quoting Jubilees.* the sinners, the Gentiles; But none will be saved. **25** And the heads of the children will be white with grey hair, And a child of three weeks will appear old like a man of one hundred years, And their stature will be destroyed by tribulation and oppression.

Renewed Study Of The Law Followed By a Renewal of Mankind. The Messianic Kingdom and the Blessedness of the Righteous (23:26-32; cf. Isa. 65:17 ff. [Eschatological.])

26 And in those days the children will begin to study

the laws, And to seek the commandments, And to return to the path of righteousness. **27** And the days will begin to grow many and increase amongst those children of men, Till their days draw nigh to one thousand years, And to a greater number of years than (before) was the number of the days. **28** And there will be no old man Nor one who is not satisfied with his days, For all will be (as) children and youths. **29** And all their days they will complete and live in peace and in joy, And there will be no Satan nor any evil destroyer; For all their days will be days of blessing and healing, **30** And at that time Yahuah will heal His servants, And they will rise up and see great peace, And drive out their adversaries. And the righteous will see and be thankful, And rejoice with joy for ever and ever, And will see all their judgments and all their curses on their enemies. **31** And their bones will rest in the earth, And their spirits will have much joy, And they will know that it is Yahuah who executeth judgment, And showeth mercy to hundreds and thousands and to all that love Him. **32** And do thou, Moses, write down these words; for thus are they written, and they record (them) on the heavenly tables for a testimony for the generations for ever.

The span of life originally designed for mankind. Adam fell short of this because of his sin.

Cf. Is. 65:20

Cf. Is. 55:14

Cf. Assumpt. Moses 10:1.
Origin of Rv. 20:10
Cf. 1:29
Origin of Rv. 21:4

1 En. 91-104
Origin of Rv. 21:3-8

Prophecy says believers will receive new heavenly bodies on the Day of Judgment. Cf. 1 Cor. 15:51-52, 42-44; 2 Cor. 5:1-5;Phl. 3:21. This remains consistent and such concept is not new to the New Testament.

Cf. 2 Esd. 7:132 ff

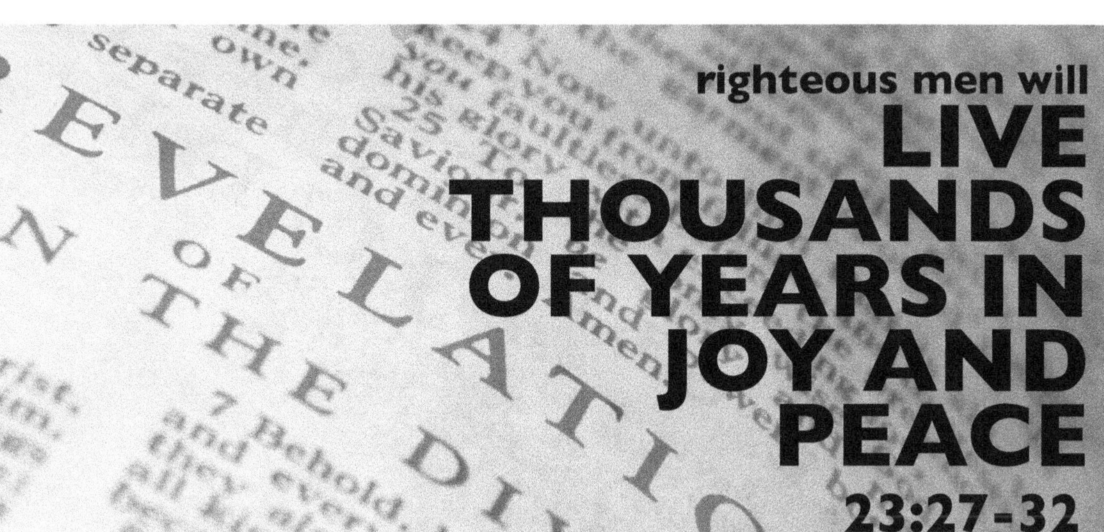

CHAPTER 24:

Isaac At The Well Of Vision: Esau Sells His Birthright

(24:1-7; cf. Gen. 25:11, 29-34)

i.e. Beer-lahai-roi ("the well of the Living One that seeth me"); Gn. 25:3.

1 And it came to pass after the death of Abraham, that Yahuah blessed Isaac his son, and he arose from Hebron and went and dwelt at the Well of the Vision in the first *2073 A.M.* year of the third week of this jubilee, seven years. **2** And in the first year of the fourth *2080 A.M.* week a famine began in the land, besides the first famine, which had been in the days of Abraham. **3** And Jacob sod lentil pottage, and Esau came from the field hungry. And he said to Jacob his brother: "Give me of this red pottage." And Jacob said to him: "Sell to me thy [primogeniture, this] birthright and I will give thee bread, and also some of this lentil pottage." **4** And Esau said in his heart: "I shall die; of what profit to me is this birthright?" And he said to Jacob: "I give it to thee." **5** And Jacob said "Swear to me, this day," and he sware unto him. **6** And Jacob gave his brother Esau bread and pottage, and he ate till he was satisfied, and Esau despised his birthright; for this reason was Esau's name called

i.e. lentil pottage = "red soup" Cf. Gn. 26:11

Cf. Gn. 25:30 i.e. lentil pottage = "red soup"

Edom, on account of the red pottage which Jacob gave him for his birthright. **7** And Jacob became the elder, and Esau was brought down from his dignity.

Edom = "red." Esau was named for the color of the soup for which he disrespected the value of his birthright. He did have red skin at birth which is medium brown but not red hair just lots of it. This is used to inject the Synagogue of Satan as Hebrews falsely and it fails.

Isaac's Sojourn In Gerar And Dealings With Abimelech *(24:8-27; cf. Gen. 26)*

8 And the famine was over the land, and Isaac departed to go down into Egypt in the second year of this week, and went to the king of the Philistines to Gerar, unto Abimelech.

9 And Yahuah appeared unto him and said unto him: "Go not down into Egypt; dwell in the land that I shall tell thee of, and sojourn in this land, and I shall be with thee and bless thee. **10** For to thee and to thy seed shall I give all this land, and I shall establish My oath which I sware unto Abraham thy father, and I shall multiply thy seed as the stars of heaven, and shall give unto thy seed all this land. **11** And in thy seed will all the nations of the earth be blessed, because thy father obeyed My voice, and kept My charge and My commandments, and My laws, and My ordinances, and My covenant; and now obey My voice and dwell in this land." **12** And he dwelt

For 9-12 cf. Gn. 26:2-6

2080-2101 A.M.

Cf. Gn. 26:2. Notice that no reference is made in our text to Isaac's deception about Rebecca.

in Gerar three weeks of years. **13** And Abimelech charged concerning him, and concerning all that was his, saying: "Any man that shall touch him or aught that is his shall surely die." **14** And Isaac waxed strong among the Philistines, and he got many possessions, oxen and sheep and camels and asses and a great household. **15** And he sowed in the land of the Philistines and brought in a hundred-fold, and Isaac became exceedingly great, and the Philistines envied him. **16** Now all the wells which the servants of Abraham had dug during the life of Abraham, the Philistines had stopped them after the death of Abraham, and filled them with earth. **17** And Abimelech said unto Isaac: "Go from us, for thou art much mightier than we"; and

2101 A.M.

Isaac departed thence in the first year of the seventh week, and sojourned in the valleys of Gerar. **18** And they digged again the wells of water which the servants of Abraham, his father, had digged, and which the Philistines had closed after the death of Abraham his father, and he called their names as Abraham his father had named them. **19** And the servants of Isaac dug a well in the valley, and found living water, and the shepherds of Gerar strove with the shepherds of Isaac, saying: "The water is ours "; and Isaac called the name of the well "Perversity," because they had been perverse with us. **20** And they dug a second well, and they strove for that also, and he called its name "Enmity." And he arose from thence and they digged another well, and for that they strove not, and he called the name of it "Room," and Isaac said: "Now Yahuah hath made room for us, and we have increased in the land."

21 And he went up from thence to the Well of the Oath in the first year of the first week in the forty-fourth jubilee.

22 And Yahuah appeared to him that night, on the new moon of the first month, and said unto him: "I am the Elohim of Abraham thy father; fear not, for I am with thee, and shall bless thee and shall surely multiply thy seed as the sand of the earth, for the sake of Abraham my servant." **23** And he built an altar there, which Abraham his father had first built, and he called upon the name of

Esek; cf. Gn. 26:20

= Sinai; cf. Gn. 26:21

= Rehoboth; cf. Gn. 26:22

i. e. Beersheba.

2108 A.M.

YHWH, Yahuah in Hebrew. Abraham, Isaac and Jacob knew and used the true name of God many times. A doctrine hiding the name of YHWH is of Samaritan, pagan origin not the Bible.

In Gn. 26:32 the MT does not read not; but LXX agrees with our text in so reading. It is implied here that their failure to find water was due to the covenant made with Abimelech.

and he offered sacrifice to the Elohim of Abraham his father. **24** And they digged a well and they found living water. **25** And the servants of Isaac digged another well and did not find water, and they went and told Isaac that they had not found water, and Isaac said: "I have sworn this day to the Philistines and this thing hath been announced to us." **26** And he called the name of that place the "Well of the Oath"; for there he had sworn to Abimelech and Ahuzzath his friend and Phicol the prefect of his host. **27** And Isaac knew that day that under constraint he had sworn to them to make peace with them.

Cf. Gn. 26:31, 33

The Philistines are a long-time enemy of Israel even housing Nephilim among them such as Goliath.

Isaac Curses Philistines
(24:28-33)

Kittim is often associated with Greece and the Roman Empire. These are associated in the War Scroll in league with those who will oppose Israel until the very final battle. It is also part of the Psalm 83 enemies.

28 And Isaac on that day cursed the Philistines and said: "Cursed be the Philistines unto the day of wrath and indignation from the midst of all nations; may Yahuah make them a derision and a curse and an object of wrath and indignation in the hands of the sinners the Gentiles and in the hands of the Kittim. **29** And whoever escapeth the sword of the enemy and the Kittim, may the righteous nation root out in judgment from under heaven; for they

The righteous nation is Israel, the people, not a land necessarily.

will be the enemies and foes of my children throughout their generations upon the earth. **30** And no remnant will be left to them, Nor one that will be saved on the day of the wrath of judgment; For for destruction and rooting out and expulsion from the earth is the whole seed of the Philistines (reserved), And there will no longer be left for these Caphtorim a name or a seed on the earth.

The Philistines came originally from Caphtor according to Am. 9:7 (Dt. 2:23; Jr. 47:4). LXX Gn. 10:14 renders the ancestor of the Philistines as the Chasmoniim or Hasmonean. That faction from Modi'in, Samaria cannot be inserted into Jubilees as the authors nor favorable.

31 For though he ascend unto heaven, Thence will he be brought down, And though he make himself strong on earth, Thence will he be dragged forth, And though he hide himself amongst the nations, Even from thence will he be rooted out; And though he descend into Sheol, There also will his condemnation be great, And there also he will have no peace. **32** And if he go into captivity, By the hands of those that seek his life will they slay him on the way, And neither name nor seed will be left to him on all the earth; For into eternal malediction will he depart." **33** And thus is it written and engraved concerning him on the heavenly tables, to do unto him on the day of judgment, so that he may be rooted out of the earth.

The basis of 31-32 seems to be Am. 9:2-4.

Edom = "red."

Esau was named for the color of the
soup for which he disrespected the
value of his birthright.He did have red
skin at birth which is medium brown
but not red hair just lots of it.
No leaven here!

24:6

CHAPTER 25:

Rebecca Admonishes Jacob Not To Marry A Canaanitish Woman. Rebecca's Blessing

(25:1-23; cf. Gen. 28:1-4). 1

2109 A.M.

With this section also compare 27 of our Book.

1 And in the second year of this week in this jubilee, Rebecca called Jacob her son, and spake unto him, saying: "My son, do not take thee a wife of the daughters of Canaan, as Esau, thy brother, who took him two wives of the daughters of Canaan, *Cf. Gn. 26:34* and they have embittered my *Cf. Gn. 27:46, 26:35* soul with all their unclean deeds: for all their deeds are fornication and lust, and there is no righteousness with them, for (their deeds) are evil. 2 And I, my son, love thee exceedingly, and my heart and my affection bless thee every hour of the day and watch of the night. 3 And now, my son, hearken to my voice, and do the will of thy mother, and do not take thee a wife of the daughters of this land, but only of the house of my father, and of my father's kindred. Thou wilt take thee a wife of the house of my father, and the Most High Elohim will bless thee, and thy children will be a righteous generation and a holy seed."

4 And then spake Jacob to Rebecca, his mother, and said unto her: "Behold, mother, I am nine weeks of years old, *i.e. 63.* and I neither know nor have I touched any woman, nor have I betrothed myself to any, nor even think of taking me a wife of the daughters of Canaan. 5 For I remember, mother, the words of Abraham, our father, for he commanded me not to take a wife of the daughters of Canaan, but to take me a wife from the seed of my father's house and from my kindred. 6 I have heard before that daughters have been born to Laban, thy brother, and I have set my heart on them to take a wife from amongst them. 7 And for this reason I have guarded myself in my spirit against sinning or being corrupted in all my ways throughout all the days of my life; for with regard to lust and fornication, Abraham, my father, gave me many commands. 8 And, despite all that he hath commanded me, *Cf. 20:4, 39:6.* these two and twenty years my brother hath striven with me, and spoken frequently to me and said: 'My brother, take to wife a sister of my two wives'; but I refuse to do as he hath done. 9 I swear before thee, mother, that all the days of my

life I will not take me a wife from the daughters of the seed of Canaan, and I will not act wickedly as my brother hath done. **10** Fear not, mother; be assured that I shall do thy will and walk in uprightness, and not corrupt my ways for ever." **11** And thereupon she lifted up her face to heaven and extended the fingers of her hands, and opened her mouth and blessed the Most High Elohim, who had created the heaven and the earth, and she gave Him thanks and praise. **12** And she said: "Blessed be the Yahuah Elohim, and may His holy name be blessed for ever and ever, who hath given me Jacob as a pure son and a holy seed; for He is Thine, and Thine shall his seed be continually and throughout all the generations for evermore. **13** Bless him, O Yahuah, and place in my mouth the blessing of righteousness, that I may bless him." **14** And at that hour, when the spirit of righteousness descended into her mouth, she placed both her hands on the head of Jacob, and said: **15** "Blessed art thou, Yahuah of righteousness and Elohim of the ages; And may He bless thee beyond all the generations of men. May He give thee, my son, the path

of righteousness, And reveal righteousness to thy seed. **16** And may He make thy sons many during thy life, And may they arise according to the number of the months of the year. And may their sons become many and great beyond the stars of heaven, And their numbers be more than the sand of the sea. **17** And may He give them this goodly land -- as He said He would give it to Abraham and to his seed after him alway -- And may they hold it as a possession for ever. **18** And may I see (born) unto thee, my son, blessed children during my life, And a blessed and holy seed may all thy seed be. **19** And as thou hast refreshed thy mother's spirit during †my† life, The womb of her that bare thee blesseth thee, [My affection] and my breasts bless thee And my mouth and my tongue praise thee greatly. **20** Increase and spread over the earth, And may thy seed be perfect in the joy of heaven and earth for ever; And may thy seed rejoice, And on the great day of peace may it have peace. **21** And may thy name and thy seed endure to all the ages, And may the Most High Yahuah be their Elohim, And may the Elohim

Cf. Jn. 14:17, 15:26, 16:13 (τὸ πλεῦμα τῆς ἀληθείας) variant reading here is "Holy Spirit." This is reminiscent of a New Testament application of the Holy Spirit.

Cf. Lk. 1:55

†Read "thy" (Charles).

of righteousness dwell with them, And by them may His *Cf. 1:29* sanctuary be built unto all the ages. **22** Blessed be he that blesseth thee, And all flesh that curseth thee falsely may it *Cf. Gn. 27:29* be cursed." **23** And she kissed him, and said to him "May Yahuah of the world love thee As the heart of thy mother and her affection rejoice in thee and bless thee." And she ceased from blessing.

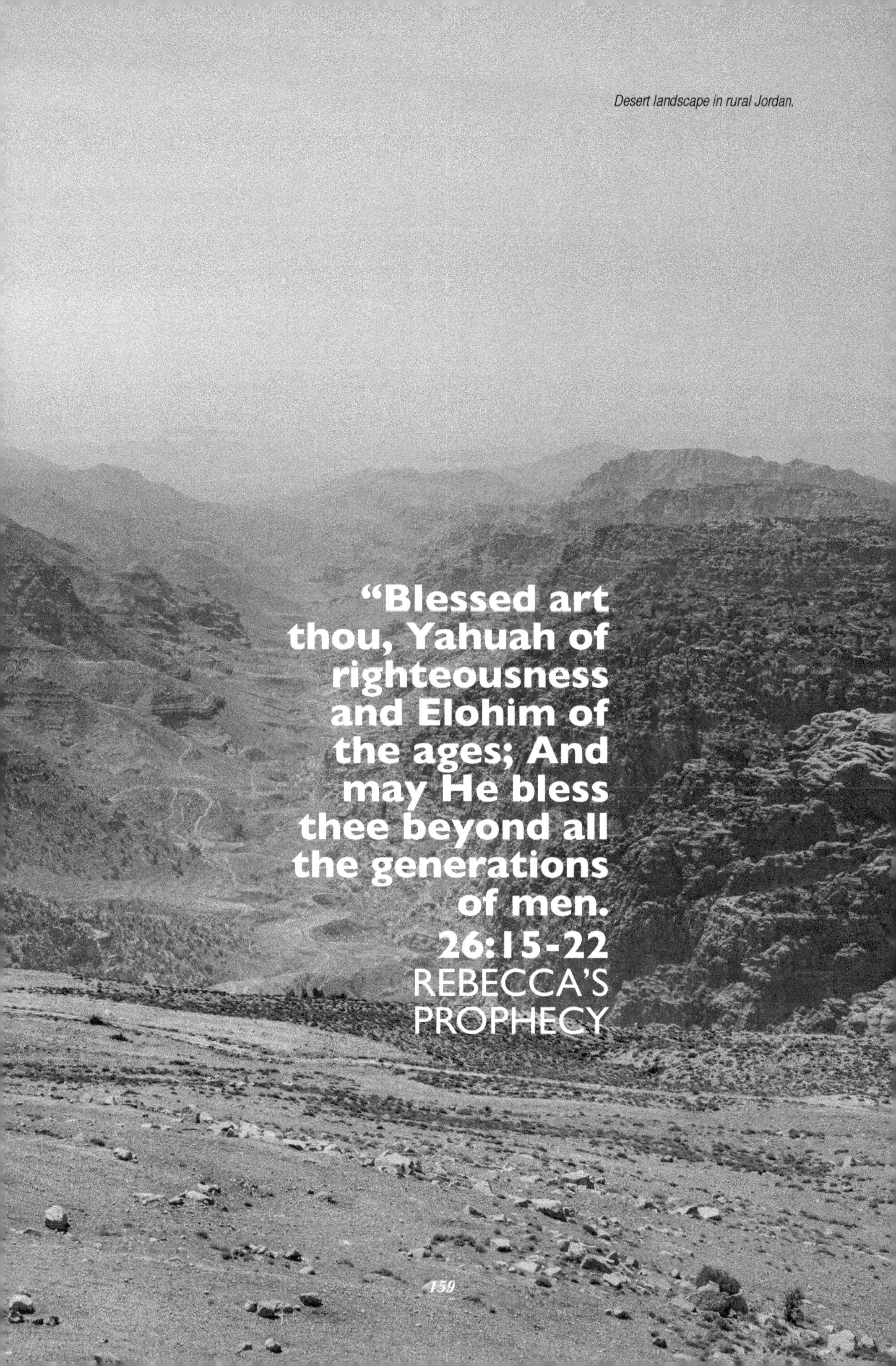

Desert landscape in rural Jordan.

"Blessed art thou, Yahuah of righteousness and Elohim of the ages; And may He bless thee beyond all the generations of men.

26:15-22

REBECCA'S PROPHECY

CHAPTER 26:

Jacob Obtains The Blessing Of The Firstborn
(26:1-35; cf. Gen. 27)

2114 A.M. **1** And in the seventh year of this week Isaac called Esau, his elder son, and said unto him: "I am old, my son, and behold my eyes are dim in seeing, and I know not the day of my death. **2** And now take thy hunting weapons, thy quiver and thy bow, and go out to the field, and hunt and catch me (venison), my son, and make me savoury meat, such as my soul loveth, and bring it to me that I may eat, and that my soul may bless thee before I die." **3** But Rebecca heard Isaac speaking to Esau. **4** And Esau went forth early to the field to hunt and catch and bring home to his father. **5** And Rebecca called Jacob, her son, and said unto him: "Behold, I heard Isaac, thy father, speak unto Esau, thy brother, saying: 'Hunt for me, and make me savoury meat, and bring (it) to me that I may eat and bless thee before Yahuah before I die.' **6** And now, my son, obey my voice in that which I command thee: Go to thy flock and fetch me two good kids of the goats, and I will make them savoury meat for thy father, such as he loveth, and thou shalt bring (it) to thy father that he may eat and bless thee before Yahuah before he die, and that thou mayst be blessed." **7** And Jacob said to Rebecca his mother: "Mother, I shall not withhold anything which my father would eat, and which would please him: only I fear, my mother, that he will recognise my voice and wish to touch me. **8** And thou knowest that I am smooth, and Esau, my brother, is hairy, and I shall appear before his eyes as an evildoer, and shall do a deed which he had not commanded me, and he will be wroth with me, and I shall bring upon myself a curse, and not a blessing." **9** And Rebecca, his mother, said unto him: "Upon me be thy curse, my son, only obey my voice." **10** And Jacob obeyed the voice of Rebecca, his mother, and went and fetched two good and fat kids of the goats, and brought them to his mother, and his mother made them (savoury meat) such as he loved. **11** And Rebecca took the goodly raiment of Esau, her elder son, which was with her in the house, and she clothed Jacob, her younger son, (with them), and she put the skins of the kids upon his hands and on the exposed parts of his neck. **12** And she gave the meat and the bread which she had prepared into the hand of her son Jacob. **13** And Jacob went in to his father and said: "I am thy son: I have done according as thou badest me: arise and sit and eat of that which I have caught, father, that thy soul may bless me." **14** And Isaac said to his son: "How hast thou found so quickly, my son?" **15** And Jacob said: "Because (Yahuah) thy Elohim caused me to find." **16** And Isaac said unto him: "Come near, that I may feel thee, my son, if thou art my son Esau or not." **17** And Jacob went near to Isaac, his father, and he felt him and said: **18** "The voice is Jacob's voice, but the hands are the hands of Esau," and he discerned him not, because it was a dispensation from heaven to remove his power of perception and Isaac discerned not, for his hands were hairy as (his brother) Esau's, so that he blessed him. **19** And he said: "Art thou my son Esau?" and he said: "I am thy son and he said, "Bring near to me that I may eat of that which thou hast caught, my son, that my soul may bless thee." **20** And he brought near to him, and he did eat, and he brought him wine and he drank. **21** And Isaac, his father, said unto him: "Come near and kiss me, my son." And he came near and kissed him. **22** And he smelled the smell of his raiment, and he blessed him and said: "Behold, the smell of my son is as the smell of a (full) field which Yahuah hath blessed. **23** And may Yahuah give thee of the dew of heaven And of the dew of the earth, and plenty of corn and oil: Let nations serve thee, And peoples bow down to thee. **24** Be lord over thy brethren, And let thy mother's sons bow down to thee; And may all the blessings wherewith Yahuah hath blessed me and blessed Abraham, my father, Be imparted to thee and to thy seed for ever Cursed be he that curseth thee, And blessed be he that blesseth thee." **25** And it came to pass as soon as Isaac had made an end of blessing his son Jacob, and Jacob had gone forth from Isaac his father †the hid himself and† Esau, his brother, came in from his hunting. **26** And he also made savoury meat, and brought (it) to his father, and said unto his father: "Let

So Latin here, and Sam. LXX and Vulg. in Gn. 27:27: MT omits.

Text of Gn. 27:28 has "fatness."

Text of Gn. has "wine."

Cf. Gn; 28:4

Cf. 1 Ki. 12:15

†Charles suspects this to be an addition to the text: read "that."

my father arise, and eat of my venison that thy soul may bless me." **27** And Isaac, his father, said unto him: "Who art thou?" And he said unto him: "I am thy first born, thy son Esau: I have done as thou hast commanded me."

28 And Isaac was very greatly astonished, and said: "Who is he that hath hunted and caught and brought (it) to me, and I have eaten of all before thou camest, and have blessed him: (and) he shall be blessed, and all his seed for ever."

29 And it came to pass when Esau heard the words of his father Isaac that he cried with an exceeding great and bitter cry, and said unto his father: "Bless me, (even) me also, father." **30** And he said unto him: "Thy brother came with guile, and hath taken away thy blessing." And he said: "Now I know why his name is named Jacob: behold, he hath supplanted me these two times: he took away my birthright, and now he hath taken away my blessing." **31** And he said: "Hast thou not reserved a blessing for me, father?" and Isaac answered and said

unto Esau: "Behold, I have made him thy lord, And all his brethren have I given to him for servants, And with plenty of corn and wine and oil have I strengthened him: And what now shall I do for thee, my son?" **32** And Esau said to Isaac, his father: "Hast thou but one blessing, O father? Bless me, (even) me also, father": And Esau lifted up his voice and wept.

33 And Isaac answered and said unto him: "Behold, far from the dew of the earth shall be thy dwelling, And far from the dew of heaven from above. **34** And by thy sword wilt thou live, And thou wilt serve thy brother. And it shall come to pass when thou becomest great, And dost shake his yoke from off thy neck, Thou wilt sin a complete sin unto death, And thy seed will be rooted out from under heaven." **35** And Esau kept threatening Jacob because of the blessing wherewith his father blessed him, and he said in his heart: "May the days of mourning for my father now come, so that I may slay my brother Jacob."

So Sam. of Gn. 27:40: MT "when Thou shalt break loose."

This line is a complete departure from the original text, which has: "thou shalt shake his yoke from off thy neck." The interpretation here given in the text has no support elsewhere.

...she put the
SKINS OF
THE KIDS
upon his hands and
on the exposed
parts of his neck.
26:11

CHAPTER 27:

Rebecca Induces Isaac To Send Jacob To Mesopotamia. Jacob's Dream And View At Bethel *(27:1-27; cf. Gen. 28)*

1 And the words of Esau, her elder son, were told to Rebecca in a dream, and Rebecca sent and called Jacob her younger son, and said unto him: 2 "Behold Esau thy brother will take vengeance on thee so as to kill thee. 3 Now, therefore, my son, obey my voice, and arise and flee thou to Laban, my brother, to Haran, and tarry with him a few days until thy brother's anger turneth away, and he remove his anger from thee, and forget all that thou hast done; then I will send and fetch thee from thence." 4 And Jacob said: "I am not afraid; if he wisheth to kill me, I will kill him." 5 But she said unto him: "Let me not be bereft of both my sons on one day." 6 And Jacob said to Rebecca his mother: "Behold, thou knowest that my father hath become old, and doth not see because his eyes are dull, and if I leave him it will be evil in his eyes, because I leave him and go away from you, and my father will be angry, and will curse me. I will not go; 1 when he sendeth me, then only will I go."

7 And Rebecca said to Jacob: "I will go in and speak to him, and he will send thee away." 8 And Rebecca went in and said to Isaac: "I loathe my life because of the two daughters of Heth, whom Esau hath taken him as wives; and if Jacob take a wife from among the daughters of the land such as these, for what purpose do I further live; for the daughters of Canaan are evil." 9 And Isaac called Jacob and blessed him, and admonished him and said unto him: 10 "Do not take thee a wife of any of the daughters of Canaan; arise and go to Mesopotamia, to the house of Bethuel, thy mother's father, and take thee a wife from thence of the daughters of Laban, thy mother's brother. 11 And Yahuah Almighty bless thee and increase and multiply thee that thou mayest become a company of nations, and give thee the blessings of my father Abraham, to thee and to thy seed after thee, that thou mayest inherit the land of thy sojournings and all the land which Yahuah gave to Abraham: go, my son, in peace." 12 And Isaac sent

Cf. Gn. 27:46

Jacob away, and he went to Mesopotamia, to Laban the son of Bethuel the Syrian, the brother of Rebecca, Jacob's mother. **13** And it came to pass after Jacob had arisen to go to Mesopotamia that the spirit of Rebecca was grieved after her son, and she wept. **14** And Isaac said to Rebecca: "My sister, weep not on account of Jacob, my son; for he goeth in peace, and in peace will he return. **15** The Most High Elohim will preserve him from all evil, and will be with him; for He will not forsake him all his days; **16** For I know that his ways will be prospered in all things wherever he goeth, until he return in peace to us, and we see him in peace.

17 Fear not on his account my sister, for he is on the upright path and he is a perfect man: and he is faithful and will not perish. Weep not." **18** And Isaac comforted Rebecca on account of her son Jacob, and blessed him. **19** And Jacob went from the Well of the Oath to go to Haran on the first year of the second week in the forty-fourth Jubilee, and he came to Luz on the mountains, that is, Bethel, on the new moon of the first

month of this week, and he came to the place at even and turned from the way to the west of the road that night: and he slept there; for the sun had set. **20** And he took one of the stones of that place and laid it (at his head) under the tree, and he was journeying alone, and he slept. **21** And he dreamt that night, and behold a ladder set up on the earth, and the top of it reached to heaven, and behold, the angels of Yahuah ascended and descended on it: and behold, Yahuah stood upon it. **22** And He spake to Jacob and said: "I am Yahuah Elohim of Abraham, thy father, and the Elohim of Isaac; the land whereon thou art sleeping, to thee shall I give it, and to thy-seed after thee. **23** And thy seed will be as the dust of the earth, and thou wilt increase to the west and to the east, to the north and the south, and in thee and in thy seed will all the families of the nations be blessed. **24** And behold, I shall be with thee, and shall keep thee whithersoever thou goest, and I shall bring thee again into this land in peace; for I shall not leave thee until I do everything that I told thee of." **25** And Jacob awoke from his sleep, and said, "Truly this place is the house of Yahuah, and I knew it not."

And he was afraid and said:" Dreadful is this place which is none other than the house of God, and this is the gate of heaven." **26** And Jacob arose early in the morning, and took the stone which he had put under his head and set it up as a pillar for a sign, and he poured oil upon the top of it. And he called the name of that place Bethel; but the name of the place was Luz at the first. **27** And Jacob vowed a vow unto Yahuah, saying: "If Yahuah will be with me, and will keep me in this way that I go, and give me bread to eat and raiment to put on, so that I come again to my father's house in peace, then shall Yahuah be my Elohim, and this stone which I have set up as a pillar for a sign in this place, shall be Yahuah's house, and of all that thou givest me, I shall give the tenth to thee, my Elohim."

And he dreamt that night, and behold
a ladder set up on the earth, and the
top of it reached to heaven, and behold,
the angels of Yahuah ascended and
descended on it: and behold,

YAHUAH STOOD UPON IT.

27:21

CHAPTER 28:

Jacob's Marriage to Leah and Rachel; His Children and Riches

(28:1-30; cf. Gen. 24, 30, 31:1-2)

1 And he went on his journey, and came to the land of the east, to Laban, the brother of Rebecca, and he was with him, and served him for Rachel his daughter one week. 2 And in the first year of the third week he said unto him: "Give me my wife, for whom I have served thee seven years;" and Laban said unto Jacob. "I will give thee thy wife."

3 And Laban made a feast, and took Leah his elder daughter, and gave (her) to Jacob as a wife, and gave her Zilpah his handmaid for an handmaid; and Jacob did not know, for he thought that she was Rachel.

4 And he went in unto her, and behold, she was Leah; and Jacob was angry with Laban, and said unto him: "Why hast thou dealt thus with me? Did not I serve thee for Rachel and not for Leah? Why hast thou wronged me? Take thy daughter, and I will go; for thou hast done evil to me."

5 For Jacob loved Rachel more than Leah; for Leah's eyes were weak, but her form was very handsome; but Rachel had beautiful eyes and a beautiful and very handsome form. 6 And Laban said to Jacob: "It is not so done in our country, to give the younger before the elder." And it is not right to do this; for thus it is ordained and written in the heavenly tables, that no one should give his younger daughter before the elder--but the elder one giveth first and after her the younger--and the man who doeth so, they set down guilt against him in heaven, and none is righteous that doeth this thing, for this deed is evil before Yahuah.

7 And command thou the children of Israel that they do not this thing; let them neither take nor give the younger before they have given the elder, for it is very wicked.

8 And Laban said to Jacob: "Let the seven days of the feast of this one pass by, and I shall give thee Rachel, that thou mayest serve me another seven years, that thou mayest pasture my sheep as thou didst in the former week." 9 And on the day when the seven days of the feast of Leah had passed, Laban gave Rachel to Jacob, that he might serve him another seven years, and

i. e. seven years. For 1 cf. Gn. 29:1, 20

For 2-4 cf. Gn. 29:21-25

2122 A.M.

Cf. Gn. 29:17-18a

Cf. Gn. 29:26

Cf. 1 En. 81:1, 93:2, 103:2,106:19 mention "Tablets of Heaven" which he read and copied every fact. Cf. Acts 7:53 "received the law (Torah) by the disposition of angels."

For 8-10 cf. Gn. 29:27-29

The marriage of two living sisters to the same man is expressly forbidden in the Mosaic Law which came after this; cf. Lv. 18:18. This is over 400 years before Moses however.

According to Test. Naphtali 1 also, Bilhah and Zilpah were sisters.

2122 A.M.

Gn. 29:32 has "she called."

The twelve sons of Jacob appear in our text in the same order as in Gn. 29:32-34, 30:1-24, 35:17-18, viz. (1) Reuben; (2) Simeon; (3) Levi; (4) Judah; (5) Dan; (6) Naphtali; (7) Gad;

2124 A.M.

Cont.'d: (8) Asher; (9) Issachar; (10) Zebulon; (11) Joseph; (12)Benjamin A different order is given in Gn. 49 and in the Test. 12 Patriarchs.

2127 A.M.

Cont.'d: The order of birth, as given in Jubilees, is complicated by textual difficulties; see Charles ad loc.

2128 A.M.

he gave to Rachel, Bilhah, the sister of Zilpah as a handmaid. **10** And he served yet other seven years for Rachel, for Leah had been given to him for nothing. **11** And Yahuah opened the womb of Leah, and she conceived and bare Jacob a son, and he called his name Reuben, on the fourteenth day of the ninth month, in the first year of the third week. **12** But the womb of Rachel was closed, for Yahuah saw that Leah was hated and Rachel loved. **13** And again Jacob went in unto Leah, and she conceived, and bare Jacob a second son, and he called his name Simeon, on the twenty-first of the tenth month, and in the third year of this week. **14** And again Jacob went in unto Leah, and she conceived, and bare him a third son, and he called his name Levi, in the new moon of the first month in the sixth year of this week. **15** And again Jacob went in unto her, and she conceived, and bare him a fourth son, and he called his name Judah, on the fifteenth of the third month, in the †first† year of the †fourth† week. **16** And on account of all this Rachel envied Leah, for she did not bear, and she said to Jacob:

"Give me children"; and Jacob said: "Have I withheld from thee the fruits of thy womb? Have I forsaken thee?" **17** And when Rachel saw that Leah had borne four sons to Jacob, Reuben and Simeon and Levi and Judah, she said unto him: "Go in unto Bilhah my handmaid, and she will conceive, and bear a son unto me." **18** (And she gave (him) Bilhah her handmaid to wife.) And he went in unto her, and she conceived, and bare him a son, and he called his name Dan, on the ninth of the sixth month, in the †sixth† year of the †third† week. **2129 A.M.**

19 And Jacob went in again unto Bilhah a second time, and she conceived, and bare Jacob another son, and Rachel called his name Naphtali, on the fifth of the seventh month, in the second year of the fourth week. **20** And when Leah saw that she had become sterile and did not bear, she envied (Rachel) and she also gave her handmaid Zilpah to Jacob to wife, and she conceived, and bare a son, and Leah called his name Gad, on the twelfth of the eighth month, in the third year of the fourth week. **2131 A.M.**

21 And he went in again unto her, and she conceived, and bare him a second son, and **2132 A.M.**

2133 A.M.

Leah called his name Asher, on the second of the eleventh month, in the †fifth† year of the fourth week. **22** And Jacob went in unto Leah, and she conceived, and bare a son, and she called his name Issachar, on the fourth of the fifth month, in the †fourth† year of the fourth week, and she gave him to a nurse.

2134 A.M.

23 And Jacob went in again unto her, and she conceived, and bare two (children), a son and a daughter, and she called the name of the son Zebulon, and the name of the daughter Dinah, in the seventh of the seventh month, in the sixth year of the fourth week.

2134 A.M.

24 And Yahuah was gracious to Rachel, and opened her womb, and she conceived, and bare a son, and she called his name Joseph, on the new moon of the fourth month, in the †sixth† year in this fourth week. **25** And in the days when Joseph was born, Jacob said to Laban: "Give me my wives and sons, and let me go to my father Isaac, and let me

2135 A.M.

make me an house; for I have completed the years in which I have served thee for thy two daughters, and I will go to the house of my father." **26** And Laban said to Jacob: "†Tarry with me for thy wages†, and pasture my flock for me again, and take thy wages." **27** And they agreed with one another that he should give him as his wages those of the lambs and kids which were born black and spotted and white, (these) were to be his wages. **28** And all the sheep brought forth spotted and speckled and black, variously marked, and they brought forth again lambs like themselves, and all that were spotted were Jacob's and those which were not were Laban's. **29** And Jacob's possessions multiplied exceedingly, and he possessed oxen and sheep and asses and camels, and menservants and maidservants. **30** And Laban and his sons envied Jacob, and Laban took back his sheep from him, and he observed him with evil intent.

†Gn. 30:28 has "appoint me thy wages."

A wrong rendering of the Hebrew (Gn. 30:32), which means "speckled" (nakŏd).

Speckled and black, variously marked LXX ποικίλα καὶ σποδοιεδῆ ῥαντά does not represent σποδοειδῆ.

And sheep so LXX (Gn. 30:43); but MT and other versions omit.

The Tribes of Jacob (Israel) are born

CHAPTER 29:

Jacob's Flight With His Family: His Covenant With Laban
(29:1-12; cf. Gen, 31)

1 And it came to pass when Rachel had borne Joseph, that Laban went to shear his sheep; for they were distant from him a three days' journey. **2** And Jacob saw that Laban was going to shear his sheep, and Jacob called Leah and Rachel, and spake kindly unto them that they should come with him to the land of Canaan. **3** For he told them how he had seen everything in a dream, even all that He had spoken unto him that he should return to his father's house; and they said: "To every place whither thou goest we will go with thee." **4** And Jacob blessed the Elohim of Isaac his father, and the Elohim of Abraham his father's father, and he arose and mounted his wives and his children, and took all his possessions and crossed the river, and came to the land of Gilead, and Jacob hid his intention from Laban and told him not. **5** And in the seventh year of the fourth week Jacob turned (his face) toward Gilead in the first month, on the twenty-first thereof. And Laban pursued after him and overtook Jacob in the mountain of Gilead in the third month, on the thirteenth thereof. **6** And Yahuah did not suffer him to injure Jacob; for He appeared to him in a dream by night. And Laban spake to Jacob, **7** And on the fifteenth of those days Jacob made a feast for Laban, and for all who came with him, and Jacob sware to Laban that day, and Laban also to Jacob, that neither should cross the mountain of Gilead to the other with evil purpose. **8** And he made there a heap for a witness; wherefore the name of that place is called: "The Heap of Witness," after this heap. **9** But before they used to call the land of Gilead the land of the Rephaim; for it was the land of the Rephaim, and the Rephaim were born (there), giants whose height was ten, nine, eight down to seven cubits. **10** And their habitation was from the land of the children of Ammon to Mount Hermon, and the seats of their kingdom were Karnaim and Ashtaroth, and Edrei, and Mîsûr, and Beon. **11** And Yahuah destroyed them because of the evil of their deeds; for they were very malignant, and the

So LXX (Gn. 31:20) and Targ. Onkelos; but MT Sam., Vulg., "stole" (the heart of Laban).

2135 A.M.

Sivan 15 is Shavuot/ Pentecost which Jacob celebrated long before Moses.

Cf. Gn. 31:47 ("Galeed" = "Heap of Witness").

Cf. Gn. 14:5 At least 15 ft. – 10 ft. tall in estimation. These are Nephilim. This is why Israel was told to wipe out even the women, children and animals of certain tribes in Canaan. They were not human. In MT of Gn. 14:5, Asheroth-karnaim is one place; but Syr. and some MSS. of LXX support our text. Cf. Dt. 3:10

Amorites dwelt in their stead, wicked and sinful, and there is no people today which hath wrought to the full all their sins, and they have no longer length of life on the earth. **12** And Jacob sent away Laban, and he departed into Mesopotamia, the land of the East, and Jacob returned to the land of Gilead.

Israel did all but wipe out some tribes but not all.

Cf. Gn. 31:22

Jacob, Reconciled With Esau, Dwells In Canaan And Supports His Parents
(29:13-20; Cf. Gen. 32, 33)

13 And he passed over the Jabbok in the ninth month, on the eleventh thereof. And on that day Esau, his brother, came to him, and he was reconciled to him, and departed from him unto the land of Seir, but Jacob dwelt in tents. **14** And in the first year of the fifth week in this jubilee he crossed the Jordan, and dwelt beyond the Jordan, and he pastured his sheep from the sea †of the heap† unto Bethshan, and unto Dothan and unto the †forest† of Akrabbim. **15** And he sent to his father Isaac of all his substance, clothing, and food, and meat, and drink, and milk, and butter, and cheese, and some

2136 A.M.

†Text corrupt. Latin has "from the Salt Sea."

†? read "ascent" (cf. Nm. 34:4; Jos. 15:3)

dates of the valley, **16** And to his mother Rebecca also four times a year, between the times of the months, between ploughing and reaping, and between autumn and the rain (season) and between winter and spring, to the tower of Abraham. **17** For Isaac had returned from the Well of the Oath and gone up to the tower of his father Abraham, and he dwelt there apart from his son Esau. **18** For in the days when Jacob went to Mesopotamia, Esau took to himself a wife Mahalath, the daughter of Ishmael, and he gathered together all the flocks of his father and his wives, and went up and dwelt on Mount Seir, and left Isaac his father at the Well of the Oath alone.

Cf. Gn. 28:9, 36:6, 8. In contrast with Jacob's conduct to his parents, Esau's is unfilial.

19 And Isaac went up from the Well of the Oath and dwelt in the tower of Abraham his father on the mountains of Hebron, **20** And thither Jacob sent all that he did send to his father and his mother from time to time, all they needed, and they blessed Jacob with all their heart and with all their soul.

CHAPTER 30:

Dinah Ravished. Slaughter Of The Shechemites. Laws Against Intermarriage Between Israel And The Heathen. The Choice Of Levi *(30:1-26; cf. Gen. 34)*

2143 A.M.

Based upon 33:18 (cf. R.V. marg.). Our text combines two readings ("Shalem," the name of a city, and shalōm, "peace"). Salem is not Jerusalem which is not named until over 400 years later.

Jubilees does not record the anger of Jacob especially towards Simeon and Levi. That does not mean he was not and does not disagree with Gn. Cf. Gn. 49:5-7

1 And in the first year of the sixth week he went up to Salem, to the east of Shechem, in peace, in the fourth month. **2** And there they carried off Dinah, the daughter of Jacob, into the house of Shechem, the son of Hamor, the Hivite, the prince of the land, and he lay with her and defiled her, and she was a little girl, a child of twelve years.

3 And he besought his father and her brothers that she might be given to him to wife. And Jacob and his sons were wroth because of the men of Shechem; for they had defiled Dinah, their sister, and they spake to them with evil intent and dealt deceitfully with them and beguiled them.

4 And Simeon and Levi came unexpectedly to Shechem and executed judgment on all the men of Shechem, and slew all the men whom they found in it, and left not a single one remaining in it: they slew all in torments because they had dishonoured their sister Dinah. **5** And thus let it not again be done from henceforth that a daughter of Israel be defiled; for judgment is ordained in heaven against them that they should destroy with the sword all the men of the Shechemites because they had wrought shame in Israel.

6 And Yahuah delivered them into the hands of the sons of Jacob that they might exterminate them with the sword and execute judgment upon them, and that it might not thus again be done in Israel that a virgin of Israel should be defiled. **7** And if there is any man who wisheth in Israel to give his daughter or his sister to any man who is of the seed of the Gentiles he shall surely die, and they shall stone him with stones; for he hath wrought shame in Israel; and they shall burn the woman with fire, because she *Cf. Lv. 21:9* hath dishonoured the name of the house of her father, and she shall be rooted out of Israel. **8** And let not an adulteress and no uncleanness be found in Israel throughout all the days of the generations of the earth; for Israel is holy unto Yahuah, and every man who hath defiled (it) shall surely die: they shall stone him with stones. **9** For thus hath it been ordained and written in the heavenly tables regarding all the seed of Israel: he who defileth (it) shall surely die, and he shall be stoned with stones. **10** And to this law there is no limit of days, and no remission, nor any atonement: but the man who hath defiled his daughter shall be rooted out in the midst of all Israel, because he hath given of his seed to Moloch, and wrought impiously so as to defile it. **11** And do thou, Moses, command the children of Israel and exhort them not to give their daughters to the Gentiles, and not to take for their sons any of the daughters of the Gentiles, for this is abominable before Yahuah. **12** For this reason I have written for thee in the words of the Law all the deeds of the Shechemites, which they wrought against Dinah, and how the sons of Jacob spake, saying: "We shall not give our daughter to a man who is uncircumcised; for that were a reproach unto us." **13** And it is a reproach to Israel, to those who give, and to those who take the daughters of the Gentiles; for this is unclean and abominable to Israel. **14** And Israel will not be free from this uncleanness if it hath a wife of the daughters of the Gentiles, or hath given any of its daughters to a man who is of any of the Gentiles. **15** For there will be plague upon plague, and curse upon curse, and every judgment and plague and curse will come (upon him): if he do this thing, or hide his eyes from those who commit uncleanness, or those who defile the sanctuary of Yahuah, or those who profane His holy name, (then) will the whole nation together be judged for all the uncleanness and profanation of this (man). **16** And there will be no respect of persons [and no consideration of persons], and no receiving at his hands of fruits and offerings and burnt-offerings and fat, nor the fragrance of sweet savour, so as to accept it: and so fare every man or woman in Israel who defileth the sanctuary. **17** For this reason I have commanded thee, saying: "Testify this testimony to Israel: see how the Shechemites fared and their sons: how they were delivered into the hands of two sons of Jacob, and they slew them under tortures, and it was (reckoned) unto

Moloch, Molech, Adram-melech is the name of Ba'al. Ba'al means "lord." 6,800 times the Pharisees and Catholic Church replaced the name of YHWH , Yahuah, with Lord or Ba'al in Hebrew. It is Samaritan doctrine not to pronounce nor recognize the name of their god but to call him lord and that same practice continues in modern Judaism which originated from the Pharisees/ Hasmoneans of Samaria not Israel.

14-15 are based upon Lv. 20:2-4

i. e. "ignore"; cf. Lv. 20:4

Cf. Lv. 20:3

In Lv. 20:5, only the guilty man's family is involved.

Bracketed as a dittograph.

them for righteousness, and it is written down to them for righteousness. **18** And the seed of Levi was chosen for the priesthood, and to be Levites, that they might Cf. 32:3, Jacob chooses Levi as priest; cf. also Test. Levi 4:2, Yahuah chooses Levi as priest. This is Levi's reason and there are no conflicts. minister before Yahuah, as we, continually, and that Levi and his sons may be blessed for ever; for he was zealous to execute righteousness and judgment and vengeance on all those who arose against Israel. **19** And so they inscribe as a testimony in his favour on the heavenly tables blessing and righteousness before the Elohim of all: **20** And we remember the righteousness which the man fulfilled during his life, at all periods of the year; until a thousand generations they will record it, and it will come to him and to his descendants after him, and he hath been recorded on sc. of God. This is the second such mention. The likely origin of "Friend of God" in James 2:23. the heavenly tables as a friend and a righteous man. **21** All this account I have written for thee, and have commanded thee to say to the children of Israel, that they should not commit sin nor transgress the ordinances nor break the covenant which hath been ordained for them, (but) that they should fulfil it and be sc. of God. recorded as friends. **22** But if they transgress and work uncleanness in every way, they will be recorded on the Cf. Ps. 69:28; Ex. 32:32; Rev. 3:5, 13:8, etc.; 1 En. 47:3. In all cases, being written in the book of life is salvation and being blotted out means not saved. Jubilees appears the direct origin of this doctrine of the Book of Life mentioned several times in the New Testament. heavenly tables as adversaries, and they will be destroyed out of the book of life, and they will be recorded in the book of those who will be destroyed and with those who will be rooted out of the earth. **23** And on the day when the sons of Jacob slew Shechem a writing was recorded in their favour in heaven that they had executed righteousness and uprightness and vengeance on the sinners, and it was written for a blessing.

24 And they brought Dinah, their sister, out of the house of Shechem, and they took captive everything that was in Shechem, their sheep and their oxen and their asses, and all their wealth, and all their flocks, and brought them all to Jacob their father. **25** And he Cf. Test. Levi 6 reproached them because they had put the city to the sword; for he feared those who dwelt Cf. Gn. 35:5 in the land, the Canaanites and the Perizzites. **26** And the dread of Yahuah was upon all the cities which are around about Shechem, and they did not rise to pursue after the sons of Jacob; for terror had fallen upon them.

"But if they transgress and work uncleanness in every way, they will be recorded on the heavenly tables as adversaries, and they will be...

destroyed out of the book of life..."

30:22

CHAPTER 31:

Jacob's Journey To Bethel And Hebron. Isaac Blesses Levi And Judah
(31:1-25; cf. Gen. 35)

1 And on the new moon of the month Jacob spake to all the people of his house, saying: "Purify yourselves and change your garments, and let us arise and go up to Bethel, where I vowed a vow to Him on the day when I fled from the face of Esau my brother, because He hath been with me and brought me into this land in peace, and put ye away the strange gods that are among you." **2** And they gave up the strange gods and that which was in their ears and which *†Corrupt.* was †on their necks,† and the idols which Rachel stole from Laban her brother she gave wholly to Jacob. And he burnt and brake them to pieces and destroyed them, and hid them under an oak which is in the land of Shechem. **3** And he went up on the new moon of the seventh month to Bethel. And he built an altar at the place where he had slept, and he set up a pillar there, and he *Isaac refused to go to Bethel; cf. Test. Levi 9:2.* sent word to his father Isaac to come to him to his sacrifice, and to his mother Rebecca.

4 And Isaac said: "Let my son Jacob come, and let me see *i. e. to Hebron.* him before I die." **5** And Jacob went to his father Isaac and to his mother Rebecca, to the house of his father Abraham, and he took two of his sons with him, Levi and Judah, and he came to his father Isaac and to his mother Rebecca.

6 And Rebecca came forth from the tower to the front of it to kiss Jacob and embrace him; for her spirit had revived when she heard: "Behold Jacob thy son hath come"; and she kissed him. **7** And she saw his two sons, and she recognised them, and said unto him: "Are these thy sons, my son?" and she embraced them and kissed them, and blessed them, saying: "In you shall the seed of Abraham become illustrious, and ye will prove a blessing on the earth." **8** And Jacob went in to Isaac his father, to the chamber where he lay, and his two sons were with him, and he took the hand of his father, and stooping down he kissed him, and Isaac clung to the neck of Jacob his son, and wept upon his neck. **9** And the darkness left the eyes of Isaac, and he saw the two sons of Jacob, Levi and Judah, and he said: "Are these thy sons, my son? for they are like thee." **10** And he said unto him that they were truly his sons: "And thou hast truly seen that they are truly my sons." **11** And they came near to him, and he turned and kissed them and embraced them both together. **12** And the spirit of prophecy came down into his mouth, and he took Levi by his right hand and Judah by his left.

Cf. Test. Levi 9:1 f. The primacy of Levi is here marked.

13 And he turned to Levi first, and began to bless him first, and said unto him:, 'May the Elohim of all, the very Yahuah of all the ages, bless thee and thy children throughout all the ages. **14** And may Yahuah give to thee and to thy seed †greatness and great glory|, and cause thee and thy seed,

Levi is to serve in the sanctuary as the two highest orders of angels serve in the highest heaven.

from among all flesh, to approach Him to serve in His sanctuary as the angels of the presence and as the holy ones. (Even) as they, will the seed of thy sons be for glory and greatness and holiness, and may He make them great unto all the ages. **15** And they will be princes and judges, and chiefs of all the seed of the sons of Jacob; They will

Cf. Test. Levi 8:2 ff

speak the word of Yahuah in righteousness, And they will judge all His judgments in righteousness. And they will declare My ways to Jacob And My paths to Israel. The blessing of Yahuah will be given in their mouths to bless all the seed of the beloved.

i. e. the priestly blessing; cf. Ecclus. 50:20.

16 Thy mother hath called thy name Levi, And justly hath she called thy name; Thou wilt be joined to Yahuah And be the companion of all the sons of Jacob; Let His table be thine, And do thou and thy sons eat thereof; And may thy table be full unto all generations, And thy food fail not unto all the ages.

i. e. of Abraham.

A play on the name "Levi" (= attaché); cf. Gn. 29:34 (R.V. marg.); also Nm. 18:2, 4.

Cf. Test. Levi 8:16 ("and the table of the Lord shall thy seed apportion").

17 And let all who hate thee fall down before thee, And let all thy adversaries be rooted out and perish; And blessed be he that blesseth thee, And cursed be every nation that curseth thee. **18** And to Judah he said: May Yahuah give thee strength and power To tread down all that hate thee; A prince shalt thou be, thou and one of thy sons, over the sons of Jacob; May thy name and the name of thy sons go forth and traverse every land and region. Then will the Gentiles fear before thy face, And all the nations will quake And all the peoples will quake]. **19** In thee shall be the help of Jacob, And in thee be found the salvation of Israel. **20** And when thou sittest on the throne of the honour of thy righteousness, There will be great peace for

i. e.? the Messiah who is to spring from Judah: but if so the expression of the hope is somewhat vague. More probably the reference is to the historical David.

i. e. the name of the Hebrew people. Yahudim.

Bracketed as a dittograph.

i. e. of Abraham. all the seed of the sons of the beloved, And blessed will he be that blesseth thee; And all that hate thee and afflict thee and curse thee Shall be rooted out and destroyed from the earth and accursed."

21 And turning he kissed him again and embraced him, and rejoiced greatly; for he had seen the sons of Jacob his son in very truth. 22 And he went forth from between his feet and fell down and worshipped him. And he blessed them. And (Jacob) rested there with Isaac his father that night, and they ate and drank with joy.

23 And he made the two sons of Jacob sleep, the one on his right hand and the other on his left and it was counted to him for righteousness.

24 And Jacob told his father everything during the night, how Yahuah had shown him great mercy, and how He had prospered (him in) all his ways, and protected him from all evil.

25 And Isaac blessed the Elohim of his father Abraham, who had not withdrawn His mercy and His righteousness from the sons of His servant Isaac.

Rebecca Journeys With Jacob To Bethel *(31:26-32)*

26 And in the morning Jacob told his father Isaac the vow which he had vowed to Yahuah, and the vision which he had seen, and that he had built an altar, and that everything was ready for the sacrifice to be made before Yahuah as he had vowed, and that he had come to set him on an ass. 27 And Isaac said unto Jacob his son: "I am not able to go with thee; for I am old, and not able to bear the way: go, my son, in peace; for I am one hundred and sixty-five years this day; I am no longer able to journey, set thy mother (on an ass) and let her go with thee. 28 And I know, my son, that thou hast come on my account, and may this day be blessed on which thou hast seen me alive, and I also have seen thee, my son. 29 Mayest thou prosper and fulfil the vow which thou hast vowed, and put not off thy vow; for thou wilt be called to account as touching the vow; now therefore make haste to perform it, and may He be pleased who hath made all things, to whom thou hast vowed the vow." 30 And he said to Rebecca: "Go with Jacob thy son"; and Rebecca went with Jacob her son, and Deborah with her, and they

At Bethel; cf. Gn. 28:18-22.

Note the emphasis on the obligation to keep a vow. Cf. Gn. 28:20; Nm. 30:2; Lv. 27:2; Dt. 23:21-23; Zc. 8:17

came to Bethel. **31** And Jacob remembered the prayer with which his father had blessed him and his two sons, Levi and Judah, and he rejoiced and blessed the Elohim of his fathers, Abraham and Isaac. **32** And he said: "Now I know that I have an eternal hope, and my sons also, before the Elohim of all;" and thus is it ordained concerning the two; and they record it as an eternal testimony unto them on the heavenly tables how Isaac blessed them.

Feild near Metar, a comunity village northen Ber-Sheva, Israel.

CHAPTER 32:

Levi's Dream At Bethel; He Is appointed To The Priesthood. Jacob Celebrates The Feast Of Tabernacles And Offers Tithes. The Institution Of Tithes.

(32:1-15; cf. Gen. 35)

Cf. Test. Levi 8 (which describes Levi's dream-vision of seven men in white as having taken place at Bethel); also 5 of the same work (in 9:3 Jacob has this dream also).

1 And he abode that night at Bethel, and Levi dreamed that they had ordained and made him the priest of the Most High Elohim, him and his sons for ever; and he awoke from his sleep and blessed Yahuah. **2** And Jacob rose early in the morning, on the fourteenth of this month, and he gave a tithe of all that came with him, both of men and cattle, both of gold and every vessel and garment, yea, he gave tithes of all. **3** And in those days Rachel became pregnant with her son Benjamin. And Jacob counted his sons from him upwards and Levi fell to the portion of Yahuah, and his father clothed him in the garments of the priesthood and filled his hands. **4** And on the fifteenth of this month, he brought to the altar fourteen oxen from amongst the cattle, and twenty-eight rams, and forty-nine sheep, and seven lambs, and twenty-one kids of

Hasmonean Priest Kings were not Levites nor even Israelites but Samaritans. They usurped this title from the Levites whom they ousted from the High Priesthood. There is no Biblical justification for such.

Levi, as the tenth son (counting backwards from Benjamin), fell, under the law of tithe, to the Lord, and was consecrated to the priesthood. cf. Lv. 27:32

A technical expression meaning appointment to the priesthood; cf. Ex. 28:41 (R.V. marg.); 29:9.

the goats as a burnt-offering on the altar of sacrifice, well pleasing for a sweet savour before Yahuah. **5** This was his offering, in consequence of the vow which he had vowed that he would give a tenth, with their fruit-offerings and their drink-offerings. **6** And when the fire had consumed it, he burnt incense on the fire over the fire, and for a thank-offering two oxen and four rams and four sheep, four he-goats, and two sheep of a year old, and two kids of the goats; and thus he did daily for seven days. **7** And he and all his sons and his men were eating (this) with joy there during seven days and blessing and thanking Yahuah, who had delivered him out of all his tribulation and had given him his vow. **8** And he tithed all the clean animals, and made a burnt sacrifice, but the unclean animals he gave (not) to Levi his son, and he gave him all the souls of the men. **9** And Levi discharged the priestly office at Bethel before Jacob his father in preference to his ten brothers, and he was a priest there, and Jacob gave his vow: thus he tithed again the tithe to Yahuah and sanctified it, and it became holy unto Him.

The number of victims does not agree with the prescriptions of the Mosaic Law regarding the Feast of Tabernacles; cf. Nm. 29:12-40; Lv. 23:34-36, 39-44.

Cf. Gn. 28:22

Cf. Test. Levi 9:3 ("And he [Jacob] paid tithes of all to the Lord through me").

i. e. the second tithe; cf. Nm. 18:26.

Cf. Dt. 14:23 (Tobit 1:7)

10 And for this reason it is ordained on the heavenly tables as a law for the tithing again the tithe to eat before Yahuah from year to year, in the place where it is chosen that His name should dwell, and to this law there is no limit of days for ever.

11 This ordinance is written that it may be fulfilled from year to year in eating the second tithe before the Lord in the place where it hath been chosen, and nothing shall remain over from it from this year to the year following. **12** For in its year shall the seed be eaten till the days of the gathering of the seed of the year, and the wine till the days of the wine, and the oil till the days of its season.

13 And all that is left thereof and becometh old, let it be regarded as polluted: let it be burnt with fire, for it is unclean. **14** And thus let them eat it together in the sanctuary, and let them not suffer it to become old.

Cf. Lv. 27:32; 2 Chr. 31:6.

These tithes are not otherwise attested in the O.T.

15 And all the tithes of the oxen and sheep shall be holy unto Yahuah, and shall belong to His priests, which they will eat before Him from year to year; for thus is it ordained and engraven regarding the tithe on the heavenly tables.

Jacob's Visions. He Celebrates The Eighth Day Of Tabernacles. The Birth of Benjamin And Death Of Rachel
(32:16-34; cf. Gen. 35)

16 And on the following night, on the twenty-second day of this month, Jacob resolved to build that place, and to surround the court with a wall, and to sanctify it and make it holy for ever, for himself and his children after him. **17** And Yahuah appeared to him by night and blessed him and said unto him: "Thy name shall not be called Jacob, but Israel shall they name thy name." **18** And He said unto him again: "I am Yahuah who created the heaven and the earth, and I shall increase thee and multiply thee exceedingly, and kings will come forth from thee, and they will judge everywhere wherever the foot of the sons of men hath trodden. **19** And I shall give to thy seed all the earth which is under heaven, and they will judge all the nations according to their desires, and after that they will get possession of the whole earth and inherit it for ever." **20** And He finished speaking with him, and He went up from him, and Jacob looked till He had ascended

For 17-18 cf. Gn. 35:10-12. Notice that the whole inhabited earth (not merely Palestine, as in Gn. 35:12 which is a different oontoxt) is here promised to Israel in the context of the end times. This is when believers are promised the earth forever. Israel always included the "stranger among you" (gentiles) from the Exodus forward. It still does. This definitively defines Israel as a people not a land. Gog of Magog does not inherit Israel's blessings when he takes the land. They follow a seed in which gentiles are grafted into for those who choose.

Cf. Gn. 35:13 into heaven. **21** And he saw in a vision of the night, and behold an angel descended from heaven with seven tablets in his hands, and he gave them *Cf. 2 Esd. 14:24* to Jacob, and he read them and knew all that was written therein which would befall him and his sons through-out all the ages.

22 And he showed him all that *Cf. 45:4* was written on the tablets, and *The sanctuary at Bethel was not to be the one central shrine, where alone acceptable worship was to be offered. As with the second Temple, it would not house Yahuah's presence.* said unto him: "Do not build this place, and do not make it an eternal sanctuary, and do not dwell here; for this is not the place. Go to the house of Abraham thy father and dwell with Isaac thy father until the day of the death of thy father. **23** For in Egypt thou wilt die in peace, and in this land thou wilt be buried with honour in the sepulchre of thy fathers, with Abraham and Isaac. **24** Fear not, for as thou hast seen and read it, thus will it all be; and do thou write down everything as thou hast seen and read." **25** And Jacob said: "Lord, how can I remember all that I have read and seen?" And he said unto him: "I will bring all things to thy remembrance." **26** And he went up from him, and he awoke from his sleep, and he remembered everything which he had read and seen, and he wrote down all the words which he had read and seen. **27** And he celebrated there yet another day, and he sacrificed thereon according to all that he sacrificed on the former days, and called its name †"Addition,"† for †this day was added,† and

*Cf. Jn. 14:26. "bring all things to your remembrance." **Exact quote from Jubilees.** Also, in 2 Esd. 14:40, Ezra's memory is said to have been miraculously strengthened after he had received the cup of inspiration; Jubilees is the likely origin of both.*

i. e. the eighth day of the Feast of Tabernacles.

† The Hebrew name is 'asereth ('asarta), from a root meaning "detain" ('aṣar). Hence, perhaps, we may emend here "keeping back," for on that day he was kept back (Charles).

the former days he called "The Feast." **28** And thus it was manifested that it should be, and it is written on the heavenly tables: wherefore it was revealed to him that he should celebrate it, and add it to the seven days of the feast. **29** And its name was called †"Addition," † †because that† it was recorded amongst the days of the feast days, †according to† the number of the days of the year. **30** And in the night, on the twenty-third of this month, Deborah Rebecca's nurse died, and they buried her beneath the city under the oak of the river, and he called the name of this place, "The river of Deborah," and the oak, "The oak of the mourning of Deborah." **31** And Rebecca

29 is very corrupt. Charles suggests that it should be read: "And its name was called 'a keeping back' (i.e. 'aṣereth) when it was recorded amongst the days of the feast days in the number of the days of the year."

Cf. Gn. 35:8

went and returned to her house to his father Isaac, and Jacob sent by her hand rams and sheep and he-goats that she should prepare a meal for his father such as he desired. **32** And he went after his mother till he came to the land of Kabrâtân, and he dwelt there. **33** And Rachel bare a son in the night, and called his name "Son of my sorrow"; for she suffered in giving him birth: but his father called his name Benjamin, on the eleventh of the eighth month in the first of the sixth week of this jubilee. **34** And Rachel died there and she was buried in the land of Ephrath, the same is Bethlehem, and Jacob built a pillar on the grave of Rachel, on the road above her grave.

i. e. the eighth day of the Feast. Due to a misunderstanding of the words rendered "some distance" (kibrath hā'ares) in Gn. 35:16. The LXX also took kibrath to be a proper name (Χιβραθο).

2143 A.M.

"On the way to" in the text of Gn. 35:19.

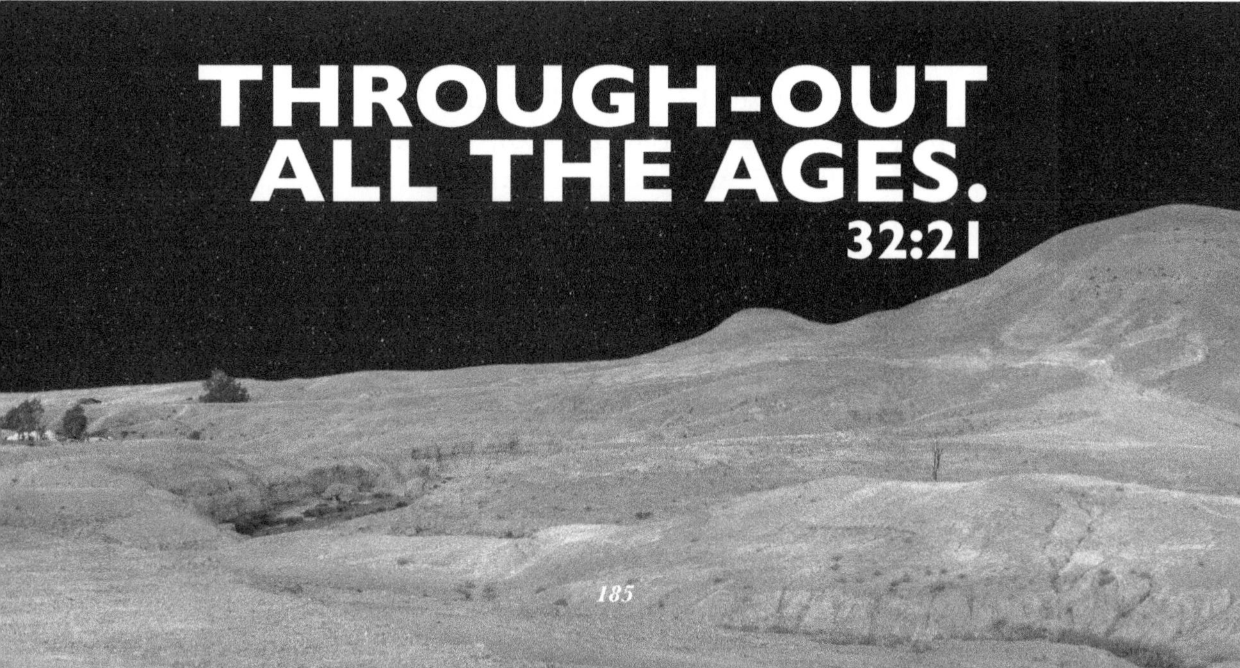

CHAPTER 33:

Reuben's Sin With Bilhah. Laws Regarding Incest. Jacob's Children

(33:1-23; Cf. Gen. 35:21-27)

1 And Jacob went and dwelt to the south of Magdalâdrâ'êf. And he went to his father Isaac, he and Leah his wife, on the new moon of the tenth month. **2** And Reuben saw Bilhah, Rachel's maid, the concubine of his father, bathing in water in a secret place, and he loved her.

A compound of migdal 'eder 'ephrāth ("the tower of Eder of Ephrath"); cf. Gn. 35:21, also Test. Reuben 3:9-15, where the same incident is narrated.

3 And he hid himself at night, and he entered the house of Bilhah [at night], and he found her sleeping alone on a bed in her house. **4** And he lay with her, and she awoke and saw, and behold Reuben was lying with her in the bed, and she uncovered the border of her covering and seized him, and cried out, and discovered that it was Reuben. **5** And she was ashamed because of him, and released her hand from him, and he fled. **6** And she lamented because of this thing exceedingly, and did not tell it to any one. **7** And when Jacob returned and sought her, she said unto him: "I am not clean for thee, for I have been defiled as regards thee; for Reuben hath defiled me, and hath lain with me in the night, and I was asleep, and did not discover until he uncovered my skirt and slept with me."

8 And Jacob was exceedingly wroth with Reuben because he had lain with Bilhah, because he had uncovered his father's skirt. **9** And Jacob did not approach her again because Reuben had defiled her. And as for any man who uncovereth his father's skirt his deed is wicked exceedingly, for he is abominable before Yahuah.

Cf. Dt. 22:30

10 For this reason it is written and ordained on the heavenly tables that a man should not lie with his father's wife, and should not uncover his father's skirt, for this is unclean: they shall surely die together, the man who lieth with his father's wife and the woman also, for they have wrought uncleanness on the earth.

Cf. Lv. 20:11

11 And there shall be nothing unclean before our Elohim in the nation which He hath chosen for Himself as a possession.

12 And again, it is written a second time: "Cursed he be who lieth with the wife of his father, for he hath uncovered his father's shame"; and all the holy ones of Yahuah said "So be it; so be it." **13** And do thou, Moses, command

Cf. Dt. 27:20

the children of Israel that they observe this word; for it (entaileth) a punishment of death; and it is unclean, and there is no atonement for ever to atone for the man who hath committed this, but he is to be put to death and slain, and stoned with stones, and rooted out from the midst of the people of our Elohim. **14** For to no man who doeth so in Israel is it permitted to remain alive a single day on the earth, for he is abominable and unclean. **15** And let them not say: to Reuben was granted life and forgiveness after he had lain with his father's concubine, and to her also though she had a husband, and her husband Jacob, his father, was still alive. **16** For until that time there had not been revealed the ordinance and judgment and law in its completeness for all, but in thy days (it hath been revealed) as a law of seasons and of days, and an everlasting law for the everlasting generations. **17** And for this law there is no consummation of days, and no atonement for it, but they must both be rooted out in the midst of the nation: on the day whereon they committed it they shall slay them. **18** And do thou, Moses, write (it) down for Israel that they may observe it, and do according to these words, and not commit a sin unto death; for Yahuah our Elohim is judge, who respecteth not persons and accepteth not gifts. **19** And tell them these words of the covenant, that they may hear and observe, and be on their guard with respect to them, and not be destroyed and rooted out of the land; for an uncleanness, and an abomination, and a contamination, and a pollution are all they who commit it on the earth before our Elohim. **20** And there is no greater sin than the fornication which they commit on earth; for Israel is a holy nation unto Yahuah its Elohim, and a nation of inheritance, and a priestly and royal nation and for (His own) possession; and there shall no such uncleanness appear in the midst of the holy nation. **21** And in the third year of this sixth week Jacob and all his sons went and dwelt in the house of Abraham, near Isaac his father and Rebecca his mother. **22** And these were the names of the sons of Jacob: the first-born Reuben, Simeon, Levi, Judah, Issachar, Zebulon, the

"Where there is no law there is no transgression" (Rom. 4:15).

Cf. 21:22

Cf. 5:16, 40:8

Cf. 16:18 (note).

2145 A.M.

For 22 cf. Gn. 35:23-27

sons of Leah; and the sons of Rachel, Joseph and Benjamin; and the sons of Bilhah, Dan and Naphtali, and the sons of Zilpah, Gad and Asher; and Dinah, the daughter of Leah, the only daughter of Jacob. **23** And they came and bowed themselves to Isaac and Rebecca, and when they saw them they blessed Jacob and all his sons, and Isaac rejoiced exceedingly, for he saw the sons of Jacob, his younger son, and he blessed them.

THE Levite BIBLE
LeviteBible.com

Isaac rejoiced exceedingly,
for he saw the sons of Jacob,
his younger son, and

HE BLESSED THEM.
33:23

CHAPTER 34:

War Of The Amorite Kings Against Jacob And His Sons. Joseph Sold Into Egypt *(cf. Gen. 37)*. The Death Of Bilhah And Dinah *(34:1-19)*

2148 A.M. **1** And in the sixth year of this week of this forty-fourth jubilee Jacob sent his sons to pasture their sheep, and his servants with them, to the pastures of Shechem. **2** And *[More detail in Test. Judah 3-7. Gn. 48:22 "Jacob's conquest of Shechem"]* the seven kings of the Amorites assembled themselves together against them, to slay them, hiding themselves under the trees, and to take their cattle as a prey. **3** And Jacob and Levi and Judah and Joseph were in the house with Isaac their father; for his spirit was sorrowful, and they could not leave him: and Benjamin was the youngest, and for this reason remained with his father. **4** And there came the king of Tâphû, *[Read "king." = Tappuah (Jos. 15:53, 16:8)]* and the king of †'Arêsa,† and the king of Sêragân, *[i. e. Shiloh.]* and the king of Sêlô, and the king of Gâ'as, *[=? Gaash (Jos. 24:30).]* and the king of Bêthôrôn, and the king of †Ma'anîsâkîr,† *[†Corrupt for "Shakir-Maani."]* and all those who dwell in these mountains (and) who dwell in the woods in the land of Canaan. **5** And they announced this to Jacob saying: "Behold, the kings of the Amorites have surrounded thy sons, and plundered their herds." **6** And he arose from his house, he and his three sons and all the servants of his father, and his own servants, and he went against them with *[Another reading is "800."]* six thousand men, who carried swords. **7** And he slew them in the pastures of Shechem, and *[Six out of the seven kings are slain; so Test. Judah 4 [For the names see notes on 4 above.]]* pursued those who fled, and he slew them with the edge of the sword, and he slew †'Arêsa † and Tâphû and Sarêgân and Sêlô and †'Amânîsakîr† and Gâ[gâ]'as, and he recovered his herds.

8 And he prevailed over them, and imposed tribute on them that they should pay him tribute, five fruit products of their land, and he built Rôbêl *[= Timnath-heres (Jud. 2:9).]* and Tamnâtârês **9** And he returned in peace, and made peace with them, and they became his servants, until the day that he and his sons went down into Egypt. **10** And in *2149 A.M.* the seventh year of this week he sent Joseph to learn about *[For 10-11 cf. Gn. 37:12 ff]* the welfare of his brothers from his house to the land of Shechem, and he found them in the land of Dothan.

11 And they dealt treacherously with him, and formed a plot against him to slay him, but changing their minds, they sold him to Ishmaelite merchants, and they brought him down into Egypt, and they sold him to Potiphar, the eunuch of Pharaoh, the chief of the cooks, priest of the city of 'Êlêw. **12** And the sons of Jacob slaughtered a kid, and dipped the coat of Joseph in the blood, and sent (it) to Jacob their father on the tenth of the seventh month. **13** And he mourned all that night, for they had brought it to him in the evening, and he became feverish with mourning for his death, and he said: "An evil beast hath devoured Joseph"; and all the members of his house [mourned with him that day, and they] were grieving and mourning with him all that day. **14** And his sons and his daughter rose up to comfort him, but he refused to be comforted for his son.

15 And on that day Bilhah heard that Joseph had perished, and she died mourning him, and she was living in †Qafrâtêf† and Dinah also, his daughter, died after Joseph had perished. And there came these three mournings upon Israel in one month. **16** And they buried Bilhah over against the tomb of Rachel, and Dinah also, his daughter, they buried there. **17** And he mourned for Joseph one year, and did not cease, for he said "Let me go down to the grave mourning for my son." **18** For this reason it is ordained for the children of Israel that they should afflict themselves on the tenth of the seventh month -- on the day that the news which made him weep for Joseph came to Jacob his father -- that they should make atonement for themselves thereon with a young goat on the tenth of the seventh month, once a year, for their sins; for they had grieved the affection of their father regarding Joseph his son. **19** And this day hath been ordained that they should grieve thereon for their sins, and for all their transgressions and for all their errors, so that they might cleanse themselves on that day once a year.

The Wives of Jacob's Sons (34:20-21)

20 And after Joseph perished, the sons of Jacob took unto themselves wives. The name of Reuben's wife is 'Adâ and the name of Simeon's wife is 'Adîbâ'a, a Canaanite; and the name of Levi's wife is Mêlkâ, of the daughters of Aram, of the seed of the sons of Terah; and the name of Judah's wife, Bêtasû'êl, a Canaanite; and

Or "court official."

So LXX of Gn. 37:36 (ἀρχιμά-γειρος), misunderstanding the Hebrew (= "captain of the guard").

i. e. Heliopolis (LXX Ἡλίου πόλεωσ, Gn. 41:45, 50), i. e. "On."

Bracketed as a dittograph.

†? = "Kabrâtân," 32:32.

Cf. Gn. 37:35 The reason here given for the institution of the Day of Atonement (cf. Lv. 16) = "fast," cf. Lv. 16:31, etc.

Cf. Gn. 46:10. Cf. 30:7 ff such a marriage (with a Canaanitish woman) punishable by death.

Cf. Test. Levi 11:1

Cf. 41:7. The name goes back to "Bathshua" (i. e. "daughter of Shua"); cf. Test. Judah 8:2, etc.; cf. Gn. 38:2.

the name of Issachar's wife, Hêzaqâ; and the name of Zebulon's wife, †Nî'îmân†; and the name of Dan's wife, 'Êglâ; and the name of Naphtali's wife, Rasû'û, of Mesopotamia; and the name of Gad's wife, Mâka; and the name of Asher's wife, 'Îjônâ; and the name of Joseph's wife, Asenath, the Egyptian; and the name of Benjamin's wife, 'Îjasaka. **21** And Simeon repented, and took a second wife from Mesopotamia as his brothers.

Cf. Gn. 41:45

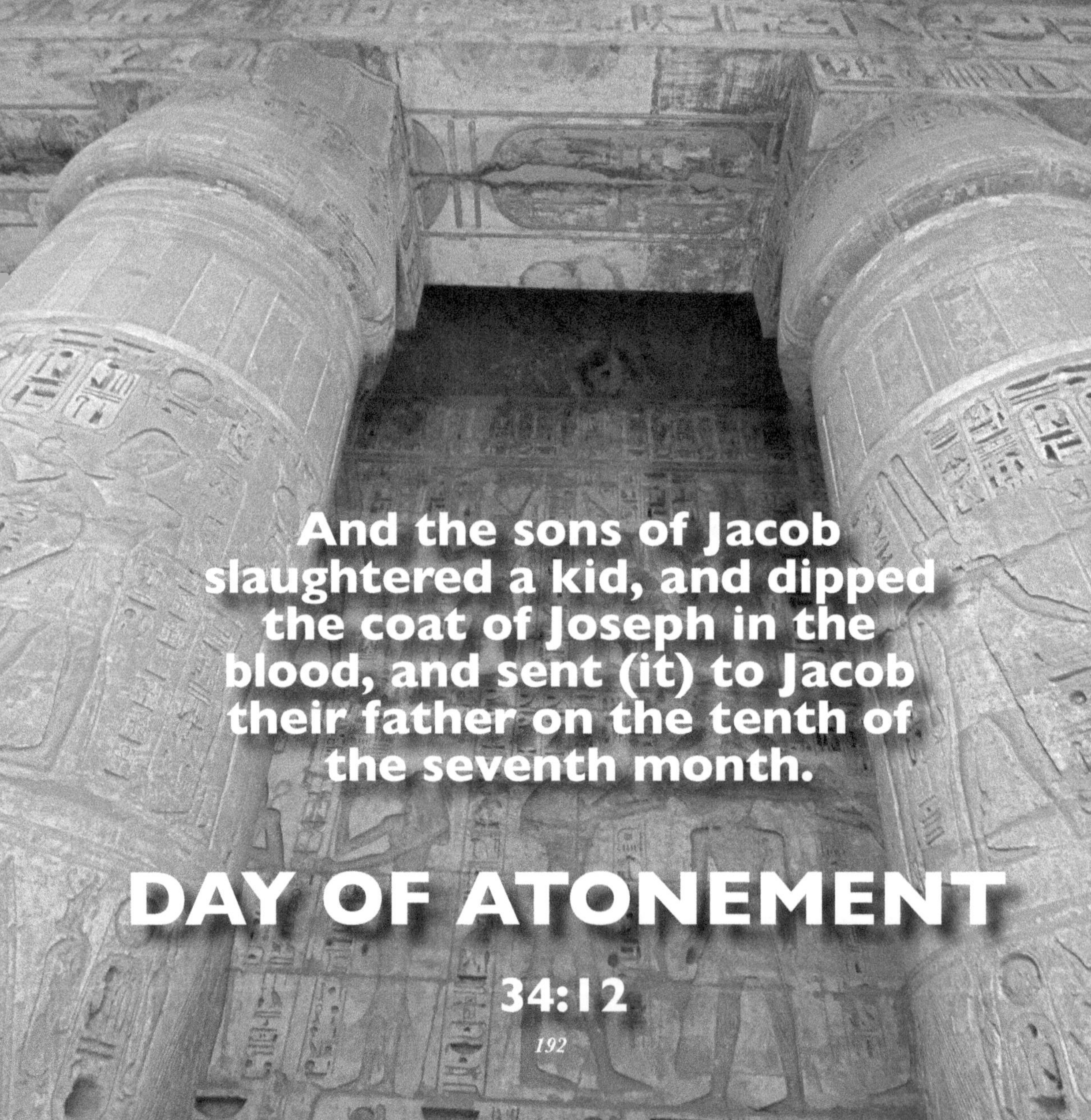

CHAPTER 35:

Rebecca's Last Admonitions And Death
(35:1-27)

2157 A.M.

1 And in the first year of the first week of the forty-fifth jubilee Rebecca called Jacob, her son, and commanded him regarding his father and regarding his brother, that he should honour them all the days of his life. **2** And Jacob said: "I will do everything as thou hast commanded me; for this thing will be honour and greatness to me, and righteousness before Yahuah, that I should honour them. **3** And thou too, mother, knowest from the time I was born until this day, all my deeds and all that is in my heart, that I always think good concerning all. **4** And how should I not do this thing which thou hast commanded me, that I should honour my father and my brother! **5** Tell me, mother, what perversity hast thou seen in me and I shall turn away from it, and mercy will be upon me."

6 And she said unto him: "My son, I have not seen in thee all my days any perverse but (only) upright deeds. And yet I shall tell thee the truth, my son: I shall die this, year, and I shall not survive this year in my life; for I have seen in a dream the day of my death, that I should not live beyond a hundred and fifty-five years: and behold I have completed all the days of my life which I am to live." **7** And Jacob laughed at the words of his mother, because his mother had said unto him that she should die; and she was sitting opposite to him in possession of her strength, and she was not infirm in her strength; for she went in and out and saw, and her teeth were strong, and no ailment had touched her all the days of her life. **8** And Jacob said unto her: "Blessed am I, mother, if my days approach the days of thy life, and my strength remain with me thus as thy strength: and thou wilt not die, for thou art jesting idly with me regarding thy death." **9** And she went in to Isaac and said unto him: "One petition I make unto thee: make Esau swear that he will not injure Jacob, nor pursue him with enmity; for thou knowest Esau's thoughts that they are perverse from his youth, and there is no goodness in him; for he desireth after thy death to kill him. **10** And thou knowest all that he hath done since the day Jacob his brother went to Haran until this day; how he hath forsaken us with his whole heart, and hath done evil to us; thy flocks he hath taken to himself, and carried off all thy possessions from before thy face. **11** And when we implored and besought him for what was our own, he did as a man who was taking pity on us. **12** And he is bitter against thee because thou didst bless Jacob thy perfect and upright son; for there is no evil but only goodness in him, and since he came from Haran unto this day he hath not robbed us of aught, for he bringeth us everything in its season always, and rejoiceth with all his heart when we take at his hands, and he blesseth us, and hath not parted from us since he came from Haran until this day, and he remaineth with us continually at home honouring us."

13 And Isaac said unto her: "I, too, know and see the deeds of Jacob who is with us, how that with all his heart he honoureth us; but I loved Esau formerly more than Jacob, because he was the first-born; but now I love Jacob more than Esau, for he hath done manifold evil deeds, and there is no righteousness in him, for all his ways are unrighteousness and violence, [and there is no righteousness around him].[a] **14** And now my heart is troubled because of all his deeds, and neither he nor his seed is to be saved, for they are those who will be destroyed from the earth, and who will be rooted out from under heaven, for he hath forsaken the Elohim of Abraham and gone after his wives and after their uncleanness and after their error, he and his children. **15** And thou dost bid me make him swear that he will not slay Jacob, his brother; even if he swear he will not abide by his oath, and he will not do good but evil only. **16** But if he desireth to slay Jacob, his brother, into Jacob's hands will he be given, and he will not escape from his hands, [for he will descend into his hands.][b] **17** And fear thou not on account of Jacob; for the guardian of Jacob is great and powerful and honoured, and praised more than the guardian of Esau."[c] **18** And Rebecca sent and called Esau, and he came to her, and she said unto him: "I have a petition, my son, to make unto thee, and do thou promise to do it, my son." **19** And he said: "I will do everything that

[a] *? a dittograph.*

[b] *? bracketed words a gloss; cf. 36:9.*

[c] *? the guardian-angel; cf. Mt. 18:10; Acts 12:15; Heb. 1:14.*

thou sayest unto me, and I will not refuse thy petition."

20 And she said unto him: "I ask you that the day I die, thou wilt take me in and bury me near Sarah, thy father's mother, and that thou and Jacob will love each other, and that neither will desire evil against the other, but mutual love only, and (so) ye will prosper, my sons, and be honoured in the midst of the land, and no enemy will rejoice over you, and ye will be a blessing and a mercy in the eyes of all those that love you." **21** And he said: "I will do all that thou hast told me, and I shall bury thee on the day thou diest near Sarah, my father's mother, as thou hast desired that her bones may be near thy bones. **22** And Jacob, my brother, also, I shall love above all flesh; for I have not a brother in all the earth but him only: and this is no great merit for me if I love him; for he is my brother, and we were sown together in thy body, and together came we forth from thy womb, and if I do not love my brother, whom shall I love? **23** And I, myself, beg thee to exhort Jacob concerning me and concerning my sons, for I know that he will assuredly be king over me and my sons, for

on the day my father blessed him he made him the higher and me the lower. **24** And I swear unto thee that I shall love him, and not desire evil against him all the days of my life but good only." And he sware unto her regarding all this matter. **25** And she called Jacob before the eyes of Esau, and gave him commandment according to the words which she had spoken to Esau.

26 And he said: "I shall do thy pleasure; believe me that no evil will proceed from me or from my sons against Esau, and I shall be first in naught save in love only." **27** And they ate and drank, she and her sons that night, and she died, three jubilees and one week and one year old, on that night, and her two sons, Esau and Jacob, buried her in the double cave near Sarah, *i. e. Machpelah.* their father's mother.

CHAPTER 36:
Isaac's Last Words and Admonitions: his Death. The Death of Leah *(36:1-24)*

2162 A.M. 1 And in the sixth year of this week Isaac called his two sons, Esau and Jacob, and they came to him, and he said unto them: "My sons, I am going the way of my fathers, to the eternal house where my fathers are. 2 Wherefore bury me near Abraham my father, in the double cave in the field of Ephron the Hittite, where Abraham purchased a sepulchre to bury in; in the sepulchre which I digged for myself, there bury me. 3 And this I command you, my sons, that ye practise righteousness and uprightness on the earth, so that Yahuah may bring upon you all that Yahuah said that he would do to Abraham and to his seed. 4 And love one another, my sons, your brothers as a man who loveth his own soul, and let each seek in what he may benefit his brother, and act together on the earth; and let them love each other as their own souls. 5 And concerning the question of idols, I command and admonish you to reject them and hate them, and love them not; for they are full of deception for those that worship them and for those that bow down to them.

6 Remember ye, my sons, the Yahuah Elohim of Abraham your father, and how I too worshipped Him and served Him in righteousness and in joy, that He might multiply you and increase your seed as the stars of heaven in multitude, and establish you on the earth as the plant of righteousness which will not be rooted out unto all the generations for ever. 7 And now I shall make you swear a great oath--for there is no oath which is greater than it by the name glorious and honoured and great and splendid and wonderful and mighty, which created the heavens and the earth and all things together -- that ye will fear Him and worship Him. 8 And that each will love his brother with affection and righteousness, and that neither will desire evil against his brother from henceforth for ever all the days of your life, so that ye may prosper in all your deeds and not be destroyed. 9 And if either of you deviseth evil against his brother, know that from henceforth every one that deviseth evil against his brother will fall into his hand, and will be rooted out of the

Cf. Eccles. 12:5 ("man goeth to his long home," lit. "to his eternal house").

"Your brothers" probably a gloss.

Cf. 1:16, 16:26, 21:24 Only Messiah, Jacob's seed, fits this plant of righteousness.

land of the living, and his seed will be destroyed from under heaven. **10** But on the day of turbulence and execration and indignation and anger, with flaming devouring fire as He burnt Sodom, so likewise will He burn his land and his city and all that is his, and he will be blotted out of the book of the discipline of the children of men, and not be recorded in the book of life, but in that which is appointed to destruction, and he will depart into eternal execration; so that their condemnation may be always renewed in hate and in execration and in wrath and in torment and in indignation and in plagues and in disease for ever. **11** I say and testify to you, my sons, according to the judgment which will come upon the man who wisheth to injure his brother." **12** And he divided all his possessions between the two on that day, and he gave the larger portion to him that was the first-born, and the tower and all that was about it, and all that Abraham possessed at the Well of the Oath. **13** And he said, "This larger portion I shall give to the first-born." **14** And Esau said, "I have sold to Jacob and given my birthright to Jacob; to him let it be given, and I have not

Cf. 30:22 Book of Life. This divine title occurs frequently in our Book, and in Ecclus. (48 times), and Daniel (13 times). In the Pentateuch, outside Gn. 14 (where it occurs four times), it is only found twice. Its use was revived in Ap. Bar. (23 times), and in 2 Esd.

a single word to say regarding it, for it is his." **15** And Isaac said, "May a blessing rest upon you, my sons, and upon your seed this day, for ye have given me rest, and my heart is not pained concerning the birthright, lest thou shouldest work wickedness on account of it. **16** May the Most High Elohim 1 bless the man that worketh righteousness, him and his seed for ever." **17** And he ended commanding them and blessing them, and they ate and drank together before him, and he rejoiced because there was one mind between them, and they went forth from him and rested that day and slept. **18** And Isaac slept on his bed that day rejoicing; and he slept the eternal sleep, and died one hundred and eighty years old. He completed twenty-five weeks and five years; and his two sons Esau and Jacob buried him.

Cf. Gn. 35:29

19 And Esau went to the land of Edom, to the mountains of Seir, and dwelt there. **20** And Jacob dwelt in the mountains of Hebron, in the tower of the land of the sojournings of his father Abraham, and he worshipped Yahuah with all his heart and according to the visible commands according as He had divided the days of

These commands had been made visible to Jacob on the seven tables which the angel had shown him in a vision; Cf. 32:21.

his generations. **21** And Leah his wife died in the fourth year of the second week of the forty-fifth jubilee, and he buried her in the double cave near Rebecca his mother, to the left of the grave of Sarah, his father's mother. **22** And all her sons and his sons came to mourn over Leah his wife with him, and to comfort him regarding her, for he was lamenting her. **23** For he loved her exceedingly after Rachel her sister died; for she was perfect and upright in all her ways and honoured Jacob, and all the days that she lived with him he did not hear from her mouth a harsh word, for she was gentle and peaceable and upright and honourable. **24** And he remembered all her deeds which she had done during her life, and he lamented her exceedingly; for he loved her with all his heart and with all his soul.

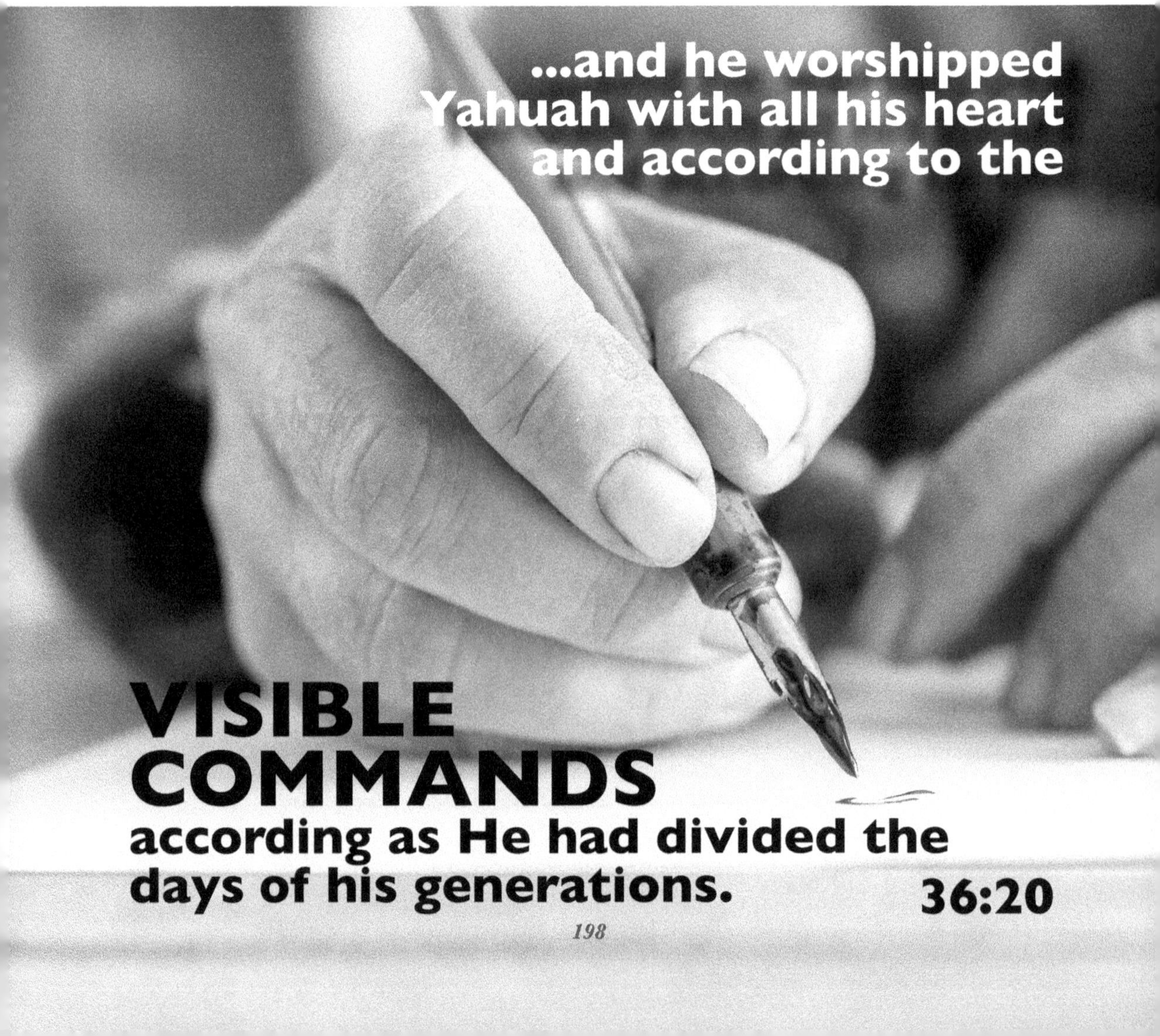

2167 A.M.

...and he worshipped Yahuah with all his heart and according to the

VISIBLE COMMANDS
according as He had divided the days of his generations.

36:20

CHAPTER 37:

Esau And His Sons Wage War With Jacob *(37:1-25)*

2162 A.M.

The legend of the wars between the sons of Jacob and Esau contained in chaps. 37-38 here seems to be ancient. It is also found in Test. Judah 9 and in the Jewish Midrashic literature. Our text contains the oldest form.

This explains how Edom and Israel became rivals after the brothers reconciled. Edom is at odds with Israel after Jacob all the way until the very end times. Now we know what happened.

1 And on the day that Isaac the father of Jacob and Esau died, the sons of Esau heard that Isaac had given the portion of the elder to his younger son Jacob and they were very angry. 2 And they strove with their father, saying: "Why hath thy father given Jacob the portion of the elder and passed over thee, although thou art the elder and Jacob the younger?" 3 And he said unto them "Because I sold my birthright to Jacob for a small mess of lentils; and on the day my father sent me to hunt and catch and bring him something that he should eat and bless me, he came with guile and brought my father food and drink, and my father blessed him and put me under his hand. 4 And now our

This represent-ation gives a favourable view of Esau's own attitude. In the later form of the legend (in the Yalkut) this is altered to Esau's dis-advantage. An example of Pharisees changing the Bible.

father hath caused us to swear, me and him, that we shall not mutually devise evil, either against his brother, and that we shall continue in love and in peace each with his brother and not make our ways corrupt." 5 And they said unto him, "We shall not hearken unto thee to make peace with him; for our strength is greater than his strength, and we are more powerful than he; we shall go against him and slay him, and destroy him and his sons. And if thou wilt not go with us, we shall do hurt to thee also. 6 And now hearken unto us: Let us send to Aram and Philistia and Moab and Ammon, and let us choose for ourselves chosen men who are ardent for battle, and let us go against him and do battle with him, and let us exterminate him from the earth before he groweth strong." 7 And their father said unto them, "Do not go and do not make war with him lest ye fall before him." 8 And they said unto him, "This too, is exactly thy mode of action from thy youth until this day, and thou art putting thy neck under his yoke. We shall not hearken to these words." 9 And they sent to Aram, and to 'Adurâm to the friend of their father, and they hired along with them one thousand fighting men, chosen men of war. 10 And there came to them from Moab and from the children of Ammon, those who were hired, one thousand chosen men, and from Philistia, one thousand chosen men of war, and from Edom and from the Horites one thousand chosen

Philistia with Nephilim among them were long-time enemies. Moab and Ammon, the sons of lot were also nto allies much of the time.

An Aramaean; cf. 38:3.

Cf. Gn. 6 "mighty men of old, men of renown" Nephilim. Giants lived among Horites, Kittim (Cf. 24:28) and Edom. The D.S.S. refer to the Kittim as the great enemy in the very end.

fighting men, and from the Kittim mighty men of war. **11** And they said unto their father: "Go forth with them and lead them, else we shall slay thee." **12** And he was filled with wrath and indignation on seeing that his sons were forcing him to go before (them) to lead them against Jacob his brother. **13** But afterward he remembered all the evil which lay hidden in his heart against Jacob his brother; and he remembered not the oath which he had sworn to his father and to his mother that he would devise no evil all his days against Jacob his brother. **14** And notwithstanding all this, Jacob knew not that they were coming against him to battle, and he was mourning for Leah, his wife, until they approached very near to the tower with four thousand warriors and chosen men of war. **15** And the men of Hebron sent to him saying, "Behold thy brother hath come against thee, to fight thee, with four thousand girt with the sword, and they carry shields and weapons"; for they loved Jacob more than Esau. So they told him; for Jacob was a more liberal and merciful man than Esau. **16** But Jacob would not believe until they came very near to the tower.

17 And he closed the gates of the tower; and he stood on the battlements and spake to his brother Esau and said, "Noble is the comfort wherewith thou hast come to comfort me for my wife who hath died. Is this the oath that thou didst swear to thy father and again to thy mother before they died? Thou hast broken the oath, and on the moment that thou didst swear to thy father wast thou condemned." **18** And then Esau answered and said unto him, "Neither the children of men nor the beasts of the earth have any oath of righteousness which in swearing they have sworn (an oath valid) for ever; but every day they devise evil one against another, and how each may slay his adversary and foe. **19** And thou dost hate me and my children for ever. And there is no observing the tie of brotherhood with thee. **20** Hear these words which I declare unto thee, If the boar can change its skin and make its bristles as soft as wool, Or if it can cause horns to sprout forth on its head like the horns of a stag or of a sheep, Then shall I observe the tie of brotherhood with thee. [And if the breasts separated themselves from their mother; for thou hast not

Charles thinks the bracketed words may be out of place or corrupt.

been a brother to me.] **21** And if the wolves make peace with the lambs so as not to devour or do them violence, And if their hearts are towards them for good, Then there will be peace in my heart towards thee. **22** And if the lion becometh the friend of the ox and maketh peace with him, And if he is bound under one yoke with him and plougheth with him, Then shall I make peace with thee. **23** And when the raven becometh white as the râzâ, Then know that - I have loved thee And shall make peace with thee. Thou shalt be rooted out, And thy sons shall be rooted out, And there shall be no peace for thee." **24** And when Jacob saw that he was (so) evilly disposed towards him with his heart, and with all his soul as to slay him, and that he had come springing like the wild boar which cometh upon the spear that pierceth and killeth it, and recoileth not from it; **25** Then he spake to his own and to his servants that they should attack him and all his companions.

"A large white bird which eats grasshoppers" (Isenberg, quoted by Charles).

CHAPTER 38:

The War Between Jacob And Esau At The Tower of Hebron. The Death Of Esau And Overthrow Of His Forces *(38:1-4)*

1 And after that Judah spake to Jacob, his father, and said unto him: "Bend thy bow, father, and send forth thy arrows and cast down the adversary and slay the enemy; and mayest thou have the power, for we shall not slay thy brother, for he is such as thou, and he is like thee: let us give him (this) honour." **2** Then Jacob bent his bow and sent forth the arrow and struck Esau, his brother, (on his right breast) and slew him. **3** And again he sent forth an arrow and struck 'Adôrân the Aramaean, on the left breast, and drove him backward and slew him. *Cf. 37:9* **4** And then went forth the sons of Jacob, they and their servants, dividing themselves into companies on the four sides of the tower. **5** And Judah went forth in front, and Naphtali and Gad with him and fifty servants with him on the south side of the tower, and they slew all they found before them, and not one individual of them

escaped. **6** And Levi and Dan and Asher went forth on the east side of the tower, and fifty (men) with them, and they slew the fighting men of Moab and Ammon. **7** And Reuben and Issachar and Zebulon went forth on the north side of the tower, and fifty men with them, and they slew the fighting men of the Philistines. **8** And Simeon and Benjamin and Enoch, Reuben's son, went forth on the west side of the tower, and fifty (men) with them, and they slew of Edom and of the Horites four hundred men, stout warriors; and six hundred fled, and four of the sons of Esau fled with them, and left their father lying slain, as he had fallen on the hill which is in 'Adûrâm. *A city in Idumaea (Edom) identical with the "Adora" mentioned in 1 Macc. 8:20* **9** And the sons of Jacob pursued after them to the mountains of Seir. And Jacob buried his brother on the hill which is in 'Adûrâm, and he returned to his house. **10** And the sons of Jacob pressed hard upon the sons of Esau in the mountains of Seir, and bowed their necks so that they became servants of the sons of Jacob. **11** And they sent to their father (to inquire) whether they should make peace with them or slay them. **12** And Jacob sent word to his sons that they should make peace, and they made peace with them, and placed the yoke of servitude upon them, so that they paid tribute to Jacob and to his sons always. **13** And they continued to pay tribute to Jacob until the day that he went down into Egypt.

For 11-13 cf. Test. Judah 9:7-8. 37:9

14 And the sons of Edom have not got quit of the yoke of servitude which the twelve sons of Jacob had imposed on them until this day.

In the fulfillment of the Ps. 83 war in 165 B.C., Edom joined forces to conquer the Temple.

The Kings Of Edom
(38:15-24; cf. Gen. 36:31-39)

15 And these are the kings that reigned in Edom before there reigned any king over the children of Israel [until this day] in the land of Edom. **16** And Bâlâq, the son of Beor, reigned in Edom, and the name of his city was Danâbâ. **17** And Bâlâq died, and Jobab, the son of Zârâ of Bôsêr, reigned in his stead.

LXX (Gn. 36:22) Βάλακ= Heb. Belă.

MT Dinhabah.

MT Bozrah.

18 And Jobab died, and 'Asâm, of the land of Têmân, reigned in his stead. **19** And 'Asâm died, and 'Adâth, the son of Barad, who slew Midian in the field of Moab, reigned in his stead, and the name of his city was Avith.

LXX Ἀσόμ, MT Husham.

MT Hadad. LXX Βαράθ, MT Bedad.

20 And 'Adâth died, and Salman, from 'Amâsêqâ, reigned in his stead.

LXX Σαλαμά, MT Samlah.

MT Masrekah.

21 And Salman died, and Saul of Râ'abôth (by the) river, reigned in his stead. **22** And Saul died, and Ba'êlûnân, the son of Achbor, reigned in his stead. **23** And Ba'êlûnân, the son of Achbor, died, and 'Adâth reigned in his stead, and the name of his wife was Maiṭabîth, the daughter of Mâṭarat, the daughter of Mêtabêdzâ'ab. **24** These are the kings who reigned in the land of Edom.

LXX Ῥωβώθ, MT Rehoboth.

LXX Βαλαεννάν, MT Baal-hanan.

MT Hadar.

MT Mehetabel.

MT Matred (LXX Ματαρείθ).

MT Me-zahab

CHAPTER 39:

Joseph's Service With Potiphar; His Purity And Imprisonment
(39:1-13; cf. Gen. 39)

1 And Jacob dwelt in the land of his father's sojournings in the land of Canaan. 2 These are the generations of Jacob. And Joseph was seventeen years old when they took him down into the land of Egypt, and Potiphar, an eunuch of Pharaoh, the chief cook bought him. 3 And he set Joseph over all his house, and the blessing of Yahuah came upon the house of the Egyptian on account of Joseph, and Yahuah prospered him in all that he did. 4 And the Egyptian committed everything into the hands of Joseph; for he saw that Yahuah was with him, and that Yahuah prospered him in all that he did. 5 And Joseph's appearance was comely and very beautiful was his appearance, and his master's wife lifted up her eyes and saw Joseph, and she loved him, and besought him to lie with her. 6 But he did not surrender his soul, and he remembered Yahuah and the words which Jacob, his father, used to read from amongst the words of Abraham, that no man should commit fornication with a woman who hath a husband; that for him the punishment of death hath been ordained in the heavens before the Most High Elohim, and the sin will be recorded against him in the eternal books continually before Yahuah. 7 And Joseph remembered these words and refused to lie with her. 8 And she besought him for a year, but he refused and would not listen. 9 But she embraced him and held him fast in the house in order to force him to lie with her, and closed the doors of the house and held him fast; but he left his garment in her hands and broke through the door and fled without from her presence. 10 And the woman saw that he would not lie with her, and she calumniated him in the presence of his lord, saying: "Thy Hebrew servant, whom thou lovest, sought to force me so that he might lie with me; and it came to pass when I lifted up my voice that he fled and left his garment in my hands when I held him, and he brake through the door." 11 And the Egyptian saw the garment of Joseph and the broken door, and heard the words of his wife, and cast Joseph into prison into the place where the

prisoners were kept whom the king imprisoned. **12** And he was there in the prison; and Yahuah gave Joseph favour in the sight of the chief of the prison guards and compassion before him, for he saw that Yahuah was with him, and that Yahuah made all that he did to prosper. **13** And he committed all things into his hands, and the chief of - the prison guards knew of nothing that was with him, for Joseph did everything, and Yahuah perfected it.

Cf. Gn. 39:8

Joseph Interprets the Dreams of the Chief Butler and the Chief Baker *(39:14-18; cf. Gen. 40)*

14 And he remained there two years. And in those days Pharaoh, king of Egypt, was wroth against his two eunuchs,

Cf. Gn. 41:1

against the chief butler and against the chief baker, and he put them in ward in the house of the chief cook, in the prison where Joseph was kept. **15** And the chief of the prison guards appointed Joseph to serve them; and he served before them.

Cf. 34:11 (note).

16 And they both dreamed a dream, the chief butler and the chief baker, and they told it to Joseph. **17** And as he interpreted to them so it befell them, and Pharaoh restored the chief butler to his office, and the (chief) baker he slew, as Joseph had interpreted to them. **18** But the chief butler forgot Joseph in the prison, although he had informed him what would befall him, and did not remember to inform Pharaoh how Joseph had told him for he forgot.

CHAPTER 40:

Pharaoh's Dreams And Their Interpretation. Joseph's Elevation And Marriage *(40:1-13; cf. Gen. 41)*

1 And in those days Pharaoh dreamed two dreams in one night concerning a famine which was to be in all the land, and he awoke from his sleep and called all the interpreters of dreams that were in Egypt, and magicians, and told them his two dreams, and they were not able to declare (them). **2** And then the chief butler remembered Joseph and spake of him to the king, and he brought him forth from the prison, and he told his two dreams before him. **3** And he said before Pharaoh that his two dreams were one, and he said unto him: "Seven years will come (in which there will be) plenty over all the land of Egypt, and after that seven years of famine, such a famine as hath not been in all the land. **4** And now let Pharaoh appoint overseers in all the land of Egypt, and let them store up food in every city throughout the days of the years of plenty, and there will be food for the seven years of famine, and the land will not perish through the famine, for it will be very severe." **5** And Yahuah gave Joseph favour and mercy in the eyes of Pharaoh, and Pharaoh said unto his servants: "We shall not find such a wise and discreet man as this man, for the spirit of Yahuah is with him." **6** And he appointed him the second in all his kingdom and gave him authority over all Egypt, and caused him to ride in the second chariot of Pharaoh. **7** And he clothed him with byssus garments, and he put a gold chain upon his neck, and (a herald) proclaimed before him "'Êl 'Êl wa' Abîrĕr," and he placed a ring on his hand and made him ruler over all his house, and magnified him, and said unto him: "Only on the throne shall I be greater than thou." **8** And Joseph ruled over all the land of Egypt, and all the princes of Pharaoh, and all his servants, and all who did the king's business loved him, for he walked in uprightness, for he was without pride and arrogance, and he had no respect of persons, and did not accept gifts, but he judged in uprightness all the people of the land. **9** And the land of Egypt was at peace before Pharaoh because of Joseph,

Cf. Gn. 41:34

'Êl 'Êl wa' Abîrĕr = Heb. 'el 'el wa'ăbîr 'el, "God, God, the mighty one of God." This is a peculiar amplification of the Hebrew 'abrēk (R.V. "bow the knee ") of Gn. 41:43. "Mighty one of God" may be a technical term for a great magician; cf. Acts 8:10.

Cf. 46:15-16 Satan will influence Pharaoh and the Egyptians later but there was no rise of evil opposition to Israel yet.

for Yahuah was with him, and gave him favour and mercy for all his generations before all those who knew him and those who heard concerning him, and Pharaoh's kingdom was well ordered, and there was no Satan and no evil person (therein). **10** And the king called Joseph's name Sĕphânṭîphâns, and gave Joseph to wife the daughter of Potiphar, the daughter of the priest of Heliopolis, the chief cook. **11** And on the day that Joseph stood before Pharaoh he was thirty years old [when he stood before Pharaoh].

= Zaphnath-Paaneah "treasury of the glorious rest" Cf. Gn. 41:45

Cf. 34:11 (note).

12 And in that year Isaac died. And it came to pass as Joseph had said in the interpretation of his two dreams, according as he had said it, there were seven years of plenty over all the land of Egypt, and the land of Egypt produced abundantly, one measure (producing) eighteen hundred measures. **13** And Joseph gathered food into every city until they were full of corn until they could no longer count and measure it for its multitude.

CHAPTER 41:

Judah's Incest With Tamar; His Repentance And Forgiveness
(41:1-28; Cf. Gen. 38)

2165 A.M.

Cf. Test. Judah 10 ("from Meso- potamia"). . 34:11 (note).

1 And in the forty-fifth jubilee, in the second week, (and) in the second year, Judah took for his first-born Er, a wife from the daughters of Aram, named Tamar. 2 But he hated, and did not lie with her, because his mother was of the daughters of Canaan, and he wished to take him a wife of the kinsfolk of his mother, but Judah, his father, would not permit him. 3 And this Er, the first-born of Judah, was wicked, and Yahuah slew him. 4 And Judah said unto Onan, his brother: "Go in unto thy brother's wife and perform

Cf. Gn. 38:8; Dt. 25:5

the duty of a husband's brother unto her, and raise up seed unto thy brother." 5 And Onan knew that the seed would not be his, (but) his brother's only, and he went into the house of his brother's wife, and spilt the seed on the ground, and he was wicked in the eyes of Yahuah, and He slew him. 6 And Judah said unto Tamar, his daughter-in-law: "Remain in thy father's house as a widow till Shelah my son be grown up, and I shall give thee to him to

wife." 7 And he grew up; but Bêdsû'êl, the wife of Judah, did not permit her son Shelah to marry. And Bêdsû'êl, the wife of Judah, died in the fifth year of this week. 8 And in the sixth year Judah went up to shear his sheep at Timnah. And they told Tamar: "Behold thy father-in-law goeth up to Timnah to shear his sheep." 9 And she put off her widow's clothes, and put on a veil, and adorned herself, and sat in the gate adjoining the way to Timnah. 10 And as Judah was going along he found her, and thought her to be an harlot, and he said unto her: "Let me come in unto thee"; and she said unto him: "Come in," and he went in. 11 And she said unto him: "Give me my hire"; and he said unto her: "I have nothing in my hand save my ring that is on my finger, and my necklace, and my staff which is in my hand." 12 And she said unto him: "Give them to me until thou dost send me my hire"; and he said unto her: "I will send unto thee a kid of the goats"; and he gave them to her, (and he went in unto her,) and she conceived by him. 13 And Judah went unto his sheep, and she went to her father's house. 14 And Judah sent a kid of the goats

i. e. Bathshua; Cf. 34:20

2168 A.M.

2169 A.M.

by the hand of his shepherd, an Adullamite, and he found her not; and he asked the people of the place, saying: "Where is the harlot who was here?" And they said unto him: "There is no harlot here with us." **15** And he returned and informed him, and said unto him that he had not found her; "I asked the people of the place, and they said unto me: 'There is no harlot here.'" And he said: "Let her keep (them) lest we become a cause of derision." **16** And when she had completed three months, it was manifest that she was with child, and they told Judah, saying: "Behold Tamar, thy daughter-in-law, is with child by whoredom."

The punishment appointed for such an offence on the part of a priest's daughter (Lev. 21:9). **17** And Judah went to the house of her father, and said unto her father and her brothers: "Bring her forth, and let them burn her, for she hath wrought uncleanness in Israel." **18** And it came to pass when they brought her forth to burn her that she sent to her father-in-law the ring and the necklace, and the staff, saying: "Discern whose are these, for by him am I with child."

19 And Judah acknowledged, and said: "Tamar is more righteous than I am. And

therefore let them burn her not." **20** And for that reason she was not given to Shelah, and he did not again approach her. **21** And after that she bare two sons, Perez and Zerah, in the seventh year of this second week. **22** And thereupon the seven years of fruitfulness were accomplished, of which Joseph spake to Pharaoh.

23 And Judah acknowledged that the deed which he had done was evil, for he had lain with his daughter-in-law, and he esteemed it hateful in his eyes, and he acknowledged that he had transgressed and gone astray; for he had uncovered the skirt of his son, and he began to lament and to supplicate before Yahuah because of his transgression. **24** And we told him in a dream that it was forgiven him because he supplicated earnestly, and lamented, and did not again commit it. **25** And he received forgiveness because he turned from his sin and from his ignorance, for he transgressed greatly before our Elohim; and every one that acteth thus, every one who lieth with his mother-in-law, let them burn him with fire that he may burn therein, for there is uncleanness and pollution upon them; with fire

2170 A.M.
Perez = Phares. Ancestor of Messiah thru Judah. This account is important as Messiah chose this bloodline from Shem not from Shua the Canaanite. Thamar was from Aram. Cf. Mt. 1:3; Lk. 3:33

Cf. Gn. 41:53

Cf. Lv. 20:14

let them burn them. **26** And do thou command the children of Israel that there be no uncleanness amongst them, for every one who lieth with his daughter-in-law or with his mother-in-law hath wrought uncleanness; with fire let them burn the man who hath lain with her, and likewise the woman, and He will turn away wrath and punishment from Israel.

Cf. Lv. 18:15, 20:12 (mode of death not specified; but Gn. 38:24 presupposes burning by fire).

27 And unto Judah we said that his two sons had not lain with her, and for this reason his seed was established for a second generation, and would not be rooted out. **28** For in singleness of eye he had gone and sought for punishment, namely, according to the judgment of Abraham, which he had commanded his sons, Judah had sought to burn her with fire.

Cf. 20:4 (note).

And it came to pass when they brought her forth to burn her that she sent to her father-in-law the ring and the necklace, and the staff, saying: "Discern whose are these, for by him am I with child."

41:18

CHAPTER 42:

The Two Journeys of the Sons of Jacob to Egypt
(42:1-25; cf. Gen. 42, 43)

2171 A.M. 1 And in the first year of the third week of the forty-fifth jubilee the famine began to come into the land, and the rain refused to be given to the earth, for none whatever fell. 2 And the earth grew barren, but in the land of Egypt there was food, for Joseph had gathered the seed of the land in the seven years of plenty *Cf. Gn. 41:54* and had preserved it. 3 And the Egyptians came to Joseph that he might give them food, and he opened the storehouses where was the grain of the first year, and he sold it to the *Cf. Gn. 41:56* people of the land for gold. 4 (Now the famine was very sore in the land of Canaan), and Jacob heard that there was food in Egypt, and he sent his ten sons that they should procure food for him in Egypt; but Benjamin he did not send, and (the ten sons of Jacob) arrived (in Egypt) among those that went (there.) 5 And Joseph recognized them, but they did not recognize him, and he spake unto them and questioned them, and he said unto them: "Are ye not spies, and have ye not come to explore the approaches of the land?" And he put them in ward. 6 And after that he set them free again, and detained Simeon alone and sent off his nine brothers. 7 And he filled their sacks with corn, and he put their gold in their sacks, and they did not know. 8 And he commanded them to bring their younger brother, for they had told him their father was living and their younger brother. 9 And they went up from the land of Egypt and they came to the land of Canaan; and they told their father all that had befallen them, and how the lord of the country had spoken roughly to them, and had seized Simeon till they should bring Benjamin. 10 And Jacob said: "Me have ye bereaved of my children! Joseph is not and Simeon also is not, and ye will take Benjamin away. On me hath your wickedness come." 11 And he said: "My son will not go down with you lest perchance he fall sick; for their mother gave birth to two sons, and one hath perished, and this one also ye will take from me. If perchance he took a fever on the road, ye would bring down my old age with sorrow unto death." 12 For

? An interpretation of Gn. 42:36 (" All these things are against me ").

"If mischief befall him by the way in the which ye go" (Gn. 42:38).

he saw that their money had been returned to every man in his sack, and for this reason he feared to send him. **13** And the famine increased and became sore in the land of Canaan, and in all lands save in the land of Egypt, for many of the children of the Egyptians had stored up their seed for food from the time when they saw Joseph gathering seed together and putting it in storehouses and preserving it for the years of famine.

14 And the people of Egypt fed themselves thereon during the first year of their famine. **15** But when Israel saw that the famine was very sore in the land, and there was no deliverance, he said unto his sons: "Go again, and procure food for us that we die not." **16** And they said: "We shall not go; unless our youngest brother go with us, we shall not go." **17** And Israel saw that if he did not send him with them, they should all perish by reason of the famine. **18** And Reuben said: "Give him into my hand, and if I do not bring him back to thee, slay my two sons instead of his soul." And he said unto him He will not go with thee." **19** And Judah came near and said: "Send him with me, and if I do not bring him back to thee, let me bear the blame before thee all the days of my life." **20** And he sent him with them in the second year of this week on the first day of the month, and they came to the land of Egypt with all those who went, and (they had) presents in their hands, stacte and almonds and terebinth nuts and pure honey.

2172 A.M.

21 And they went and stood before Joseph, and he saw Benjamin his brother, and he knew him, and said unto them: "Is this your youngest brother?" And they said unto him: "It is he." And he said: "Yahuah be gracious to thee, my son!"

22 And he sent him into his house and he brought forth Simeon unto them and he made a feast for them, and they presented to him the gift which they had brought in their hands. **23** And they ate before him and he gave them all a portion, but the portion of Benjamin was seven times larger than that of any of theirs. **24** And they ate and drank and arose and remained with their asses. **25** And Joseph devised a plan whereby he might learn their thoughts as to whether thoughts of peace prevailed amongst them, and he said to the steward who was over his house: "Fill all their sacks with food, and return their money unto them into their vessels, and my cup, the silver cup out of which I drink, put it in the sack of the youngest, and send them away." *Cf. Gn. 44:1, 2*

CHAPTER 43:

Joseph Finally Tests His Brethren, And Then Makes Himself Known To Them *(43:1-24; cf. Gen. 44, 45)*

1 And he did as Joseph had told him, and filled all their sacks for them with food and put their money in their sacks, and put the cup in Benjamin's sack. **2** And early in the morning they departed, and it came to pass that, when they had gone from thence, Joseph said unto the steward of his house: "Pursue them, run and seize them, saying, 'For good ye have requited me with evil; you have stolen from me the silver cup out of which my lord drinks.' And bring back to me their youngest brother, and fetch (him) quickly before I go forth to my seat of judgment." **3** And he ran after them and said unto them according to these words. **4** And they said unto him: "Elohim forbid that thy servants should do this thing, and steal from the house of thy lord any utensil, and the money also which we found in our sacks the first time, we thy servants brought back from the land of Canaan. **5** How then should we steal any utensil? Behold here are we and our sacks; search, and wherever thou findest the cup in the sack of any man amongst us, let him be slain, and we and our asses will serve thy lord." **6** And he said unto them: "Not so, the man with whom I find, him only shall I take as a servant, and ye will return in peace unto your house."

7 And as he was searching in their vessels, beginning with the eldest and ending with the youngest, it was found in Benjamin's sack. **8** And they rent their garments, and laded their asses, and returned to the city and came to the house of Joseph, and they all bowed themselves on their faces to the ground before him. **9** And Joseph said unto them: "Ye have done evil." And they said: "What shall we say and how shall we defend ourselves? Our lord hath discovered the transgression of his servants; behold we are the servants of our lord, and our asses also." **10** And Joseph said unto them: "I too fear Yahuah; as for you, go ye to your homes and let your brother be my servant, for ye have done evil. Know ye not that a man delighteth in his cup as I with this cup? And yet ye have stolen it from me." **11** And Judah said: "O my

Gn. 44:15 ("Know ye not that such a man as I can indeed divine?").

lord, let thy servant, I pray thee, speak a word in my lord's ear; two brothers did thy servant's mother bear to our father; one went away and was lost, and hath not been found, and he alone is left of his mother, and thy servant our father loveth him, and his life also is bound up with the life of this (lad). **12** And it will come to pass, when we go to thy servant our father, and the lad is not with us, that he will die, and we shall bring down our father with sorrow unto death. **13** Now rather let me, thy servant, abide instead of the boy as a bondsman unto my lord, and let the lad go with his brethren, for I became surety for him at the hand of thy servant our father, and if I do not bring him back, thy servant will bear the blame to our father for ever." **14** And Joseph saw that they were all accordant in goodness one with another, and he could not refrain himself, and he told them that he was Joseph. **15** And he conversed with them in the Hebrew tongue and fell on their neck and wept. But they knew him not and they began to weep. **16** And he said unto them: "Weep not over me, but hasten and bring my father

Of course Joseph spoke the language by which he was raised. Charles claims this means this is written like the Midrash yet is it not just an obvious fact. Joseph spoke Hebrew as did his family.

to me; and ye see that it is my mouth that speaketh and the eyes of my brother Benjamin see. **17** For behold this is the second year of the famine, and there are still five years without harvest or fruit of trees or ploughing. **18** Come down quickly ye and your households, so that ye perish not through the famine, and do not be grieved for your possessions, for Yahuah sent me before you to set things in order that many people might live. **19** And tell my father that I am still alive, and ye, behold, ye see that Yahuah hath made me as a father to Pharaoh, and ruler over his house and over all the land of Egypt. **20** And tell my father of all my glory, and all the riches and glory that Yahuah hath given Me." **21** And by the command of the mouth of Pharaoh he gave them chariots and provisions for the way, and he gave them all many-coloured raiment and silver. **22** And to their father he sent raiment and silver and ten asses which carried corn, and he sent them away.

23 And they went up and told their father that Joseph was alive, and was measuring out corn to all the nations of the earth, and that he was ruler

over all the land of Egypt.
24 And their father did not believe it, for he was beside himself in his mind; but when he saw the wagons which Joseph had sent, the life of his spirit revived, and he said: "It is enough for me if Joseph liveth; I will go down and see him before I die."

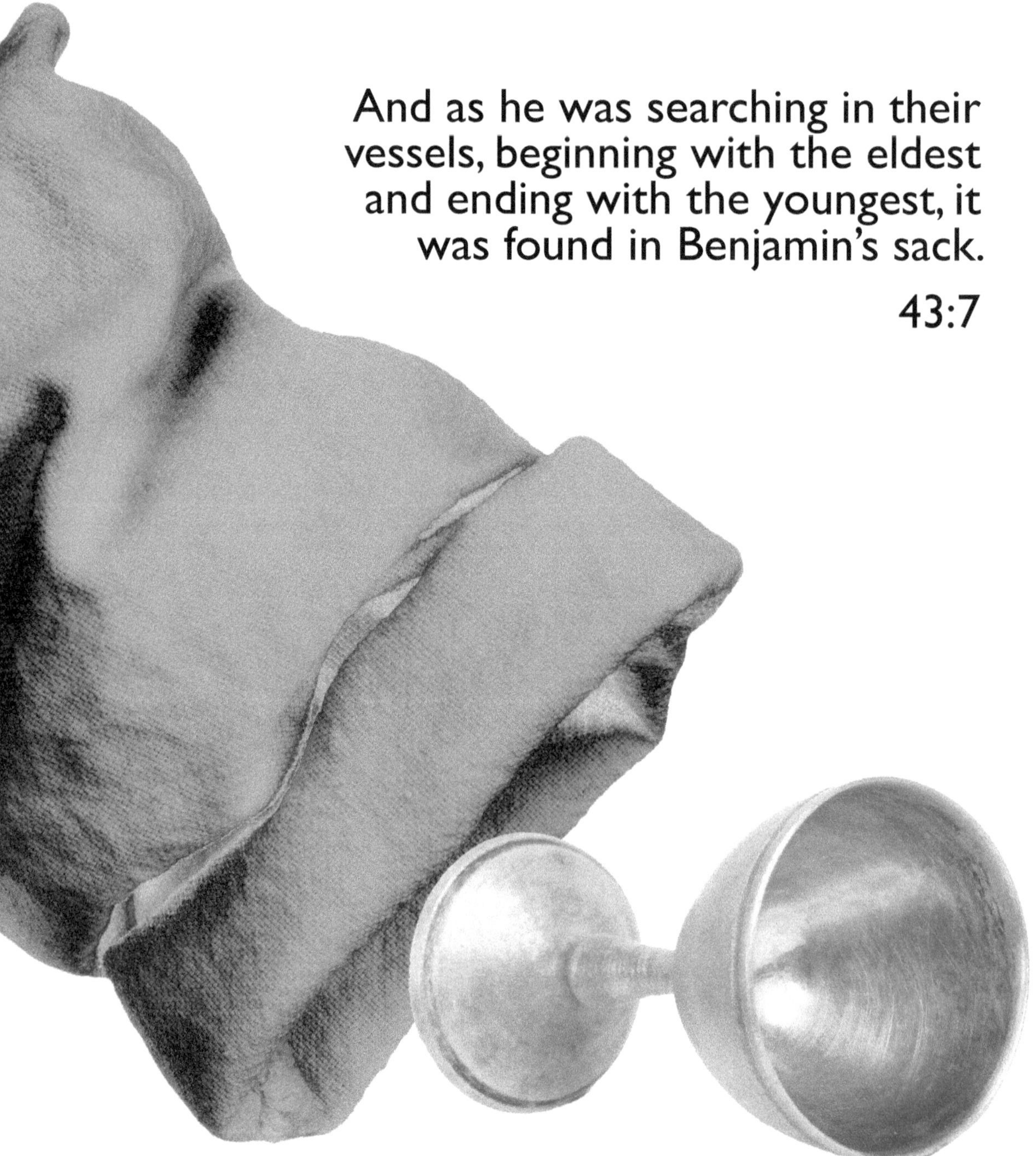

And as he was searching in their vessels, beginning with the eldest and ending with the youngest, it was found in Benjamin's sack.

43:7

CHAPTER 44:

Jacob, Celebrates The Feast Of First-fruits And Journeys To Egypt. List Of His Descendants.

(44:1-34; cf. Gen. 46:1-28)

Probably corrupt for "Hebron"; cf. Gn. 37:14

1 And Israel took his journey from †Haran† from his house on the new moon of the third month, and he went on the *Beersheba.* way of the Well of the Oath, and he offered a sacrifice to the Elohim of his father Isaac on the seventh of this month. **2** And Jacob remembered the dream that he had seen at *Cf. 27:22* Bethel, and he feared to go down into Egypt. **3** And while he was thinking of sending word to Joseph to come to him, and that he would not go down, he remained there seven days, if perchance he should see a vision as to whether he should remain or *Cf. Gn. 46:1 does not give a date for* go down. **4** And he celebrated *this Feast. It* the harvest festival of the first-*demonstrates* fruits with old grain, for in all *a reliance on* the land of Canaan there was *Jubilees for* not a handful of seed (in the *it's purpose* *of keeping* land), for the famine was over *dates, time,* all the beasts and cattle and *territories* *and details.* birds, and also over man. *Without it, the Rabbis* **5** And on the sixteenth *make up their own histories* Yahuah appeared unto him, *of a people* and said unto him, "Jacob, *that they do* *not even* Jacob"; and he said, "Here am *represent nor* I." And He said unto him: "I *know.* am the Elohim of thy fathers,

the Elohim of Abraham and Isaac; fear not to go down into Egypt, for I will there make of thee a great nation. **6** I shall go down with thee, and I shall *Cf. 27:24,* bring thee up (again), and in *32:23* this land wilt thou be buried, and Joseph will put his hands upon thy eyes. Fear not; go down into Egypt."

7 And his sons rose up, and his sons' sons, and they placed their father and their possessions upon wagons. **8** And Israel rose up from the Well of the Oath on the sixteenth of this third month, and he went to the land of Egypt. **9** And Israel sent *"To show the* Judah before him to his son *way" (Gn.* Joseph to examine the Land *46:28)* of Goshen, for Joseph had told his brothers that they should come and dwell there *The number* that they might be near him. *70, according* *to our text,* **10** And this was the goodliest *includes* (land) in the land of Egypt, *Jacob* *with his* and near to him, for all (of *descendants.* them) and also for the cattle. *Accounts* *differ even* **11** And these are the names *within the* of the sons of Jacob who went *canon and* *different* into Egypt with Jacob their *translations.* father. **12** Reuben, the first-*cf. Ex. 1:5* *and Gn.* born of Israel; and these are *46:15, 18, 21,* the names of his sons: Enoch, *25, 27. The* *number 75,* and Pallu, and Hezron and *in Acts 7:14.* *is due to the* Carmi -- five. *LXX of Ex.* *1:5 and Dt.* **13** Simeon and his sons; and *10:22.* these are the names of *The father is* *included in* *each case.*

217

his sons: Jemuel, and Jamin, and Ohad, and Jachin, and Zohar, and Shaul, the son of the Zephathite woman-- seven. **14** Levi and his sons; and these are the names of his sons: Gershon, and Kohath, and Merari -- four. **15** Judah and his sons; and these are the names of his sons: Shela, and Perez, and Zerah -- four. **16** Issachar and his sons; and these are the names of his sons: Tola, and Phûa, and Jâsûb, and Shimron -- five. **17** Zebulon and his sons; and these are the names of his sons: Sered, and Elon, and Jahleel -- four. **18** And these are the sons of Jacob, and their sons, whom Leah bore to Jacob in Mesopotamia, six, and their one sister, Dinah: and all the souls of the sons of Leah, and their sons, who went with Jacob their father into Egypt, were twenty-nine, and Jacob their father being with them, they were thirty.

19 And the sons of Zilpah, Leah's handmaid, the wife of Jacob, whom she bore unto Jacob, Gad and Asher. **20** And these are the names of their sons who went with him into Egypt: the sons of Gad: Ziphion, and Haggi, and Shuni, and Ezbon, (and Eri) and Areli, and Arodi -- eight.

21 And the sons of Asher: Imnah, and Ishvah, (and Ishvi), and Beriah, and Serah, their one sister -- six. **22** All the souls were fourteen, and all those of Leah were forty-four.

23 And the sons of Rachel, the wife of Jacob: Joseph and Benjamin. **24** And there were born to Joseph in Egypt before his father came into Egypt, those whom Asenath, daughter of Potiphar priest of Heliopolis bare unto him, Manasseh, and Ephraim -- three.

25 And the sons of Benjamin: Bela and Becher, and Ashbel, Gera, and Naaman, and Ehi, and Rosh, and Muppim, and Huppim, and Ard -- eleven. **26** And all the souls of Rachel were fourteen. **27** And the sons of Bilhah, the handmaid of Rachel, the wife of Jacob, whom she bare to Jacob, were Dan and Naphtali.

28 And these are the names of their sons who went with them into Egypt. And the sons of Dan were Hushim, and Sâmôn, and Asûdî, and 'Îjâka, and Salômôn -- six. **29** And they died the year in which they entered into Egypt, and there was left to Dan Hushim alone. 1 **30** And these are the names of the sons of Naphtali:

Cf. Gn. 46:24 and 1 Chr. 7:13: 'Iv is omitted in both texts.

Jahziel, and Guni, and Jezer, and Shallum, and 'Îv. **31** And 'Îv, who was born after the years of famine, died in Egypt. **32** And all the souls of Rachel were twenty-six. **33** And all the souls of Jacob which went into Egypt were seventy souls. These are his children and his children's children, in all seventy; but five died in Egypt before Joseph, and had no children. **34** And in the land of Canaan two sons of Judah died, Er and Onan, and they had no children, and the children of Israel buried those who perished, and they were reckoned among the seventy Gentile nations.

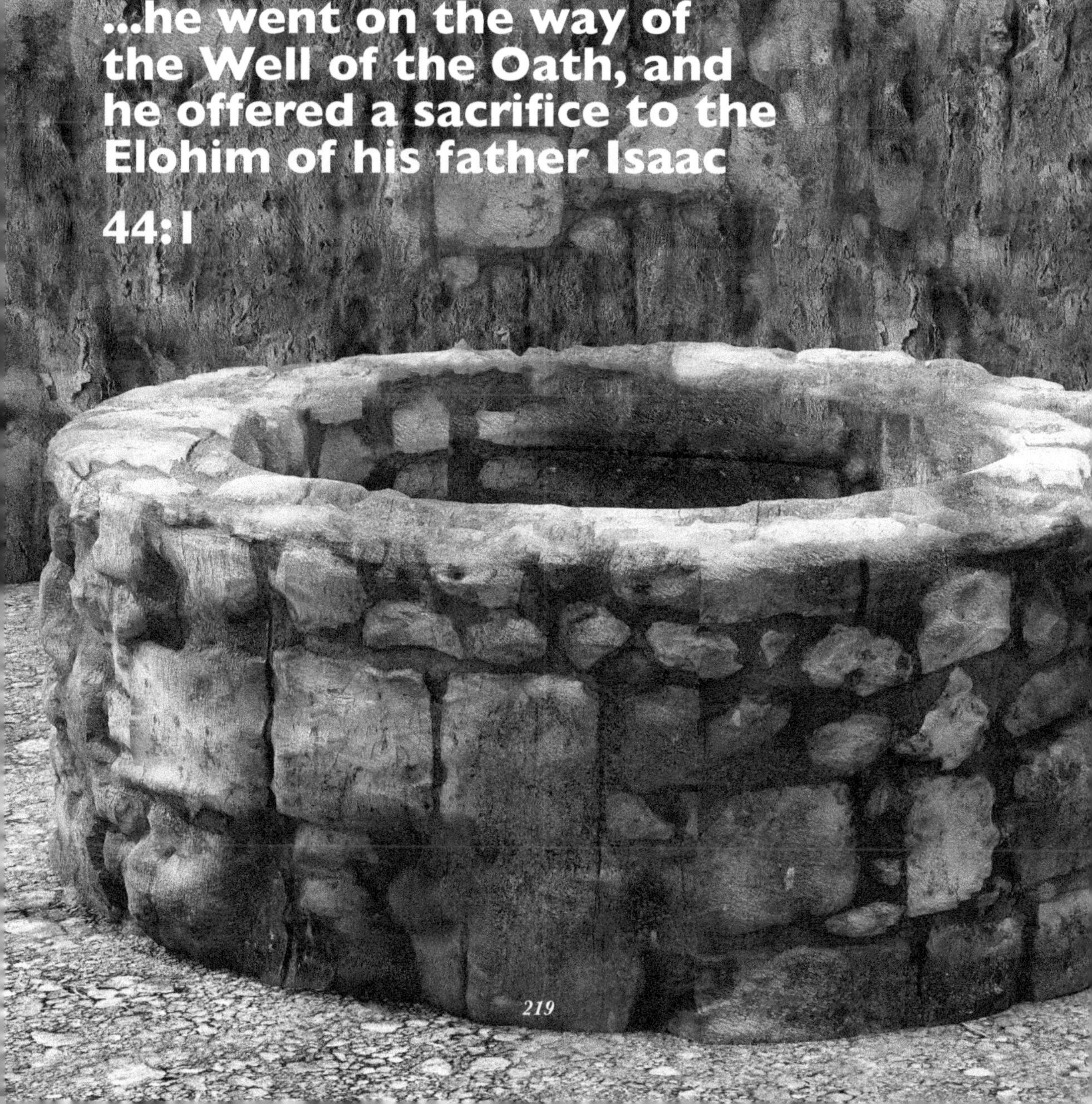

CHAPTER 45:

Joseph Receives Jacob. The Land Of Egypt Is Acquired For Pharaoh. Jacob's Death And Burial
(45:1-16; cf. Gen. 46:28 ff., 47:11 ff.)

2172 A.M. **1** And Israel went into the country of Egypt, into the land of Goshen, on the new moon of the fourth month, in the second year of the third week of the forty-fifth jubilee. **2** And Joseph went to meet his father Jacob, to the land of Goshen, and he fell on his father's neck and wept. **3** And Israel said unto Joseph: "Now let me die since I have seen thee, and now may the Yahuah Elohim of Israel be blessed, the Elohim of Abraham and the Elohim of Isaac who hath not withheld His mercy and His grace from His servant Jacob. **4** It is enough for me †MT (Gn. 46:30) "that thou art." that I have seen thy face whilst †I am† yet alive; yea, true is the vision which I saw at Bethel. Blessed be the Yahuah my Elohim for ever and ever, and blessed be His name."

5 And Joseph and his brothers ate bread before their father and drank wine, and Jacob rejoiced with exceeding great joy because he saw Joseph eating with his brothers and drinking before him, and he blessed the Creator of all things who had preserved him, and had preserved for him his twelve sons. **6** And Joseph had *Cf. Gn. 47:11* given to his father and to his brothers as a gift the right of dwelling in the land of Goshen and in Rameses and all the region round about, which he ruled over before Pharaoh. And Israel and his sons dwelt in the land of Goshen, the best part of the land of Egypt; and Israel was one hundred and thirty years old when he came into Egypt, **7** And Joseph nourished his father and his brethren and also *MT (Gn. 47:12) "according to their families."* their possessions with bread as much as sufficed them for the seven years of the famine. **8** And the land of Egypt suffered by reason of the famine, and Joseph acquired all the land of Egypt for Pharaoh in return for food, and he got possession of the people and their cattle and everything for Pharaoh. **9** And the years of the famine were accomplished, and Joseph gave to the people in the land seed and food that they might sow (the land) in the eighth year, for the river had overflowed all the land of Egypt. **10** For in the seven years of the famine it had not overflowed and had irrigated only a few places on the banks of the river, but now it overflowed and the Egyptians sowed the land, and it bore much corn that year. **11** And **2178 A.M.** this was the first year of the fourth week of the forty-fifth jubilee. **12** And Joseph took of the corn of the harvest the fifth part for the king and left four parts for them for food and for seed, and Joseph made it an ordinance for the land of Egypt until this day. **13** And Israel lived in the land of Egypt seventeen years, and all the days which he lived were three jubilees, one hundred and forty-seven years, and he **2188 A.M.** died in the fourth year of the fifth week of the forty-fifth jubilee.

14 And Israel blessed his sons before he died and told them *Cf. Gn. 49:1 ff* everything that would befall them in the land of Egypt; and he made known to them what would come upon them in the last days, and blessed them and gave to Joseph two portions in the land. **15** And *Cf. Gn. 47:22* he slept with his fathers, and he was buried in the double cave in the land of Canaan, near Abraham his father in the grave which he dug for himself in the double cave in the land of Hebron. **16** And *Cf. Gn. 50:13* he gave all his books and the books of his fathers to Levi his son that he might preserve them and renew them for his children until this day.

CHAPTER 46:

The Death Of Joseph. The Bones Of Jacob's Sons (Except Joseph) Interred At Hebron. The Oppression Of Israel By Egypt *(46:1-16; cf. Gen. 50; Ex. 1)*

1 And it came to pass that after Jacob died the children of Israel multiplied in the land of Egypt, and they became a great nation, and they were of one accord in heart, so that brother loved brother and every man helped his brother, and they increased abundantly and multiplied exceedingly, ten weeks of years, all the days of the life of Joseph.

2242 A.M.

Cf. Ex. 1

Cf. 23:29

2 And there was no Satan nor any evil all the days of the life of Joseph which he lived after his father Jacob, for all the Egyptians honoured the children of Israel all the days of the life of Joseph. **3** And Joseph died being a hundred and ten years old; seventeen years he lived in the land of Canaan, and ten years he was a servant, and three years in prison, and eighty years he was under the king, ruling all the land of Egypt. 4 And he died and all his brethren and all that generation. **5** And he commanded the children of Israel before he died that

Cf. Gn. 50:22, 26; Ex. 1:6

they should carry his bones with them when they went forth from the land of Egypt. **6** And he made them swear regarding his bones, for he knew that the Egyptians would not again bring forth and bury him in the land of Canaan, for Mâkamârôn, king of Canaan, while dwelling in the land of Assyria, fought in the valley with the king of Egypt and slew him there, and pursued after the Egyptians to the gates of 'Êrmôn. **7** But he was not able to enter, for another, a new king, had become king of Egypt, 5 and he was stronger than he, and he returned to the land of Canaan, and the gates of Egypt were closed, and none went out and none came into Egypt. **8** And Joseph died in the forty-sixth jubilee, in the sixth week, in the second year, and they buried him in the land of Egypt, and his brethren died after him. **9** And the king of Egypt went forth to war with the king of Canaan in the forty-seventh jubilee, in the second week in the second year, and the children of Israel brought forth all the bones of the children of Jacob save the bones of Joseph, and they buried them in the field in the double cave in the mountain. **10** And the most (of them)

Cf. Gn. 50:25

Cf. Test. Simeon 8:3 f. ("For the bones of Joseph the Egyptians guarded in the tombs of the kings. For the sorcerers told them that on the departure of the bones of Joseph there should be throughout all the land darkness and gloom," etc.).

i. e. Heroônpolis (close to the desert).

? Rameses III (1202-1171), founder of the 20th dynasty, who repulsed an invasion of peoples from the north and twice marched through Canaan, defeated the invaders. Cf. Test. Simeon 8:2.

2242 A.M.

Cont'd. A war between Cush and Egypt, in which Moses led the Egyptians, is referred to by Josephus (Ant. 2:10).

2263 A.M.

Jos. 24:32. 400 years later, Joseph's remains would be inhumed at the Exodus, taken with Israel and buried in the promised land.

This interesting statement apparently implies that some of the Hebrew tribes were already in Canaan before the Exodus. Or is it a reminiscence of the fact that the tribe of Judah absorbed some South Canaanitish tribes which were never in Egypt? Cf. Burney in Journal of Theological Studies, 1908, pp. 321-352.

returned to Egypt, but a few of them remained in the mountains of Hebron, and Amram thy father remained with them. **11** And the king of Canaan was victorious over the king of Egypt, and he closed the gates of Egypt. **12** And he devised an evil device against the children of Israel of afflicting them; and he said unto the people of Egypt: **13** "Behold the people of the children of Israel have increased and multiplied more than we. Come and let us deal wisely with them before they become too many, and let us afflict them with slavery before war come upon us and before they too fight against us; else they will join themselves unto our enemies and get them up out of our land, for their hearts and faces are towards the land of Canaan."

14 And he set over them taskmasters to afflict them So LXX (Ex. 1:2); MT =? "store cities." with slavery; and they built strong cities for Pharaoh, Pithom and Raamses, and they built all the walls and all the fortifications which had fallen in the cities of Egypt. **15** And they made them serve with rigour, and the more they dealt evilly with them, the more they increased and multiplied. **16** And the people

of Egypt abominated the children of Israel.

CHAPTER 47:

The Birth and Early Years of Moses
(47:1-12; cf. Exod. 2)

1 And in the seventh week, in the seventh year, in the forty-seventh jubilee, thy father went forth from the land of Canaan, and thou wast born in the fourth week, in the sixth year thereof, in the forty-eighth jubilee; this was the time of tribulation on the children of Israel.

2303 A.M.

i. e. Moses' father, Amram.

2330 A.M.

2 And Pharaoh, king of Egypt, issued a command regarding them that they should cast all their male children which were born into the river. **3** And they cast them in for seven months until the day that thou wast born. And thy mother hid thee for three months, and they told regarding her.

4 And she made an ark for thee, and covered it with pitch and asphalt, and placed it in the flags on the bank of the river, and she placed thee in it seven days, and thy mother came by night and suckled thee, and by day Miriam, thy sister, guarded thee from the birds. **5** And in those days Tharmuth, the daughter of

Thermuthis (Josephus, Ant. 2:9, 5, 7).

Pharaoh, came to bathe in the river, and she heard thy voice crying, and she told her maidens to bring thee forth, and they brought thee unto her. **6** And she took thee out of the ark, and she had compassion on thee.

7 And thy sister said unto her: "Shall I go and call unto thee one of the Hebrew women to nurse and suckle this babe for thee?" And she said (unto her): "Go." **8** And she went and called thy mother Jochebed, and she gave her wages, and she nursed thee. **9** And afterwards, when thou wast grown up, they brought thee unto the daughter of Pharaoh, and thou didst become her son, and Amram thy father taught thee writing, and after thou hadst completed three weeks they brought thee into the royal court.

Cf. Ex. 6:20; Nm. 26:59.

Contrast Acts 7:22. Moses was taught by Egyptians but Moses' father also taught him Hebrew.

10 And thou wast three weeks *2351-2372 A.M.* of years at court until the time when thou didst go forth from the royal court and didst see an Egyptian smiting thy friend who was of the children of Israel, and thou didst slay him and hide him in the sand.

11 And on the second day thou didst find two of the children of Israel striving together, and thou didst say to him who was doing the wrong: "Why dost thou smite thy brother? **12** And he was angry and indignant, and said "Who made thee a prince and a judge over us? Thinkest thou to kill me as thou killedst the Egyptian yesterday?" And thou didst fear and flee on account of these words.

CHAPTER 48:

From The Flight Of Moses To The Exodus

(48:1-19; cf. Ex. 2:15 ff., 4:19-24, 7-14)

2372 A.M. **1** And in the sixth year of the third week of the forty-ninth jubilee thou didst depart and *Cf. Ex. 2:15* dwell in the land of Midian five weeks and one year. And *Cf. Ex. 4:19* thou didst return into Egypt in *2410 A.M.* the second week in the second year in the fiftieth jubilee.

Cf. Acts 7:30 "And when forty years were expired, there appeared to him in the wilderness of mount Sina(i) an angel of the Lord in a flame of fire in a bush." **Luke quotes Jubilees.** *This timeline does not appear in the Bible otherwise.* **2** And thou thyself knowest what He spake unto thee on Mount Sinai, and what prince Mastêmâ desired to do with thee when thou wast returning into Egypt on the way when thou didst meet him at the lodging-place. **3** Did he not *Cf. 17:16 Cf. Ex. 4:24 Exodus ascribes the action to Yahuah and no doubt Satan was allowed to do so by Yahuah. The same tendency can be illustrated from 1 Chr. 21:1 compared with 2 Sa. 24:1.* with all his power seek to slay thee and deliver the Egyptians out of thy hand when he saw that thou wast sent to execute judgment and vengeance on the Egyptians? **4** And I delivered thee out of his hand, and thou didst perform the signs and wonders which thou wast sent to perform in Egypt against Pharaoh, and against all his house, and against his servants and his people. **5** And Yahuah executed a great vengeance on them for Israel's sake, and smote them through (the plagues of) blood and frogs, lice and dog-flies, and malignant boils breaking forth in blains; and their cattle by death; and by hailstones, thereby He destroyed everything that grew for them; and by locusts which devoured the residue which had been left by the hail, and by darkness; and (by the death) of the firstborn of men and animals, and on all their idols Yahuah took *An enumeration of the ten plagues.* vengeance and burned them with fire. **6** And everything was sent through thy hand, that thou shouldst declare (these things) before they were done, and thou didst speak with the king of Egypt before all his servants and before his people. **7** And everything took place according to thy words; ten great and terrible judgments came on the land of Egypt that thou mightest execute vengeance on it for Israel. **8** And Yahuah did everything for Israel's sake, and according to His covenant, which He had ordained with Abraham that He would take vengeance on them as they had brought *Cf. Gn. 15:13, 14* them by force into bondage. **9** And the prince of the Mastêmâ stood up against thee, and sought to cast thee into the hands of Pharaoh, and he helped the Egyptian sorcerers, and they stood up and wrought before thee. **10** The evils indeed we permitted them to work, but the remedies we did not allow to be wrought by their hands. **11** And Yahuah smote them with malignant ulcers, and *Cf. Ex. 9:11* they were not able to stand for we destroyed them so that they could not perform a single sign. **12** And notwithstanding all (these) signs and wonders the prince of the Mastêmâ was not put to shame because he took courage and cried to the Egyptians to pursue after thee with all the powers of the Egyptians, with their chariots, and with their horses, and with all the hosts of the *Cf. Ex. 14:8, 9* peoples of Egypt. **13** And I stood between the Egyptians and Israel, and we delivered Israel out of his hand, and out of the hand of his people, and Yahuah brought them through the midst of the sea as if it were dry land. **14** And all the peoples whom he brought to pursue after Israel, Yahuah our Elohim cast them into the midst of the sea, into the depths of the abyss beneath the children of Israel, even as the people of Egypt had cast their children into the river. He took vengeance on 1,000,000 of them, and one thousand strong and energetic men were destroyed on account of one suckling of the children of thy people which they had thrown into the river. **15** And on the fourteenth day and on the fifteenth and on the sixteenth and on the seventeenth and on the eighteenth the prince of the Mastêmâ was bound and imprisoned behind the children of Israel that he might not accuse them. **16** And on the nineteenth we let them loose that they might help the Egyptians and pursue the children of Israel. **17** And he hardened their hearts and made them stubborn, and the device was devised by Yahuah our Elohim that He might smite the Egyptians and cast them into the sea. **18** And on the fourteenth we bound him that he might not accuse the children of Israel on the day when they asked the Egyptians for vessels and garments, vessels of silver, and vessels of gold, and vessels of bronze, in order to despoil the Egyptians in return for the bondage in which they had forced them to serve. **19** And we did not lead forth the children of Israel from Egypt empty handed.

Cf. Wisdom 18:5

i. e. the prince of the Mastêmâ (substituted for Yahuah in Ex. 14:8). He was the allowed by Yahuah to oppose Israel in such manner. It was His plan.

Cf. Ex. 12:35 f

Yahuah brought them through the midst of the sea as if it were dry land

48:13

CHAPTER 49:

Regulations Regarding The Passover
(49:1-23; cf. Ex. 12)

1 Remember the commandment which Yahuah commanded thee concerning the passover, that thou shouldst celebrate it in its season on the fourteenth of the first month, that thou shouldst kill it before it is evening, and that they should eat it by night on the evening of the fifteenth from the time of the setting of the sun. **2** For on this night -- the beginning of the festival and the beginning of the joy -- ye were eating the passover in Egypt, when all the powers of Mastêmâ had been let loose to slay all the first-born in the land of Egypt, from the firstborn of Pharaoh to the first-born of the captive maidservant in the mill, and to the cattle. **3** And this is the sign which Yahuah gave them: Into every house on the lintels of which they saw the blood of a lamb of the first year, into (that) house they should not enter to slay, but should pass by (it), that all those should be saved that were in the house because the sign of the blood was on its lintels.

4 And the powers of Yahuah did everything according as Yahuah commanded them, and they passed by all the children of Israel, and the plague came not upon them to destroy from amongst them any soul either of cattle, or man, or dog. **5** And the plague was very grievous in Egypt, and there was no house in Egypt where there was not one dead, and weeping and lamentation. **6** And all Israel was eating the flesh of the paschal lamb, and drinking the wine, and was lauding and blessing, and giving thanks to the Yahuah Elohim of their fathers, and was ready to go forth from under the yoke of Egypt; and from the evil bondage. **7** And remember thou this day all the days of thy life, and observe it from year to year all the days of thy life, once a year, on its day, according to all the law thereof, and do not adjourn (it) from day to day, or from month to month. **8** For it is an eternal ordinance, and engraven on the heavenly tables regarding all the children of Israel that they should observe it every year on its day once a year, throughout all their generations; and there is no limit of days, for this is ordained for ever.

9 And the man who is free

Cf. Ex. 12:6

Cf. Heb. 11:28 (NLT) the "angel of death" killed the firstborn not Yahuah but He allowed it. Cf. Ex. 12:23 "The destroyer" strikes the first-born. Yahuah is not the destroyer. (NLT) calls it the "death angel." Cf. Ex. 12:27 says Yahuah struck the households and delivered at the same time but that is not consistent. Jubilees is. In Ex. 12:29 it is Yahuah Himself who smites all the first-born but again the agent used was the angel of death who is Satan. Man's mis-application of Exodus does not make Jubilees wrong. Here Exodus is the same really.

The use of wine at the Passover feast is attested here for the first time and remains in the custom.

For 7-8 cf. 6:20, 22

from uncleanness, and doth not come to observe it on occasion of its day, so as to bring an acceptable offering before Yahuah, and to eat and to drink before Yahuah on the day of its festival, that man who is clean and close at hand will be cut off; because he offered not the oblation of Yahuah in its appointed season, he will take the guilt upon himself. **10** Let the children of Israel come and observe the passover on the day of its fixed time, on the fourteenth day of the first month, between the evenings, from the third part of the day to the third part of the night, for two portions of the day are given to the light, and a third part to the evening.

Cf. Nm. 9:13

Jubilees expresses day has 2 parts and evening has 1. Notice the progression of a day and the counting. The 2 portions of day are first and second and the night is third because the Biblical day begins at sunrise, then afternoon and then evening. In the Creation account it was day that was created and listed first then the night. The sun was created first and then the moon. Pharisees are rebuked in this book for following the moon.

11 That is that which Yahuah commanded thee that thou shouldst observe it between the evenings. **12** And it is not permissible to slay it during any period of the light, but during the period bordering on the evening, and let them eat it at the time of the evening until the third part of the night, and whatever is leftover of all its flesh from the third part of the night and onwards, let them burn it with fire.

"Between the two evenings" is explained here. The lamb was to be roasted at sundown and eaten before sunrise when the sacrifice remains must be burnt. One cannot eat the next day what has already disappeared.

13 And they shall not cook it with water, nor shall they eat it raw, but roast on the fire: they shall eat it with diligence, its head with the inwards thereof and its feet they shall roast with fire, and not break any bone thereof; for †of the children of Israel no bone shall be crushed†. **14** For this reason Yahuah commanded the children of Israel to observe the passover on the day of its fixed time, and they shall not break a bone thereof; for it is a festival day, and a day commanded, and there may be no passing over from day to day, and month to month, but on the day of its festival let it be observed. **15** And do thou command the children of Israel to observe the passover throughout their days, every year, once a year on the day of its fixed time, and it will come for a memorial well pleasing before Yahuah, and no plague will come upon them to slay or to smite in that year in which they celebrate the passover in its season in every respect according to His command. **16** And they shall not eat it outside the sanctuary of Yahuah, but before the sanctuary of Yahuah, and all the people of the congregation of Israel shall celebrate it in its appointed season.

Cf. LXX (σπου-δαίως): Heb. (Ex. 12:2), "in haste."

Cf. Ex. 12:9

Cf. Ex. 12:46

Cf. Ex. 12:46; Nm. 9:12; Ps. 34:20. John says Messiah's crucifixion fulfilled this same command as the Passover Lamb as no bone of His was broken. Cf. Jn. 19:36

Cf. Ex. 12:13

Cf. 20

i. e. the age when maturity is first attained; cf. Ex. 30:14; Nm. 1:32.

17 And every man who hath come upon its day shall eat it in the sanctuary of your Elohim before Yahuah from twenty years old and upward; for thus is it written and ordained that they should eat it in the sanctuary of Yahuah. **18** And when the children of Israel come into the land which they are to possess, into the land of Canaan, and set up the tabernacle of Yahuah in the midst of the land in one of their tribes until the sanctuary of Yahuah hath been built in the land, let them come and celebrate the passover in the midst of the tabernacle of Yahuah, and let them slay it before Yahuah from year to year. **19** And in the days when the house hath been built in the name of Yahuah in the land of their inheritance, they shall go there and slay the passover in the evening, at sunset, at the third part of the day.

20 And they will offer its blood on the threshold of the altar, and shall place its fat on the fire which is upon the altar, and they shall eat its flesh roasted with fire in the court of the house which hath been sanctified in the name of Yahuah.

Cf. Dt. 16:7

In later times the Passover lamb was slaughtered in the Temple, but eaten at home, i. e. in a house in Jerusalem. The vast numbers of pilgrims present necessitated this extension (cf. Josephus, War, vi. 9,3. ii. 14, 3).

21 And they may not celebrate the passover in their cities, nor in any place save before the tabernacle of Yahuah, or before His house where His name hath dwelt; and they will not go astray from Yahuah. **22** And do thou, Moses, command the children of Israel to observe the ordinances of the passover, as it was commanded unto thee; declare thou unto them every year †and the day of its days, and† the festival of unleavened bread, that they should eat unleavened bread seven days, (and) that they should observe its festival, and that they bring an oblation every day during those seven days of joy before Yahuah on the altar of your Elohim. **23** For ye celebrated this festival with haste when ye went forth from Egypt till ye entered into the wilderness of Shur; for on the shore of the sea ye completed it.

† "during its days and during." (Charles)

Cf. 49:13
Cf. Ex. 12:11

Cf. Ex. 15:22

...Ye were eating the passover in Egypt, when all the powers of Mastêmâ had been let loose to slay all the first-born in the land of Egypt

49:2

CHAPTER 50:

Laws Regarding The Jubilees And The Sabbath *(50:1-13)*

1 And after this law I made known to thee the days of the Sabbaths in the desert of *Cf. Ex. 16:1* Sin[ai], which is between Elim and Sinai. **2** And I told thee of the Sabbaths of the land on Mount Sinai, and I told *Cf. Lv. 25:8* thee of the jubilee years in the sabbaths of years: but the year thereof have I not told thee till ye enter the land which ye are to possess. **3** And the land also will keep its sabbaths while *Cf. Lv. 26:34* they dwell upon it, and they will know the jubilee year. *i.e. seven years.* **4** Wherefore I have ordained for thee the year-weeks and the years and the jubilees: there are forty-nine jubilees from the days of Adam until *2410 A.M.* this day, and one week and two years and there are yet forty *2450 A.M.* years to come (lit. "distant for learning the commandments of Yahuah, until they pass over into the land of Canaan, crossing the Jordan to the west. **5** And the jubilees will pass by, until Israel is cleansed from all guilt of fornication, and uncleanness, and pollution, and sin, and error, and dwelleth with confidence in all the land, and there will be no more a Satan or any evil one, and the land will be clean from *Cf. 1:29 (note), 23:26-29 (note)* that time for evermore. **6** And behold the commandment regarding the Sabbaths -- I have written (them) down for thee and all the judgments of its laws. **7** Six days wilt thou labour, but on the seventh day *Cf. Ex. 20:9, 10* is the Sabbath of Yahuah your Elohim. In it ye shall do no manner of work, ye and your sons, and your men-servants and your maid-servants, and all your cattle and the sojourner also who is with you. **8** And the man that doeth any *Cf. Ex. 35:2* work on it shall die: whoever desecrateth that day, whoever *Cf. Is. 58:13 Turn away "from doing thy pleasure on my holy day." We are not to find "our own pleasure" on Sabbath.* lieth with (his) wife or whoever saith he will do something on it, that he will set out on a journey thereon in regard to any buying or selling: and *Cf. Ex. 16:29* whoever draweth water *Cf. Nh. 10:31, 13:16-17* thereon which he had not prepared for himself on the sixth day, and whoever taketh up any burden to carry it out *Cf. 2:30 (note).* of his tent or out of his house shall die. **9** Ye shall do no work whatever on the Sabbath day save that ye have prepared for yourselves on the sixth day, so as to eat, and drink, and rest, and keep Sabbath from all work on that day, and to bless Yahuah your Elohim, who has given you a day of festival, and a holy day: and a day of the holy kingdom for all Israel is this day among their days for ever. **10** For great is the honour which Yahuah hath given to Israel that they should eat and drink and be satisfied on this festival day, and rest thereon from all labour which belongeth to the labour of the children of men, save burning frankincense and bringing oblations and sacrifices before Yahuah for days and for Sabbaths. **11** This work alone shall be done on the Sabbath-days in the sanctuary of Yahuah your Elohim; that they may atone for Israel with sacrifice continually from day to day for a memorial well-pleasing before Yahuah, and that He may receive them always from day to day according as thou hast been commanded. **12** And every man who doeth any work

thereon, or goeth a journey, or tilleth (his) farm, whether in his house or any other place, and whoever lighteth a fire, or rideth on any beast, or travelleth by ship on the sea, and whoever striketh or killeth anything, or slaughtereth a beast or a bird, or whoever catcheth an animal or a bird or a fish, or whoever fasteth or maketh war on the Sabbaths: **13** The man who doeth any of these things on the Sabbath shall die, so that the children of Israel shall observe the Sabbaths according to the commandments regarding the Sabbaths of the land, as it is written in the tables, which He gave into my hands that I should write out for thee the laws of the seasons, and the seasons according to the division of their days.

Herewith is completed the account of the division of the days.

Cf. 2:29 (note).

Cf. 2:29 (note). Cf. Ex. 35:3, Nm. 15:32, 33

Cf. Ex. 16:29

Cf. Ex. 34:21

Cf. Ex. 16:29

Cf. 50:9 Israel is to "eat and drink" on the Sabbath. Elijah, Messiah and others fast for more than 7 days but that is a different Hebrew word.

...there are forty-nine jubilees
from the days of Adam until
this day, and one week and two
years and there are yet forty
years to come for learning the
commandments of Yahuah

50:4

Here is the patience of the saints: here are they that keep the commandments of God (Yahuah), and the faith of Jesus (Yahusha).

Revelation 14:12 KJV

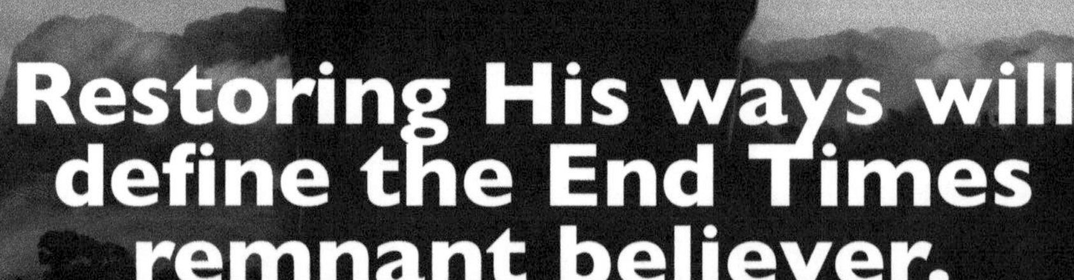

UNDERSTANDING THE BOOK OF JUBILEES

THE TORAH CALENDAR

By Timothy Schwab
Research By The God Culture Team

Not Just Useful. This is Torah.

INSIGHTS INTO DEEPER RESEARCH

HOLY BIBLE
ANSWERS
Q A
IN JUBILEES
The Key to
Understanding
Torah

SOME BIBLE QUESTIONS ANSWERED BY JUBILEES:

When Were Angels Created?

First Day of Creation. Jub. 2:2.

Did Yahuah Create Evil and Sin?

No. Evil is the antithesis of good. To do evil is to choose not to do good. Sin is lawlessness or choosing not to abide by His law. Yahuah did not create these things, they are the choice to rebel against Him and His ways. Angels were created good. Fallen Angels chose to break the law of Creation. Even the darkness at Creation is called good as Yahuah saw it was. The spirits of their offspring have no place to go after physical death thus they roam the dry places. They are the origin of demons which are not a Creation of Yahuah but the consequence of sin. This is why they are pure evil. The entire infrastructure of evil did not exist before Creation.

Was Cain the Seed of the Serpent?

Not possible. Cain was not born until 7 years after the Garden of Eden. Genesis also obliterates that doctrine of men when it says after the Garden, Adam knew his wife and she conceived. When Eve births Cain, she thanks Yahuah not Satan. He was not the serpent's seed nor could be. That doctrine is illiterate and unbiblical. Jub. 4:1.

Who Did Cain Marry?

His sister, Awan, who was the first daughter 14 years younger than he. No, incest was not forbidden in the era of the first people nor would it need to be. DNA would be far more pure in those days with no risk of complications. Jub. 4:9.

Was Cain a Twin?

No. Cain was born 7 years, Abel birthed 14 years and Awan 21 years after the Garden exile. No evil twins among them. Jub. 4:1-2.

Who Was Noah's Oldest Son?

Shem. Jub. 10:14.

Who was Noah's Wife?

'Ĕmzârâ, the daughter of Râkê'êl, the daughter of his father's brother. Jub. 4:33.

How did Cain die?

His house fell on him which was appropriate and the origin of the Torah doctrine of an eye for an eye or equal justice fitting the crime. Cain killed with a stone and was killed by the same. An eye for an eye cannot be about revenge because the Law of Moses forbids such. It was merely equal punishment for a crime. You murder, you are to be murdered in the same fashion. This was not new in Moses' day. Jub. 4:31.

If Jacob and Esau Reconciled, Why Were Their Sons at War Since?

After Jacob's death, Esau's sons agitated him into going to war with Jacob. This finally explains a gaping hole in theology as to how the two brothers reconciled and left it at that yet the two families are at war shortly after until the very end times. Genesis does not tell us why because Moses wrote of it here in Jubilees. Jub. 37-38

How did Esau die?

After declaring war on his brother Jacob, Jacob killed Esau with a bow and arrow. Gen. offers no detail on this so this is not a discrepancy. Jub. 38:2.

Did Esau Have Red Hair?

Esau was known as Edom or red because of the red pottage or lentil soup in which he sold his birthright to Jacob carelessly. He was born with red skin or countenance just as David was ruddy or red. In Genesis, Esau is born admoniy used 3 times in scripture.

> *Hebrew: ʿadmoniy: אדמני: Strong's #H132.*
> *red, ruddy (of Esau as infant). ruddy (2x), red (1x)*
> *Esau "came out red" (Gn. 25:25), David "was ruddy, and withal of a beautiful countenance" (1 Sa. 16:12), and "ruddy and of a fair countenance" (1 Sa. 17:42)*

The other 2 times the word is used it means ruddy which is also red but both times it is specific to countenance or skin tone. David was not black nor white but medium brown or red. So was Esau. Esau also had hair all over but it was not red as this word is specific to skin tone. It is a derivative of Adam and originates in the word (Hebrew: 'adam: אדם: Strong's #H120) which also refers to red skin tone and not hair as Adam was formed from the red soil of the ground [adamah: אדמה: H127: soil (from its general redness)]. Hebrews are red-skinned and darker. None are recorded as white in scripture. Many confuse passages which use white for purity as skin tone erroneously and some have inserted black in the same fashion especially regarding the Revelation mention of an anointed Messiah returning glowing in countenance as the sun and as bronze as it exits the furnace. Neither of those are black but glowing very bright. Revelation does not mention Messiah's skin tone.

However, only erroneous assumption attributes Esau's name of Edom to his skin tone or worse his hair which was not red. If they would not have banned Jubilees, they would have known this and would not appear foolish. In Jubilees, Esau was known as Edom or "red" because of the red pottage or soup in which he sold his birthright haphazardly. That is why he is called "red" or Edom not his skin at birth and he certainly did not have red hair.

Jubilees 24:6

"...and Esau despised his birthright; for this reason was **Esau's name called Edom, on account of the red pottage which Jacob gave him for his birthright."**

Is the Garden of Eden in Africa or the Middle East?

No. Jubilees places it on the Eastern border of Shem. Africa is Ham's territory and on Shem's Western edge not East. The Middle East is West as well. Neither is anywhere near the Garden which is in the Far East. Jub. 8 (See Garden of Eden Map)

Is Japheth to Dwell in the Tents of Shem?

No. Yahuah dwells in the tent of Shem never Japheth. This explains a century's old claim from Rabbis who attempt to claim Japheth has a right to take Shem's land. He does not and his people who do so will suffer a curse as a result. Jub. 7:11-12 says: "And he blessed Shem, and said: "Blessed be the Yahuah Elohim of Shem, and Canaan shall be his servant. Elohim shall enlarge Japheth, and Elohim shall dwell in the dwelling of Shem, and Canaan shall be his servant." Compare to Gn. 9:26-27 which is misrepresented by many today. Jubilees clarifies this.

How Many Days in a Biblical Year? *Jub. 6:38.*

364. 12 – 30-day months with an added day each quarter and based on the sun.

Where Does Gog of Magog Rule From?

Not Russia (Magog). Ezekiel 38 defines Gog of Magog's seat of power as Tubal and Meshech. The Book of Jubilees locates these territories as West and Central Europe. This would in modern terms define the Colonial Powers, Vatican, Germany, Italy, etc. Now prophecy makes sense. (see Ch. 9 Map).

Why Is Russia Split Into 2 Continents?

Noah set this boundary in his division here in Jubilees. The River Tina which is the modern Don(Tanais to Scythians) and Volga Rivers continues to divide Europe and Asia. Europe was Japheth and Asia was Shem. Essentially, follow history and you will find Russia bleeds into Shem's territory from Japheth. To this day, the people principally are from Japheth (78%) not Shem. (see Ch. 8 Commentary).

Why Is Borneo Divided Between 2 Countries?

Noah split the island in his setting of the border of Shem to the North and Ham to the South defined by the volcanoes. (see Ch. 8 Commentary).

Did the name Africa derive from Abraham's son Epher or Publius Cornelius Scipio Africanus as some claim?

Neither are remotely accurately as Jubilees uses both Afra (East Side) and Aferag (West side) to refer to the continent in the days of Moses long before either character lived. Jubilees 8. (See Map) Neither are even similar in Hebrew either.

Is the Moon the Measure for the Start of the Day in the Bible?

No. The sun is the measure for the start of the day at sunrise. The moon comes in 10 days too soon on the year and is off 22 of 52 weeks of the year for the Sabbath or week and day was first not night. Jub. 1:8 (Sun rules over Day and Night) 1:9 (Sun appointed as the sign for days, sabbaths (weeks), months, years, etc.), Jub. 6:36-40 (moon disrupts the Biblical calendar as the wrong measure for days, sabbaths (weeks), months and years). See our commentary on this as we offer abundant scripture from the modern canon which concurs.

How Did Moses Write About Events Long Before His Time?

For the Creation narrative in Genesis and Jubilees, the Angel of the Presence provided that portion as he had recorded them in the Heavenly Tablets since Creation. Acts 7:53 agrees "the law was received by the disposition of angels." Jub. 2.

Can Women Prophecy?

Yes. Rebecca did in Jubilees 25. Starts in Jub. 25:14. Miriam (Ex. 15:20), Deborah (Judg. 4:4), Huldah (2 Ki. 22:14; 2 Chr. 34:22), Noadiah (Neh. 6:14), and "the prophetess" (Isa. 8:3). Anna as a "woman prophet" (prophētis): Hebrew něbī'āh (Luke 2:36-38). Other woman prophesy in Acts 1:14; 2:17, 21:9).

How Did the Eldest Brother Rueben Lose His Birthright?

Torah does not answer this in detail yet it was taken from him and given to Ephraim, son of Joseph. Jubilees explains that Rueben raped one of his father's handmaid's. That is how he lost his birthright. This is consistent. Jub. 33.

How Did the Occult cross over the Flood?

Kainam, grandson of Shem, found stone carvings of the occult teachings of the Watchers and sinned owning to it. Oddly, he is mentioned in the lineage of Messiah in the Book of Luke, the Greek Septuagint, Samaritan Pentateuch and here in Jubilees but is omitted from our modern Genesis. This seems far more likely a change in Genesis in order to cover up the reinstitution of the occult. Jub. 8:1-4.

Is the Garden of Eden in Africa?

Shem received the Garden of Eden and Noah rejoiced over this. It is located on Shem's Eastern border and Africa is all the way on Shem's Western border. This is not even a close guess. (See Chapter 8 Garden Map).

Was the World Aware of the Americas in Ancient Times?

Yes. Noah includes them in his division of the earth to his sons. (See Ch. 8 Mapping).

Is Tarshish China?

No. This claim comes from some of the communist channels who are willing to commit fraud to lead to China and Russia. Tarshish was son of Japheth inheriting the Greek Isles with his brothers which means they became mariners, perhaps the first of significance after the Flood. Ophir, Sheba, Havilah and the sons of Joktan (from Shem) inherited the Far East area of Sephar, the Mount of the East (both Garden of Eden references) on Shem's Eastern border which we know today as the Philippines. They lived in Mesha, Iran even according to Josephus, and they migrated after Babel to the Philippines on the ships of Tarshish. Thus Tarshish also received a portion of the Philippines as payment. (See "The Search for King Solomon's Treasure" for full evidence). China is deep into Shem's territory and that fraud is almost an entire continent off in error. (Ch. 8 Shem's Mapping). It cannot be Britain/Spain either as both fail in resources, direction and even have their history saying they are not.

Is Ophir, land of gold, in Africa?

There is only 1 Ophir in the Bible and that is the one from Eber, from Shem. Chapter 8's mapping is very clear Shem only went to the coast of Africa and all of Africa is Ham's.

Did the Queen of Sheba originate in Ethiopia or Yemen?

Chapter 8 mapping affirms the full territory of Shem. It does not include Africa thus the one from Ethiopia is the wrong Queen as that is in Ham's territory and the Queen of Sheba from 1 Kings 10 descends from the other Sheba (Gn. 10:26-30) brother of Ophir, from Eber, from Shem not Ham.

Why Was It OK for the Lost Tribes of the Southern Kingdom to Migrate to Africa (Is. 11:10-12)?

The mapping of Chapter 8 identifies the West Coast known as the Slave Coast in history as the territory of Canaan. Canaan stole Israel instead and did not take his inheritance. Ancient maps indicate this became territory claimed by Cush/ Ethiopia. Judah especially married Shua the Canaanite and thus, the bloodline of Canaan remains in his tribe as well giving them the right to go to Canaan legally and Biblically. Even African maps during the era of the Transatlantic Slave Trade indicate Lost Tribes there in that area.

Is the Garden of Eden in Mesopotamia?

Chapter 8 map indicates the Garden of Eden on Shem's Eastern border which is no where near the Middle East. This claim is based on the occult Creation Myth of Sumer not the Bible and has no place in Bible interpretation. (See Chapter 8 Garden Map). The Garden is not associated with the Hiddekel and it is ludicrous to associate the Hiddekel with the Tigris. Daniel never lived there and was not there during that part of his life but in Susa, Iran. The Bible name for Tigris is never Hiddekel but 26 times Tigris is identified as "the river" because that is the river of abomination where the occult was reconstituted.

Did Noah's Ark Land in Turkey or Armenia?

See Chapter 8 map. Noah's descendants arrived in Shinar (Iraq) from the East. No matter how one attempts to do so, there is no moving Turkey nor Armenia to the East of Iraq. That is the wrong mountain in the wrong direction, 12,000 feet too short, with the wrong name, not mountains, not even the highest land in it's own area and definitively a wrong interpretation. If a ship was ever found there, and no evidence has ever been produced saying so, it is the ark of the Nephilim who claim a landing on a mountain in that area. Noah and his descendants did not live near Turkey in those days according to the Bible.

How long were Adam and Eve in the Garden of Eden?

7 years and they sinned in the beginning of the 8th on the 2nd month and 17th day which is the same day the Flood began and the ark door was shut. Jub. 3:17.

Was the Flood Only 40 Days and 40 Nights?

No. That is the marker for when the Flood was lifted. It continued to rise for a total of 150 days when the fountains were ceased and the windows of Heaven shut. Genesis concurs. Jub. 5:27-28. Gn. 7:24.

What Was the Original Language?

Hebrew was the original language of Creation (Jub. 12:25-26). It was lost at the Tower of Babel until restored by Abraham who learned it in order to read the writings of his fathers.

As the Book of Jubilees is the "Book of the Divisions of the Times into their Jubilees and Weeks" recorded by the Qumran community in full title, it truly represents the Torah Calendar of all of scripture. It is a 364-day calendar broken into (12) 30-day months with 1 day added at the end of each quarter. We can test this to confirm this scientifically in the Torah and the whole of scripture. In modern times, we are told the Lunar calendar, which is the so-called Hebrew calendar of Rabbinic Judaism, represents the Biblical calendar. However, this calendar not only disagrees with Jubilees, this book condemns it as essentially the pagan, Babylonian calendar and reveals it comes in 10 days to early on the year and disrupts the Biblical calendar which is based on the sun and not the moon.

Jubilees 6:36-38
For there will be those who will assuredly make observations of the moon -how (it) disturbs the seasons and comes in from year to year ten days too soon. For this reason the years will come upon them when they will disturb (the order), and make an abominable (day) the day of testimony, and an unclean day a feast day, and they will confound all the days, the holy with the unclean, and the unclean day with the holy; for they will go wrong as to the months and sabbaths and feasts and jubilees. For this reason I command and testify to thee that thou mayst testify to them; for after thy death thy children will disturb (them), so that they will not make the year three

hundred and sixty-four days only, and for this reason they will go wrong as to the new moons and seasons and sabbaths and festivals, and they will eat all kinds of blood with all kinds of flesh.

Even in the days of Moses, it was known that a new calendar would be launched and observed even in Israel that would "go wrong" by following the lunar calendar in error. The truly amazing thing is when one researches the cycle of the full moon it is 29.5 days. [24] Follow the math on this and half a day is lost every month thus there is not a single month in which the moon is an accurate measure. In 12 months this is off 6 days and then add the extra day at the end of each quarter for a total of 10 days too soon just as Jubilees documents in accurate science. In the year 2020 alone, a quick assessment shows this lunar cycle does in fact disrupt even the weekly Sabbath cycle 22 times in 52 weeks. That is not even close.

We are aware this represents a change in thinking today, but understand this is the ancient mindset – the one that follows the Bible. For instance, we have heard many times that the only measure in all of scripture is the Creation account which says it is evening it was morning the first day and so on. However, are we even reading the rest of the account or even the first day and especially all of scripture in attempting to determine such? Most do not including scholars who just follow Rabbi babble called leaven by Messiah. They were not following Jubilees, the Torah Calendar even then. Therefore, when a scholar says "ancient Rabbis say..." insert Pharisees and don't be deceived. The teachers of scripture in Biblical terms were the Aaronic Priests who did not refer to themselves as Rabbis. Matthew 23:8-12 clarifies we are to call no man Rabbi nor Father nor Master. It is almost as if Messiah knew what we would be dealing with today. First, let's review the Creation account in Jubilees.

Jubilees 1:8-9
And on the fourth day He created the sun [1st] and the moon and the stars, and set them in the firmament of the heaven, to give light upon all the earth, and to rule over the day and the night, and divide the light from the darkness. And God appointed the sun to be a great sign on the earth for days and for sabbaths and for months and for feasts and for years and for sabbaths of years and for jubilees and for all seasons of the years.

The sun was created as the measure for the day, sabbath (week), month and year. There is no way around that but the question remains, does scripture agree or does it actually propagate a lunar calendar. Clearly this Creation account does not and we will end this section with the Genesis account to clarify. Enoch agrees.

1 Enoch 41:6-7
And the Sun goes out first, and completes its journey at the command of the Lord of
Spirits - and his Name endures forever and ever. And after this is the hidden, and
visible, path of the Moon, and it travels the course of its journey, in that place, by
day and by night.

The sun is the measure for the day, Sabbath (week), month and year. Remember, the Qumran community of Temple Levite priests wrote that Jubilees is the Torah Calendar and Israel, controlled by the Pharisees through their synagogue network and takeover of the Temple turned "a blind eye" to this calendar even in the days of Messiah.

(For Yahuah made) a Covenant with you and all Israel; therefore a man shall bind
himself by oath to return to the Law of Moses, for in it all things are strictly defined.
As for the exact determination of their times to which Israel turns a blind eye, behold
it is strictly defined in the Book of the Divisions of the Times into their Jubilees and
Weeks. – Dead Sea Scrolls: The Damascus Document, 50 A.D. [21]

So let us review scripture first from this era in the New Testament to determine the actual Biblical calendar. In the Gospels, the time frame of Messiah's death and resurrection proves this out. Messiah arose just before sunrise, yet it was still Saturday (Sabbath) and not considered Sunday according to the Biblical calendar. This affirms the day actually begins at sunrise and not sundown because the sun is the measure and not the moon.

Matthew 28:1 KJV
*In the **end of the sabbath**, as it **began to dawn toward the first day of***
***the week**, came Mary Magdalene and the other Mary to see the sepulchre.*
John 20:1 KJV
*The **first day of the week cometh** Mary Magdalene early, when **it was yet***
***dark**, unto the sepulchre, and seeth the stone taken away from the sepulchre.*
John 20:19 KJV
*Then the **same day at evening, being the first day of the week**, when*
the doors were shut where the disciples were assembled for fear of the Jews, came Jesus
and stood in the midst...

Under what circumstances can it be just before dawn and the dark of the morning, yet still be Sabbath (Saturday)? Only if the day begins at sunrise. Even later in John, it marks the evening as still the same day after Mary had seen the stone rolled away in the morning after sunrise the same day. Evening was not a new day. The sun rose, the new day began and it was no longer Sabbath (Saturday) but now Sunday. Messiah rose just before sunrise on the Sabbath (Saturday) still. One cannot read this any other way. That evening is still the first day of the week Sunday and not a new day meaning the new day does not begin in the evening because it is the same day as it was after sunrise because sunrise begins the day according to scripture. Messiah's death also entrenches this calendar.

> *Luke 23:44-46 KJV*
> *And it was about the sixth hour, and there was a darkness over all the earth until the ninth hour. And the sun was darkened, and the veil of the temple was rent in the midst. And when Jesus had cried with a loud voice, he said, Father, into thy hands I commend my spirit: and having said thus, he gave up the ghost.*

Messiah died on the 9th hour. This cannot be during the evening because the sun was darkened from the 6th to the 9th hours meaning this is during the day. This was noon to 3 pm essentially. If the day began in the evening as we are told by the Rabbis, then, this would be midnight and somehow the sun was supposed to be out at midnight? It does not work. Luke continues as he records what happens later in the day after Messiah had died.

> *Luke 23:54-56 KJV*
> *And that day was the preparation, and the sabbath drew on. And the women also, which came with him from Galilee, followed after, and beheld the sepulchre, and how his body was laid. And they returned, and prepared spices and ointments; and rested the sabbath day according to the commandment.*

If the Sabbath drew on as Messiah's body was laid in the tomb, it is still Saturday in the evening. However, it was the day of preparation meaning the preparation for the Sabbath. How can it be both the Sabbath and preparation at the same time? This was a Feast Sabbath within the Passover/Unleavened Bread Season not the weekly Sabbath. Passover occurs in the evening and the Sabbath begins the next day at sunrise for those following the Biblical calendar. However, the Rabbis did not including Joseph of Arimathea who laid Messiah's body in the tomb. He and the Pharisees were anxious to get him in the tomb before sundown because they followed a Lunar calendar even in those days thus their Sabbath would not begin until sundown but Mary and the women who followed the Biblical calendar were already in observance of the Sabbath. Joseph was a ranking Pharisee who was saved but still following that observance. Notice, the women did not anoint the body that day in observance of the Sabbath. They would after sunrise each day even the third day when He rose from the dead. Passover was the night before Messiah's death according to Mark and all 4 Gospels.

Mark 14 KJV
1-2 After two days was the feast of the passover, and of unleavened bread: and the chief priests and the scribes sought how they might take him by craft, and put him to death. But they said, Not on the feast day, lest there be an uproar of the people. 12 And the first day of unleavened bread, when they killed the passover, his disciples said unto him, Where wilt thou that we go and prepare that thou mayest eat the passover?

It was the next morning when the Pharisees took Messiah to Pilate. Messiah was hung on the third hour and the day at what should be full sun was darkened from the 6th to the 9th hour.

Mark 15 KJV
1 And straightway in the morning the chief priests held a consultation with the elders and scribes and the whole council, and bound Jesus, and carried him away, and delivered him to Pilate.
25 And it was the third hour, and they crucified him.
33 And when the sixth hour was come, there was darkness over the whole land until the ninth hour.

Therefore, Messiah was crucified from 9 am (3rd Hour) and gave up the ghost at 3 pm (9th Hour). The day began at 6 am approximately in this chronology affirming Jubilees that the sun is in fact the measure for the day's beginning and not at sunset based on the moon which would disrupt His calendar. This has never fit the calendar of Rabbinic Judaism. This is affirmed again when one understands there are two calendars at play even in those days. Joseph was abiding by the Pharisee calendar and the Apostles and followers, the Biblical one. Everything that appears to be a discrepancy is easily explained with this understanding.

Mark 15:42-43 KJV
And now when the even was come, because it was the preparation, that is, the day before the sabbath, Joseph of Arimathaea, an honourable counsellor, which also waited for the kingdom of God, came, and went in boldly unto Pilate, and craved the body of Jesus.
Mark 16:1-2 KJV
And when the sabbath was past, Mary Magdalene, and Mary the mother of James,

*and Salome, had bought sweet spices, that they might come and anoint him. And very
early in the morning the first day of the week, they came unto the sepulchre at the
rising of the sun.*

Joseph kept the Pharisee Sabbath by placing Messiah in the tomb before sundown.
However, in the resurrections, Mark affirms that on the third day, the women wait
for sunrise to purchase their spices for anointing. Joseph purchased linens, etc.
during the day three days earlier but his Sabbath had not begun yet though the
Biblical Sabbath had. It would have violated it several times and he did violate
the Biblical one but it is apparent he is following the Pharisee calendar instead.
The women do not anoint his body on the first Sabbath which is a special Feast
Sabbath which is the only way you get two Sabbaths in one week. They did not
violate the first Sabbath but took note of where the body was laid to go back
and anoint it after sunrise the next day and on the third day, we see this same
cycle repeated as they wait until sunrise to purchase spices. That only works if
the day begins at sunrise. Messiah died on the Feast Sabbath and resurrected on
the Weekly Sabbath (Saturday). This was exactly three days and three nights just
as IIe said it would be and we can restore faith in the Word. However, we also
see this in Torah and the Old Testament as a matter of record and really is not
something that is debatable. During the Exodus, this is confirmed several times.

Exodus 10:4 KJV
*4 Else, if thou refuse to let my people go, behold, to morrow will I bring the locusts
into thy coast:*
*13 And Moses stretched forth his rod over the land of Egypt, and the LORD brought
an east wind upon the land all that day, and all that night; and when it was morning,
the east wind brought the locusts.*

The locusts are promised to come tomorrow. When is that? The next morning.

Exodus 12:6-8 KJV
*6-8 And ye shall keep it up until the fourteenth day of the same month: and the whole
assembly of the congregation of Israel shall kill it in the evening. And they shall take
of the blood, and strike it on the two side posts and on the upper door post of the
houses, wherein they shall eat it. And they shall eat the flesh in that night, roast with
fire, and unleavened bread; and with bitter herbs they shall eat it.*
*10-11 And ye shall let nothing of it remain until the morning; and that which
remaineth of it until the morning ye shall burn with fire.*
…it is the Lord's passover

Leviticus 7:15-16 KJV
And the flesh of the sacrifice of his peace offerings for thanksgiving shall be eaten the same day that it is offered; he shall not leave any of it until the morning. But if the sacrifice of his offering be a vow, or a voluntary offering, it shall be eaten the same day that he offereth his sacrifice: and on the morrow also the remainder of it shall be eaten:
Leviticus 22:30 KJV
On the same day it shall be eaten up; ye shall leave none of it until the morrow: I am the LORD.
Leviticus 7:15-16 KJV
…offerings for thanksgiving shall be eaten the same day that it is offered; he shall not leave any of it until the morning.

The Passover sacrifice is to be eaten in the evening and these passages are clear the new day begins in the morning at sunrise. The Passover account has several such confirmations within.

Exodus 12 KJV
11…For I will pass through the land of Egypt this night…
12…And this day shall be unto you for a memorial… (14th)
29 …And it came to pass, that at midnight the Lord smote all the firstborn in the land of Egypt…
30…And Pharaoh rose up in the night…
31 …And he called for Moses and Aaron by night…
Numbers 33:3 KJV
And they departed from Rameses in the first month, on the fifteenth day of the first month; on the morrow after the passover the children of Israel went out with an high hand in the sight of all the Egyptians.

Tomorrow is the next morning period. Even the Golden Calf story affirms this.

Exodus 32:5-6 KJV
And when Aaron saw it, he built an altar before it; and Aaron made proclamation, and said, To morrow is a feast to the LORD. And they rose up early on the morrow, and offered burnt offerings, and brought peace offerings; and the people sat down to eat and to drink, and rose up to play.

Also, Yahuah rained manna for Israel every morning except the Sabbath. A double portion came the sixth day to cover two days. (Ex. 16) They would gather it every morning and prepare and eat it except the sixth day, none was to remain for the next morning or it would spoil.

> *Exodus 16:23-24 KJV*
> *This is that which the LORD hath said, To morrow is the rest of the holy sabbath*
> *unto the LORD: bake that which ye will bake to day, and seethe that ye will seethe;*
> *and that which remaineth over lay up for you to be kept until the morning. And they*
> *laid it up till the morning, as Moses bade: and it did not stink, neither was there*
> *any worm therein. And Moses said, Eat that to day; for to day is a sabbath unto the*
> *LORD: to day ye shall not find it in the field.*

Again, the morning represents the beginning of tomorrow, the next day. Sunrise is the marker for the day as the sun is the measure and Jubilees is accurate to scripture. Even in Joshua, the day begins at sunrise.

> *Joshua 5:10-12 KJV*
> *And the children of Israel encamped in Gilgal, and kept the passover on the fourteenth*
> *day of the month at even in the plains of Jericho. And they did eat of the old corn of*
> *the land on the morrow after the passover, unleavened cakes, and parched corn in the*
> *selfsame day. And the manna ceased on the morrow after they had eaten of the old*
> *corn of the land; neither had the children of Israel manna any more; but they did eat*
> *of the fruit of the land of Canaan that year.*

Tomorrow in the morning at sunrise was the next day. This chronology is also the same in the story of Lot.

> *Genesis 19:34 KJV*
> *And it came to pass on the morrow, that the firstborn said unto the younger, Behold, I*
> *lay yesternight with my father: let us make him drink wine this night also; and go thou*
> *in, and lie with him, that we may preserve seed of our father.*

We see this specifically in the account of Gideon where twice he leaves the fleece at night and the morning it is to be wet one day and dry the next. In both cases, the morning was tomorrow, the next day. (Judges 6) In Joshua 7:13-14, Israel is to sanctify themselves for tomorrow and then, the morning comes and it is tomorrow at that point. The day has always begun at sunrise not midnight and not sundown. The same is accounted in the narrative of Abimelech as the morning is also tomorrow. (Judges 9:42-45) This is not an issue that the Bible leaves up for debate, it settles it. Test it for yourself. The Bible has always indicated a solar calendar exactly as Jubilees lays out. There is no fitting the Lunar one.

The final example we will cover is the story of the Levite traveler in Judges 19. It is crystal clear his travels begin in the early in the morning the 4th day. The evening is still the 4th day as is the whole night. The 5th day begins in the morning at sunrise and so does the 6th. He gets up in the morning on tomorrow. This chronology is the Bible clock and never has it been set on a lunar calendar. However, many are confused by the modern interpretation through the Talmud of the Creation account which claims Creation began in the evening. This is simple to rectify.

First, the challenge is was the universe evil before Creation? Is evil our true foundation? This is the claim of the Talmud for the darkness that existed in the beginning is referred to as evil by many. This is unbiblical and has no merit as evil as sin are antitheses not elements unto themselves. For evil is the opposite of good. Sin is the violation of the law or lawlessness. In order to have sin, you must have the law first. In order to have evil, you must have good first. Yahuah does not originate in evil and that is what one would have to believe to accept such. The void in Genesis 1:2 is simply the absence of Creation. The darkness is the absence of light. Darkness cannot exist in light, sin cannot exist in the law, evil cannot exist in good. Some attempt to inject a war in Heaven within the Creation account but this is not there. Satan cannot take one-third of the angels until Revelation 12 when he is accusing the brethren or mankind. He could not accuse man before man was created on the sixth day. This is not Bible but man's manufactured doctrine. The void was the absence of creation, that's it. Yes, it would be chaos because it was elements that were not used yet to create. On each day Yahuah saw that it was good or in other woods NOT evil including the darkness for that matter.

Genesis 1:3-5 KJV
And God said, Let there be light: and there was light. [Light was His 1st Creation]
And God saw the light, that it was good: and God divided the light from the darkness.
And God called the light Day [Day comes 1st], and the darkness he called Night.
[Night comes 2nd] [After Creating All Day]
And the evening and the morning were the first day.
[Yom - 24 hr Day or Daylight - Never Just Night]

Light was the first Creation and it was called Day as Day comes first, night comes after. Then it was evening (night) and morning (still darkness) and the next day begins at sunrise. The Creation account indicates Yahuah begins created during the day essentially at sunrise. On the fourth, He creates the sun first and then the moon following the same pattern. Again, Jubilees tells us the sun is the measure of the day, Sabbath (week), month and year not the moon. Thus, the day begins with the sun rising.

Genesis 1:17-19 KJV

And God set them in the firmament of the heaven to give light upon the earth, And to rule over the day [1st] and over the night [2nd], and to divide the light [1st] from the darkness [2nd]: and God saw that it was good. [Creation during Day] And the evening and the morning were the fourth day.

Notice, night (darkness) is also certified good, Yahuah saw that it was. It was not evil in the beginning nor is it today. Yahuah created all day, then it was evening and then it was morning as those are at the end of the day's activities not the beginning. This is the Biblical calendar set forth by Jubilees, the Torah Calendar and confirmed in Torah many times as well as the rest of the Old Testament and even the New especially the death and resurrection of Messiah. This calendar is well attested through time and our modern understanding is Pharisee leaven waiting to be exposed. Test this for yourself.

The Qumran calendar from Jubilees began on the 4th day of Creation when the sun was created. The Biblical Feasts would essentially fall on the same day of the week each year and the calendar was consistent. For instance, Messiah was captured on Passover after His Passover meal with His disciples according to scripture. That is what it says as the disciples even purchased the Passover lamb. This would be a Tuesday evening. He would be crucified the next day from 9 am - 3 pm on Wednesday, Abib 15 and this must be the case because Jacob was to be sacrificed that same day, the 15th not the 14th. He placed in the tomb before sunrise on Thursday but not anointed until the next morning at sunrise as that was the Feast Sabbath on Wednesday. He would be in the Earth for three full days and nights just as He said He would and He rose on Sabbath (Saturday) just before sunrise which would begin the day on Sunday. He rose on the Sabbath not on Sunday though on today's calendar we call that Sunday morning. It was still considered Saturday and that was Sabbath on the Biblical calendar as the Sabbath remains. There is no issue for a church to meet on Sunday however, but just do not call that the Sabbath unless you are meeting prior to 6 am. There is no conflict in any of the Gospels on this as one must reconcile our modern calendar with that of the Bible with the understanding that Joseph of Arimathea, though saved, was a prominent Pharisee following the Pharisee Lunar calendar not the Biblical one. It appears he did become a believer, however, which is most important but not the only topic of importance by far.

You will notice Shem's division begins with the North Pole affirmed as such multiple times as when you follow his directions to the end, you end up right back in the very north just as you begin. The perspective in which the Bible was written is one of a flat round disc in cosmology. We do not enter such modern debate but to attempt to understand Biblical geography without understanding the mindset in which it was written is called willing ignorance. Galileo did not write Jubilees and anyone who paid attention in science class knows the world generally believed the earth flat prior to the Renaissance in which all of the Bible was written. Anyone calling themselves a scholar who will not admit this, is operating in willing ignorance. Noah is very clearly and brilliantly setting borders thus must begin on a border. What is truly amazing is Noah set the border between Europe (Japtheth) and Asia (Shem) thousands of years ago and it divides modern Moscow to this very day. Many have wondered how Moscow was ever divided between two continents and now we know. One will also not Russia's population is 78% located on the European side of the ancient Tina River. It is important to understand Japheth's descendants have controlled Russia for some time and much of the land is in Shem's territory though the population principally in Japheth's. There is no placing Russia as a nation of Shem and Ashkenaz (Ashkenazi Jews) who conquered Russia in the Bolshevik Revolution a century ago, are from Japheth not Shem thus the name of Japheth's grandson Ashkenaz and a title from their language of Jew which word cannot exist in modern Hebrew, Aramaic, Greek, Latin, Old French, Old German nor Old English. There is a channel on YouTube attempting to claim Russia is a nation of Shem and this is propaganda.

The second description really pulls this whole mapping into perspective as Noah defines what can only be the Don and Vulga Rivers in Russia as the dividing line between Shem and Japheth. Again, he starts in the very north and heads south and no other direction makes sense. The River Tina has to run to the middle of the Mts. of Rafa or Riphaen Mountains which are the modern Ural Mountains. This is Russia. It then must run to the ocean and into 2 seas dumping into a third sea. One cannot mistake this and R.H. Charles and most others got this right.

Some then misunderstand that there are 3 tongues mentioned and the tongue pointing towards the South must be India as then it heads West to the second tongue and West again to the third. In fact, we know now that the Khirasara was an Indus Valley civilization from Noah's time even which happens to be located on the bosom of the tongue which is unimaginable wisdom but what one would expect from Noah in his 800's or so. We cannot fathom wisdom in our short lifespans on these levels. Society elevates the likes of occult infants such as Plato, Socrates, etc. who are all juvenile in comparison. The reason many cannot understand these directions is they are stuck in paradigms and they underestimate whom Noah and even Moses were as many scholars do not even believe the Bible and should not be considered Bible scholars. Next you are on the coast of Africa thus these are really incredibly specific directions one cannot mistake. How far to the East does Shem go from the East coast of Africa? Beyond India to the whole East. This will become pronounced and thoroughly defined in Ham's division when the Garden of Eden and the Southeastern border of Shem is related entirely. In the Far East, there are still mountains called the "Mountains of Fire" in Indonesia and they form a perfect geographic border even splitting modern Borneo to this day. Noah divided that island.

There were other communist YouTube channels out there claiming that China was Tarshish to attempt to melt China into the narrative of Ophir. This is fraudulent as Tarshish is a son of Javan (Greece) who inherited the Greek isles. The only reason Tarshish enters the narrative of Ophir, Sheba and Havilah who are Shemites who migrate to the Far East into the Philippines, is because he provided the ships according to very abundant scripture. He thus received a portion of Ophir's territory in payment for transporting them there along with some of his brothers. Shem principally receive almost all of Asia and there is no placing China in Japheth's territory.

Another YouTube Channel propagates Africa for practically all of history as Shem's territory which is false and they attempt to move Babylon, Assyria, Israel and even the Roman Empire into Africa in complete ignorance. These directions are very clear that Shem received no part of Africa. The reason the Lost Tribes from the Southern Kingdom could migrate to the Slave Coast on the West side of Africa is because that was Canaan's territory he gave up in order to steal Shem's Israel which is why it was called Canaan. Ham and his other sons curse Canaan a second time for this infraction demonstrating how seriously they took this.

Also Madai did not desire his inheritance in the British isles and others. He took land that would become known as Media named after him which survives history. Both of these areas would become hotbeds for Nephilim incursions which was likely due to their curse. It is the bloodline from Media who were the conquerors among the first empires and this continues. Madai's area in the British Isles would have been absorbed into Meshech's Western Europe territory.

We can now understand that when Ezekiel 38-39 prophesies of Gog of Magog, he was not talking about Russia necessarily. Yes, Magog is Russia but that is a territory in which this prince demon must have originated but it is not his seat of power. Ezekiel says his seat of powers is Tubal, Central Europe and Meshech, Western Europe. One could generally call this the EU today. When comparing Gog's allies on this map and the Mass Aliyah of modern Israel in 1948-1952, one will notice that list matches but what it does not match is that of Isaiah 11. Now we know why Pharisees hate Jubilees and always did. According to the Jewish Encyclopedia and most others, Pharisaism became Rabbinic Judaism after the second temple was destroyed. it is the same without the temple rituals. Messiah Himself rebuked their Oral Traditions in Mark 7 with scathing admonition calling their traditions against His commandments and rendering His Word of none effect. We covered in the introduction that the Qumran community including those same Pharisees as the "sons of darkness." No Pharisee wrote this book and to say so is fraud. We now know that Colonialism was the advancement of the Empire of Gog, the final Roman Empire. It no longer traded goods but followed the fruits of satan to steal, kill and destroy (Jn. 10:10). The Christianity they spread has nothing to do with the Bible but is the same brand of Pharisaism rebuked by Messiah. It is time we all awaken to this. Gog already attacked Israel and we are in the End Times right now. We must all be sober and vigilant.

When we assess Ham's territory, you will note that he begins in Africa and crosses the Gihon River. The Gihon surrounds the whole land of Ethiopia which is East to West Coast of Africa in history recorded on maps from 450 B.C. by Heroditus consistently until the 1800s. Shem's border from Asia goes to the banks of the Gihon and stops there not entering Africa. He heads to the South thus a good portion of the Indian Ocean belongs to Shem but none of Africa. The Gihon must be on the ocean floor surrounding Africa. Ham cannot cross into Shem's territory for there is a curse for either son who does so. He must head West at this point. He then goes all the way to the Right of or East of the Garden of Eden which must be on Shem's eastern border. This is nowhere near Africa and Ham must head in to the West in order to come to the right of the Garden. Noah is defining essentially the entire Southern Hemisphere as belonging to Shem.

He even divided the US into a North and South. The South never belonged to Japheth but to Ham. One must wonder how many Africa migrants from Ham had already lived in the South even before the Trans-Atlantic Slave Trade began. No doubt slaves were brought especially from the Slave Coast which is Canaan's and Lost Tribes of the Southern Kingdom of Israel are known to have migrated there. All of those of African descent, however, are not Lost Tribes and Judah did marry a Canaanite woman.

In Japheth's territory, he crosses the Atlantic into the Americas as he is in Gadir and heads into the Ocean to the West. There is no other way to interpret that. The five great islands also give this away as in the Northern Hemisphere of his territory, 5 of the 10 largest islands exist there. However, four of them are in Canada thus North America is invoked. This is why we believe Fara is Fairbanks, Alaska or similar in the area. We are unsure about the Northern portion of the Pacific as these directions for Japheth seem to end off the West coast of North America. It appears that the International Date Line may actually have an ancient precedence as it divides the Pacific right at that point and this makes sense. In fact, that date line even turns almost parallel with the border of Shem and Ham in the Far East which is odd. We are not entirely sure where the Pacific split between Shem and Japheth would be though Ham and Shem are well defined. It is incredible that Noah even included the waters in this division.

One can quickly see that Japheth, or really Gog of Magog's powers, have greatly expanded violating Noah's division drastically. Colonialism and conquest is unbiblical especially for those claiming to do so in the name of the Bible. No scripture ever says to go into all the world and conquer. There is never any justification for exhibiting the fruit of satan to steal, kill and destroy no matter how one attempts to justify such actions. They are and always will be evil and no good fruit comes from them. Many have fallen into the deception of this religion and these are the same who have and continue to censor Jubilees which rebukes them. Is it really any surprise why the Pharisees who hail from Japheth essentially and Holy Roman Empire under the powerful Pharisee called Pope would desire to cover up the find in Qumran veiling it in such illusive, scary language? It is time to restore this book and all Biblical knowledge.

As you will find in the Chapter 8 and 9 maps, we have extensively mapped all of Noah's division and it includes essentially the entire Earth. The only area not accounted for directly appears to be Antartica perhaps though it could be concluded that it falls in Ham's division most likely. This division several millennia old, remains valid and can be understood even in our time and it is brilliant on many levels. This will clarify many things we have all been taught.

The Book of Jude makes what would seem a very odd assertion in what is called modern scholarship as many do not understand Genesis 6.

Jude 1:6
And the angels which kept not their first estate, but left their own habitation, he hath reserved in everlasting chains under darkness unto the judgment of the great day.

That Apocrypha book of Jude sure does derive some strange doctrine right? Oh, no that's right, it is published in the canon of scripture. However, this strange event in which a group of angels leaving Heaven must be some arbitrary falling of angels because angels fall all the time right? Well, no they do not and when they do, it is recorded in scripture and this is the only associated with Noah period. There are angels in Enoch who were being punished for not keeping their courses, there is satan who is an angel who fell of sorts yet still has access to Heaven thus not completely fallen in a sense until Revelation 12 and then, there is this one group in all of scripture who chose as a group to leave Heaven and sin. They are locked away in everlasting chains awaiting their final judgment on the Day of Judgment. Who is this? Well, it is no mystery whatsoever though many modern scholars follow doctrines of men that shun portions of the Bible. We find this event recorded in Genesis and then they try to tell us it says something else but with Jubilees as well as Enoch, we know what Genesis means. Examine this.

Jubilees 5

1 And it came to pass when the children of men began to multiply on the face of the earth and daughters were born unto them, that the angels of Elohim saw them on a certain year of this jubilee, that they were beautiful to look upon; and they took themselves wives of all whom they chose, and they bare unto them sons and they were giants. 2 And lawlessness increased on the earth and all flesh corrupted its way, alike men and cattle and beasts and birds and everything that walketh on the earth-all of them corrupted their ways and their orders, and they began to devour each other, and lawlessness increased on the earth and every imagination of the thoughts of all men (was) thus evil continually. 3 And Elohim looked upon the earth, and behold it was corrupt, and all flesh had corrupted its orders, and all that were upon the earth had wrought all manner of evil before His eyes. 4 And He said: "I shall destroy man and all flesh upon the face of the earth which I have created."

Genesis 6 KJV

1 And it came to pass, when men began to multiply on the face of the earth, and daughters were born unto them, 2 That the sons of God saw the daughters of men that they were fair; and they took them wives of all which they chose. 3 And the Lord said, My spirit shall not always strive with man, for that he also is flesh: yet his days shall be an hundred and twenty years. 4 There were giants in the earth in those days; and also after that, when the sons of God came in unto the daughters of men, and they bare children to them, the same became mighty men which were of old, men of renown. 5 And God saw that the wickedness of man was great in the earth, and that every imagination of the thoughts of his heart was only evil continually. 6 And it repented the Lord that he had made man on the earth, and it grieved him at his heart. 7 And the Lord said, I will destroy man whom I have created from the face of the earth; both man, and beast, and the creeping thing, and the fowls of the air; for it repenteth me that I have made them.

Anyone can read this for themselves and see these are the same. Any scholar claiming Genesis is referring to human men or the sons of Seth as the sons of Elohim and human woman in this account cannot read especially the Hebrew. The same will lose debate after debate when atheists especially accuse Yahuah of being evil and sinning because without this narrative, the Flood makes no sense. Just as depicted in the occult, gnostic movie "Noah", they devise a God who hates mankind, even Noah, so much that he just has to destroy them for no good reason. Go talk to a teenager who has entered science classes into this occult realm taught right in our schools and they are getting beat over the head with how this angry God just hates us all. Why would anyone serve such a God? The answer is simple when this understanding is restored. However, when we follow much of modern scholarship on this, we find them impotent on the topic having a form of Godliness but no power thereof and easy prey for the gnostic response.

Of course, those scholars may even think they are defending the Bible yet they represent the same gnostic view really. If men procreating with women produce some new race "against their orders," how exactly could that even work nor make sense. It does not. If regular men and women multiply, where do giants enter this picture? Of course, they'll go into the Hebrew and say it's not really giants yet Jubilees clarifies this is definitively giants and the translators of Genesis knew this and render it as well. The church and scholarship is placing stumbling blocks which become impediments to people accepting Jesus(Yahusha) in such deeds. They have done more harm on this doctrine than one can imagine and all because they choose to steep themselves in the doctrines of men defending them with the sword and they are not actually studying and learning the Bible.

These two accounts mirror each other. Men and women began to multiply. That is humans. Then, the sons of God, enter the picture as something different even in language. Sons of God and daughters of men is distinctly different. Jubilees says these are angels and so does Genesis. In Hebrew, this is the ben ha elohim (בני־האלהים). This is a very specific reference in Hebrew to angels as these sons of Elohim in Job 1:6 and 2:1 represent the council of Elohim in Heaven in which no men are mentioned but angels. Job uses this again in 38:7 in the context of Creation when the firmament was created, this group shouted for joy yet man was not even created yet but angels were. This represents the only four times this phrase is used as such in Hebrew and it is always angels of high authority thus Genesis and Jubilees are certainly indicating the same here.

An English only comparison of the phrase "sons of God" by the way, is meaningless and moot and that is the sole approach of these so-called scholars who can't seem to bother to read the Hebrew on those to see those other times, are a different Hebrew phrase not an exact match and the Greek is impertinent. All four times, these are angels and Jubilees calls them angels directly because they are angels not men.

Without this understanding, one is stuck in a false paradigm with no answer as to why Yahuah would Flood the earth other than men did evil things. If this were so, why are we still here? These actions are specific to intrusions against the Law of Creation to reproduce after their kind. Those angels violated that and in doing so the result was a race in which every imagination of their heart was evil continually and the origin of demons. This is not a random rebuke of someone wishing to benefit on the backs of others, it is a murderous, manipulating breed who desires to kill, steal and destroy. The earth had not seen such evil until this.

However, they were not completely wiped out by the Flood and this breed began reasserting themselves in Daniel's warning of a final empire. Daniel's interpretation of Nebuchadnezzar's dream from Yahuah lays out the rise of the One World Empire beginning with Babylon which was conquered by Medo-Persia which was conquered by Greece which was conquered by Rome in the legs of iron. There is not a day which passed in which the One World Empire did not exist in power. However, the final empire is treated as an enigma in scholarship by many yet Daniel interprets this for us himself. It has never been a mystery but when one is not aware whom the enemy really is, they are inept in understanding what Daniel meant.

Daniel 2:43 KJV
And whereas thou sawest iron mixed with miry clay, they shall mingle themselves with the seed of men: but they shall not cleave one to another, even as iron is not mixed with clay.

The miry clay represents they who are not men as they cannot mingle their seed if they are men. That would not be mingling and we have seen this before. The final empire is Rome mixed in with Nephilim bloodlines who wish to conquer mankind which has been demonstrated thousands of times in the past millennia. Most recently this is demonstrated by Colonialism, the Trans-Atlantic Slave Trade, Communism's murder of over 100 million of their own people and this continues under different names to this day. It is getting worse not improving. Messiah warned of the same return of the Nephilim in the last days. The Flood reset the balance of power in the favor of man which was it's purpose.

Matthew 24:38 KJV
But as the days of Noah were, so shall also the coming of the Son of man be.

The battle has always been man vs. Nephilim ultimately as they are the principalities of darkness in which Paul refers (Eph. 6:12-23). It has never been between races of men and when one extreme to the other within mankind is represented by a minor fractional differential, it proves we are all essentially the same and should never be separated into groups by skin tone. This manipulation brought Yahuah's reaction in the Flood and now it will lead to the final replenishing of the earth through fire as the days of Noah have returned. These doctrines taught by the Watchers permeate our society today even in modern science, Hollywood and every aspect of life today. It is being taught in our schools as fact and indoctrination whether any of us appreciates this forced occult agenda or not.

Evil Doctrines of the Watchers

Jubilees 8:1-4

In the twenty-ninth jubilee, in the first week, in the beginning thereof Arpachshad took to himself a wife and her name was Râsû'ĕjâ, [the daughter of Sûsân,] the daughter of Elam, and she bare him a son in the third year in this week, and he called his name Kâinâm. And the son grew, and his father taught him writing, and he went to seek for himself a place where he might seize for himself a city. And he found a writing which former (generations) had carved on the rock, and he read what was thereon, and he transcribed it and sinned owing to it; for it contained the teaching of the Watchers in accordance with which they used to observe the omens of the sun and moon and stars in all the signs of heaven. And he wrote it down and said nothing regarding it; for he was afraid to speak to Noah about it lest he should be angry with him on account of it.

Arpachshad's descendants are known in part as the Chaldeans who practiced this continued occult doctrine even in the days of Abraham's father, Terah.

Jubilees 11:8

And she bare him Nahor, in the first year of this week, and he grew and dwelt in Ur of the Chaldees, and his father taught him the researches of the Chaldees to divine and augur, according to the signs of heaven.

Jubilees 7:21-24

For owing to these three things came the flood upon the earth, namely, owing to the fornication wherein the Watchers against the law of their ordinances went a whoring after the daughters of men, and took themselves wives of all which they chose: and they made the beginning of uncleanness. 22 And they begat sons the Nâphîdîm, and †they were all unlike†, and they devoured one another: and the Giants slew the Nâphîl, and the Nâphîl slew the Eljô, and the Eljô mankind, and one man another. 23 And every one sold himself to work iniquity and to shed much blood, and the earth was filled with iniquity. 24 And after this they sinned against the beasts and birds, and all that moveth and walketh on the earth: and much blood was shed on the earth, and every imagination and desire of men imagined vanity and evil continually.

For specifics on what the Watchers taught, one has to go to the Book of Enoch.

1 Enoch 10:8

And Azaz'el taught the people the art of making swords and knives, and shields, and breastplates; and he showed to their chosen ones bracelets, decorations, shadowing of the eye with antimony, ornamentation, the beautifying of the eyelids, all kinds of

precious stones, and all coloring tinctures and alchemy. And there were many wicked ones and they committed adultery and erred, and all their conduct became corrupt. Amasras taught incantation and the cutting of roots; and Armaros the resolving of incantations; and Baraqiyal astrology, and Kokarer'el the knowledge of the signs, and Tam'el taught the seeing of the stars, and Asder'el taught the course of the moon as well as the deception of man. And the people cried and their voice reached unto heaven.
1 Enoch 10:8
And the whole earth has been corrupted by Azaz'el's teaching of his own actions; and write upon him all sin.

Do we see these doctrines being employed today? By governments? By government institutions they call higher learning? Do we see this in Hollywood and the media? Unfortunately, we even see some of this in the church. Azazel taught the art of war not Sun Tzu who is merely a master of Nephilim doctrine and not one anyone should pay attention. His doctrine is what corrupted the Earth before the Flood and we are right back there today. Step back and ask the question, why are we at war? Why perpetual wars now with no end? Who benefits financially and what are they doing with the proceeds? They have and agenda and it is very public and not hidden really. He taught alchemy or pharmakeia which is sorcery in the Bible. But of course, we don't use such today right with pharmacies on every corner. He taught sexual degradation as well. These are three of the top pillars, as rotten and odious as they may be, of modern society generally world-wide. This only leads to one end which has already been prophesied. The world will need to be replenished again.

They then taught witchcraft, astrology and twisted astronomy, etc. Today, we call that science class which is mostly Kabbalah and Babylonian Mystery Religion. Enoch is rebuking these actions and their penalty is steep. They are already locked away awaiting judgment. However, how is it that today, these doctrines have returned as what is considered the status quo? Well, the church ignores the enemy with willing ignorance as to the severity of the Flood and generally, they focus little on the enemy whom we should know and prepare to do battle spiritually. Once cannot put on their full armor without this awareness. We are wrestling with principalities and powers of darkness. Satan and his demons. There are no other angels among them at least but they have thousands of years of knowledge and we are still bickering over whether or not to even read books like Jubilees because some fool said Essenes may have lived in Qumran. This is our fault because we allow them to say such things because their initials and we should not. That should require more proof as they are supposed to be smart enough to prove things not enter a phase of laziness and scoff in ignorance.

The problem is most of the church does not even know what a demon is because this narrative is being shoved under the carpet even still. This is a clear indication of the Pharisee control of church doctrine which should be no surprise as the church is following their system not the Bible.

Origin of Demons

In the New Testament, we find Messiah casting out demons exercising an authority one does not appear to witness in the Old Testament other than perhaps David playing his harp in which demons would flee from King Saul. In the entire modern Old Testament, we find little on demons especially their origins. This is not because it did not deal with the topic, but because we are missing the portions which did such as Jubilees, Enoch, Tobit and 2 Esdras which all clearly define this. There were no demons in the Creation account and Yahuah did not create them anywhere in scripture. These books found in the Levite Library at Qumran define what a demon is and where they hail from. It is important that we know our enemy and his infrastructure as well as how they operate.

Jubilees 7:26
For I see, and behold the demons have begun (their) seductions against you and against your children...
Jubilees 10
1 And in the third week of this jubilee the unclean demons began to lead astray †the children of† the sons of Noah; and to make to err and destroy them.
5 And Thou knowest how Thy Watchers, the fathers of these spirits, acted in my day: and as for these spirits which are living, imprison them and hold them fast in the place of condemnation, and let them not bring destruction on the sons of thy servant, my Elohim; for these are malignant, and created in order to destroy.
7 And Yahuah our Elohim bade us to bind all.
11 And we did according to all His words: all the malignant evil ones we bound in the place of condemnation, and a tenth part of them we left that they might be subject before Satan on the earth.

A demon is a disembodied spirit of a Nephilim who are the sons of the Watcher fallen angel union with human women defying the order of Creation. The reason their spirits do not go to rest with the rest of mankind's spirits, is because they are a manipulation and an abomination. Yahuah will not allow them to have salvation and their judgment is certain already as they will all be destroyed on the Day of Final Judgment. When the physical body of the Nephilim dies, their spirits wander the dry places until a man invites them in or they can also inhabit an animal as evidenced by the demons Messiah cast into the swine. That is reincarnation and only a demon can reincarnate not a human spirit. Thus that is a literal doctrine of demons.

This is why there were so many demons after the Flood because almost all the Nephilim died. As you read further in the chapter, 90% of these were locked away inside the Earth and only 10% remained. Satan was given control over them. All the Watcher Fallen Angels were also locked away during the Flood and we no longer deal with them. The infrastructure of evil is satan and the demons under his control known as the principalities and powers of darkness. There are no other fallen angels who have joined him. No war in Heaven has occurred yet according to scripture as even Revelation 12 defines this timeline as during the Tribulation period. One certainly cannot go back to Creation between Genesis 1:1 and 1:2 with the Gap Theory and claim they fell then as they were not even created until the first day not before. They cannot have fallen before they were created. They also did not fall the day they were created. The Bible is completely absent on any such falling of angels except the Watchers and that is because none other has occurred. Satan sinned in the Garden, Enoch mentions other angels being disciplined but no war has ever occurred. Even the Watchers did not war in Heaven ever nor will they have such opportunity.

Notice the authority over demons is not new to the New Testament but Noah was given the same authority. Abraham also exercised this authority in driving ravens out of the land. This was an event of demonic incursion in which Abraham was casting them out of the land even as a young man. Even those claiming this book was written in 150 B.C. have a major issue here as that was before Messiah and Pharisees whom they claim erroneously wrote this, do not cast out demons. The problems with that whole line of reasoning represent such a long list, we could spend many pages on how Jubilees does not fit Pharisee doctrine yet they claim it written by one in willing ignorance. It is incoherent propaganda not logic.

Therefore, we have authority over these demons and Israel defeated them. Even in their physical form as giants in many cases, though not all, they could not kill Adam, Enoch, Noah nor their holy lineages. However, by the days of Noah, he represented the last of the human race who was pure in his generations and righteous. It is time we realize the Flood was a righteous judgment reacting to this Fallen Angel incursion of mass proportion. Mankind, animals and plants were being violated in every way and Yahuah saved us. It's called the Doctrine of Grace which any such without Noah is incomplete. Israel had to face the Rephaim who were 7-10 cubits (15 ft.) tall which Jubilees calls them giants (29:9) but they won. Only in the final battle to come recorded in Revelation 12 will we see angels choose to fall again following satan and once again, they will lose.

SABBATH AND THE LAW

The Book of Jubilees places major emphasis on the Sabbath and the Law. Akin to Genesis and Exodus, this is no surprise and fits the collection very well. Jubilees represents the mechanism for keeping the Law – time and details which is likely why it begins in the first portion with Sabbath and the Law and it ends with the same in Chapter 50. This book was not written over a thousand years later but by Moses and it is Torah. Anyone keeping the Law without this portion of Torah will never get it right. What many seem to forget is the importance that Torah places on Sabbath all the way through Revelation in the end. Messiah said He did not come to abolish the Law and the Sabbath is the fourth commandment. You will find scripture aligns on this many times over and never once is there an inconsistent passage including from Paul. Many misread Paul in fragments which one cannot do. A thorough study of Paul's words will reveal he followed the Law, taught the Law and never abolished it. He would be a hypocrite if he ever did because he continued to keep the Sabbath and the Law after Messiah's ascension.

Genesis 2:2-3 KJV
And on the seventh (שביעי sh^ebîy'îy) day God ended his work which he had made; and
he rested (שבת: shâbath) on the seventh day from all his work which he had made.
And God blessed the seventh (שביעי sh^ebîy'îy) day, and sanctified it: because that in it
he had rested ((שבת: shâbath) from all his work which God created and made. [25]

Especially Catholic scholars will review this only in English and say with a straight face the word Sabbath is not even used in the passage. That is called fraud. The word is there four times in these two verses alone in the Hebrew language in which it was written and they know better. The Sabbath was set apart as holy on the 7th day of the week and no other from the 7th day of Creation. It can only follow a cycle every 7th day and not the 8th, 6th, 9th or similar. There is a Luni-Solar theory out there which does that and it leaves the 7-day cycle from the first Sabbath thus it is erroneous from the first week. This is Saturday from sunrise to what we call Sunday at sunrise based on this book. For those questioning Saturday, there are over 100 cultures around the world who title that 7th day as Sabbath in their languages such as Sabado, etc. thus Saturday has been well preserved as best we can tell. The Sabbath began at Creation and it was made for man or Adam.

Mark 2:27-28 KJV
And he said unto them, The sabbath was made for man, and not man for the sabbath:
Therefore the Son of man is Lord also of the sabbath.

Are we really supposed to believe that Messiah came and declared He was Lord of the Sabbath for the first time in this passage? Of course not. He was since the beginning (John 1) as the Creator with Yahuah which is why it says "Let us make." He created man on the 6th day and the Sabbath for man on the 7th and Adam had to keep the Sabbath to exist in the incorruptible Garden of Eden. Therefore, if we are man, we are blessed with a sanctified and holy day every Saturday. It is a major quandary to attempt to figure how exactly a day of rest has been mischaracterized so by the church as a burden. It is an oxymoron. Some even go so far as to say Messiah never decreed the Sabbath and they forget He did at Creation and He said He did not come to change that.

Matthew 5:17-18 KJV
Think not that I am come to destroy the law, or the prophets: I am not come to destroy,
but to fulfil. For verily I say unto you, Till heaven and earth pass, one jot or one tittle
shall in no wise pass from the law, till all be fulfilled. Whosoever therefore shall

> *break one of these least commandments, and shall teach men so, he shall be called*
> *the least in the kingdom of heaven: but whosoever shall do and teach them, the same*
> *shall be called great in the kingdom of heaven. For I say unto you, That except your*
> *righteousness shall exceed the righteousness of the scribes and Pharisees, ye shall in no*
> *case enter into the kingdom of heaven.*

When does Heaven and Earth pass away? The Day of Final Judgment. Not one letter passes from the law until at least that point. This is what Messiah said and any church opposing Him is not following Him. Anyone teaching men to break even the least of His commandments will be the least in His kingdom. He is saying right there the Law including the Sabbath matters to Him then, now and to the end. His commandments never change as in the Sermon on the Mount, he reinforces the 10 commandments of Moses and He better because they were written by the very finger of Yahuah not by Moses (Dt. 9:10, Ex. 24:12, 31:18, 32:16, Jub. 50:6). He just copied them. It is the only part of scripture, Yahuah physically wrote Himself and we are taught it passed away? These remain the same as even Messiah's 2 commandments that some declare as new both originate directly from the Law of Moses. They were referring to the Law of Moses and He answered from the Law of Moses not with new law. Even the Book of Hebrews, tells us after Messiah ascended to Heaven, that breaking the Sabbath is a sign of unbelief. How did that get into the New Testament? Well, the Apostles kept the Sabbath in Acts alone over 50 times.

> *Hebrews 4:9-11 KJV*
> *There remaineth therefore a rest [Sabbath] to the people of God. For he that is entered*
> *into his rest [Sabbath], he also hath ceased from his own works, as God did from his.*
> *Let us labour therefore to enter into that rest [Sabbath], lest any man fall after the*
> *same example of unbelief.*

Sabbath is a sign between us and Yahuah (Ez. 20:19-20, Jub. 2:17). He who keeps it is blessed (Is. 56:2, Jub. 2:28). It is a delight and not a burden (Is. 58:13-14, Jub. 2:28). We are to rest one day a week in His presence (Ex. 20:8-10, Jub. 2:17). No work on the Sabbath (Ex. 20:8-10, Jub. 2:17). No pleasure for our own gain on the Sabbath (Jub. 2:29, Is. 58:13). No cooking on Sabbath but prepare our food the day before (Ex. 16:13, 35:3, Jub. 2:29).

If the Sabbath were insignificant, why is it mentioned 137 times in the Bible? Jubilees mentions it 66 times. If Messiah had done away with it, why is it observed by the disciples after His ascension? (Acts 2:1-4, 13:14-16, 13:42-44, 18:4, 1 Cor. 7:19, 11:1, etc.) Why did the early church keep it as well? If it was temporary, why does scripture profess the Sabbath is forever in your generations for a perpetual and everlasting covenant by a statute forever? (Ex. 31:13, 16, Lev. 16:31, 24:8) Why did Jesus(Yahusha) say he did not come to abolish it? (Matt. 5:17-20) In fact, why does He declare Himself "Lord of the Sabbath" (Mark 2:28) only to abolish it which He says He would not? (Matt. 5:17-20) Why would He create a day for man and then eliminate that day altogether? (Mark 2:27)

For this is the Day of Rest created for man (Mark 2:27) to rejuvenate in the presence of our Creator. He knows we need that and without it, we will never have the needed fuel nor will we ever apply our full armor. (Mark 2:27) This is never a suggestion but in Israel, to defile this day in many references, would mean death (Ex. 31:14-15, 35:2, Jub. 50:13). Even when Yahuah rained manna from Heaven, He refrained on the seventh day (Ex. 16:26).

Did Messiah void the law? No (Matt. 5:17-20). Did Paul? No (Rom. 3:31, 2:13, 7:12, 7:22). Did Luke? No (Acts 24:14, 25:8). Paul's responses to gnostic teachings and Pharisees are never repudiating the law which he says is holy, just and good. His context is one of application of the law which is not the Pharisee nor gnostic way of additives and leaven.

We are told to remember the Sabbath (Ex. 20:8) because He knew we would forget and we have generally. The Book of Jubilees foretold this thousands of years ago.

> *Jubilees 1:13*
> *And they will forget all My law and all My commandments and all My judgments, and will go astray as to new moons, and sabbaths, and festivals, and jubilees, and ordinances.*

> *Jubilees 6:34*
> *And all the children of Yisrael will forget and will not find the path of the years, and will forget the new months, and seasons, and Sabbaths and they will go wrong as to all the order of the years.*

Adam kept the Sabbath in the Garden or he would be breaking the Law in Yahuah's very presence where Yahuah was keeping the Sabbath but we are told he was hiding it from Adam somehow. That defies logic and Jubilees clarifies this. Even Moses recognizes that the Sabbath was blessed and hallowed at Creation (Ex. 20:11). The Sabbath was created for ALL ages and has been kept all along though there have been those who have forgotten along the way. This was the case in Israel by the time of Moses and it was renewed not new. No scripture ever says it was new if you truly read them in context.

> *Jubilees 2:1*
>
> *And the angel of the presence spoke to Moses according to the word of the Lord (Yahuah), saying: Write the complete history of the creation, how in six days the Lord (Yahuah) ALMIGHTY finished all His works and all that He created, and kept Sabbath on the seventh day and hallowed it for all ages, and appointed it as a sign for all His works.*
>
> *Jubilees 2:22-23*
>
> *And He caused His commands to ascend as a sweet savour acceptable before Him all the days. There (were) two and twenty heads of mankind from Adam to Jacob, and two and twenty kinds of work were made until the seventh day; this is blessed and holy; and the former also is blessed and holy; and this one serves with that one for sanctification and blessing.*

Moses received the law from the "disposition of angels" according to Luke and Paul so this is not new doctrine *(Acts 7:32, Gal. 3:19)*. Heaven and Earth kept the Sabbath since Creation.

> *Jubilees 2:17-18*
>
> *And He gave us a great sign, the Sabbath day, that we should work six days, but keep Sabbath on the seventh day from all work. And all the angel of the presence, and all the angel of sanctification, these two great classes - He has bidden us to keep the Sabbath with Him in heaven and on earth.*

It began in Heaven first but shortly after on Earth.

> *Jubilees 2:30*
>
> *And they shall not bring in nor take out from house to house on that day; for that day is more holy and blessed than any jubilee day of the jubilees; on this we kept Sabbath in the heavens before it was made known to any flesh to keep Sabbath thereon on the earth.*

Enoch kept the Sabbath and the Law. He was shown all of Heaven's practices thus even for those who attempt to say Adam did not know about it, it most certainly was restored in Enoch's days. It is very odd that a scholar would ignore that Cain and Abel, Enoch, Moses, etc. knew how to offer sacrifices but had no law to do so. That is impossible and ridiculous. One cannot be found righteous without right defined in Law. Enoch was so righteous, he was taken into the Garden of Eden. One must keep the Law to remain there. It is the Holy of Holies on Earth, the permanent one, and only the High Priest can enter.

> *1st Book Of Enoch 10:17 [Book of the Watchers]*
> *And now all the righteous will be humble, and will live until they beget thousands.*
> *And all the days of their youth, and their sabbaths, they will fulfill in peace.*
> *1st Book Of Enoch 106:14 [Book of the Noah]*
> *And behold, they (Watcher fallen angels) commit sin and transgress the law...*
> *1st Book Of Enoch 106:19 [Book of the Noah]*
> *For I know the mysteries of the Holy Ones, for the Lord showed them to me and made*
> *them known to me, and I read them in the Tablets of Heaven.*

The Law of Noah

Just as Moses, Noah is on record as having Law to follow and it is very similar to that of Moses. Compare these to the 10 commandments and the 2 commandments of Messiah and all three are a match. The Law is the Law and it remains all these thousands of years since Creation. Yahuah didn't write temporary rules Himself.

> *Jubilees 7:20*
> *And in the twenty-eighth jubilee [1324-1372 A.M.] Noah began to enjoin upon his*
> *sons' sons the ordinances and commandments, and all the judgments that he knew,*
> *and he exhorted his sons to observe righteousness, and to cover the shame of their flesh,*
> *and to bless their Creator, and honor father and mother, and love their neighbour, and*
> *guard their souls from fornication and*
> *uncleanness and all iniquity.*

Notice, Noah and his sons kept this law thus it is not new in the days of Moses but a renewal. Abraham kept the Law and the Sabbath as well.

> *Genesis 26:5 KJV*
> *Because that Abraham obeyed my voice, and kept my charge, my commandments, my*
> *statutes, and my laws.*

Messiah kept the Sabbath and He never broke it as it was His custom *(Lk. 4:16, 13:10; Mk. 1:21, 6:2, 15:42 and many more)*. The Pharisee Sabbath is not His Sabbath and He rebuked them as turning Torah against His commandments which includes the Sabbath *(Mark 7:9)*. He healed on the Sabbath as a routine (Luke 13, John 5, John 9, etc.) but it has always been and always will be "lawful to do well on the Sabbath" *(Mt. 12:12)*. Healing is mercy not work.

He allowed His disciples to eat the corn they picked on the Sabbath (Mt. 12). He reminded the Pharisees He had such authority and just as David ate the showbread of the Temple in hunger which He judged permissible, He judges the disciples the same. He then reminded them that the Temple Priests also work on the Sabbath but in His service, it is not considered work and always has and always will be permissible. He called them many names and said "Ye do err, not knowing the scriptures, nor the power of God" *(Mt. 22:29)*. Pharisees know their interpretations, their Talmud. They do not know Torah nor the Bible and we should stop treating them as if they do.

Even in the Sermon on the Mount (Mt. 5) which we are told issued new law, Messiah did no such. He restored the Law of Moses regarding anger (Ex. 20:13, Lv. 19:18), lust (Ex. 20:14), divorce (Dt. 24:1-2 even setting forth the same loophole for adultery which was not new) and love (Prov. 25:21, Lv. 19:18), further defined oaths (Nm. 30:2-3, Lv. 19:12) and revenge, He added to in a sense, but revenge was never permissible under the Law of Moses either (Lv. 19:18) and the true intent likely the same. Thus, he abolished none of it but reasserted the Law of Moses including four of the ten commandments in this one sermon. How exactly can anyone say He abolished a Law He said He would not and does not.

Then, there is Paul who is found teaching the Sabbath and keeping it (Acts 17:2, 13:13, 13:14, 13:16, 13:27, 13:42-44, 15:21, 16:13, 18:3-4, etc.). The Apostles kept the Sabbath after Messiah's ascension so why don't we?

The End Times Sabbath

If the Sabbath passed away, then there should be no more mention after Messiah's ascension yet the Apostles kept it still. This would either make them disobedient, following vain practices or holy. The Apostles were holy and the other two do not apply. Messiah takes this to the next level when he tells us believers are still keeping the Sabbath in the very end times.

> *Matthew 24:3-5 KJV*
> *And as he sat upon the mount of Olives, the disciples came unto him privately, saying, Tell us, when shall these things be? and what shall be the sign of thy coming, and of the end of the world? And Jesus answered and said unto them, Take heed that no man deceive you. For many shall come in my name, saying, I am Christ; and shall deceive many.*
> *Matthew 24:20-21 KJV*
> *But pray ye that your flight be not in the winter, neither on the sabbath day: For then shall be great tribulation, such as was not since the beginning of the world to this time, no, nor ever shall be.*

Why invoke the Sabbath in this sermon? He is preserving it's meaning to the very end. It would not matter if one travels on the Sabbath if it had passed away and of all people, Jesus (Yahusha) would know that. He is saying they are still keeping the Sabbath to the end because He intends for us to do so. If He did not, He would have abolished it and not told us He would not. Even until the Day of Judgment which is the only time there will be a new heaven and new earth, Isaiah says we will still be worshipping Him on the Sabbath.

Isaiah 66:22-23 KJV
For as the new heavens and the new earth, which I will make, shall remain before me, saith the Lord, so shall your seed and your name remain. And it shall come to pass, that from one new moon to another, and from one sabbath to another, shall all flesh come to worship before me, saith the Lord.

Even in Revelation, believers are found keeping His commandments and Sabbath.

Revelation 22:14 KJV
Blessed are they that do his commandments, that they may have right to the tree of life, and may enter in through the gates into the city.
Revelation 14:12-13 KJV
Here is the patience of the saints: here are they that keep the commandments of God, and the faith of Jesus. And I heard a voice from heaven saying unto me, Write, Blessed are the dead which die in the Lord from henceforth: Yea, saith the Spirit, that they may rest from their labours; and their works do follow them.

The Bible also places great emphasis on the Sabbath and the Law and it continues through to the end times. Anyone teaching men to break His commandments will be the least in His kingdom as they do not represent His Word. This is why we must all prove all things for ourselves or we will be deceived. Notice that is how Messiah began his message in Matthew 24. The Book of Jubilees is the key to keeping His Word as it is the book of details regarding not only detail of the Law but it is the Torah Calendar which royally disagrees with the modern Hebrew calendar from Babylon.

FEAST ORIGINS

One thing which causes undo controversy with this book, is Jubilees records the origins of certain Biblical Feasts. Those who attempt to repel this book over this are simply not reading the Torah because it does not say that Shavuot for instance originates on Mt. Sinai. A Pharisee (Rabbi) did that and the opinion and doctrine is impertinent and proven wrong. Torah does not say so and again, Torah truly includes it's calendar and record of times and divisions in Jubilees. This is not strange in the slightest as why do all Feasts and the Sabbath have to originate with Israel anyway? Is this about the truth or fitting Zionist propaganda not even supported by scripture? Unfortunately, the two are mutually exclusive far too often and this is one such case.

In fact, once we all understand that Shavuot is not a minor Feast Day for instance which is the way it is treated, it will change our perspective. Again, we reject this false paradigm of claiming that if Jubilees offers any information not found in Genesis, then we must throw it out. If it was the exact same as Genesis, would it not just be called Genesis? It offers details which is it's purpose even in title. Genesis and the rest of Torah cannot serve Jubilees' purpose. Moses wrote the book for a reason and it has been hidden away from much of society waiting for the days of increasing knowledge. The knowledge you will gain from this book is monumental. How is it that we question more ancient origins of these Feasts and the Sabbath yet we full well know that Adam, Cain and Abel, Enoch, Noah,

Abraham, Isaac, Jacob and the patriarchs knew to sacrifice somehow? How could one say they did not keep the Law yet this is a clear indication they knew far more than these scholars assume? How can we say they did not know what they were doing yet they were older and smarter than we?

Shavuot: Sivan 15: Day of Covenant Renewal since Creation

In Jubilees, Shavuot is the Day of Covenant Renewal not just for Israel though. Israel was repeating an ancient cycle since Creation, in the days of Noah and Abraham and all on this same day which the Pharisees have also changed and are exposed. Why would this be an issue for those who read the Torah which never claims the origin of this day to be Mt. Sinai? Jubilees clarifies this in enhanced resolution and restores the significance of this event. This will enlighten.

Jubilees 5:32-6:2

And on the twenty-seventh thereof he opened the ark, and sent forth from it beasts, and cattle, and birds, and every moving thing. And on the new moon of the third month he went forth from the ark, and built an altar on that mountain. And he made atonement for the earth, and took a kid and made atonement by its blood for all the guilt of the earth; for everything that had been on it had been destroyed, save those that were in the ark with Noah.

Jubilees 6:10-12

And Noah and his sons swore that they would not eat any blood that was in any flesh, and he made a covenant before the Lord God for ever throughout all the generations of the earth in this month.

On this account He spake to thee (Moses) that thou shouldst make a covenant with the children of Israel in this month upon the mountain with an oath, and that thou shouldst sprinkle blood upon them because of all the words of the covenant, which the Lord made with them for ever. And this testimony is written concerning you that you should observe it continually...

Jubilees 6:16-19

He set His bow in the cloud for a sign of the eternal covenant that there should not again be a flood on the earth to destroy it all the days of the earth. For this reason it is ordained and written on the heavenly tables, that they should celebrate the feast of weeks in this month once a year, to renew the covenant every year. And this whole festival was celebrated in heaven from the day of creation till the days of Noah-twenty-six jubilees and five weeks of years: and Noah and his sons observed it for seven jubilees and one week of years, till the day of Noah's death, and from the day of Noah's death his sons did away with (it) until the days of Abraham, and they ate blood. But Abraham observed it, and Isaac and Jacob and his children observed it up to thy days, and in thy days the children of Israel forgot it until ye celebrated it anew on this mountain.

If one reviews our "When Was Jesus Born" videos, they will find this Day of Covenant Renewal is also the birth of Messiah. Now that Jubilees has restored the meaning of this day, it certainly could be no other in which He would fulfill the covenant by entering the world becoming flesh. For Adam, Noah and Abraham kept this Creation Feast since the beginning. As it also commemorates the Sabbath, this is further evidence Adam kept the Sabbath as well as this is the annual Sabbath of sort. It was the 7th day that Yahuah rested and made covenant with the man He created the previous day. In fact, Shavuot means 7 as well as oath appropriately.

Abraham celebrated Shavuot (15:1, 44:4). Isaac was born on Shavuot, the Feast of First Fruits (Jub. 16:13). Note, the First Fruits Offering begins the countdown to this First Fruits Feast (Shavuot) as they are connected but that portion did not occur until Israel's entrance into the Promised Land. Isaac and Ishmael kept this Feast with Abraham (Jub. 22). Abraham dies on Shavuot (22:1). We find Jacob observing this Feast as well on the 15th of Sivan (Jub. 44:1-5). It is not the 6th as some Rabbi claimed after Messiah in ignorance claiming "everybody knows" and he did not. We also see Jacob and Laban binding themselves with mutual vows on this date (29:7). Even Moses in our opening is called up to Mt. Sinai on the 16th the day after Shavuot but understand that was for the 40-day period. He had already celebrated Shavuot the day before when Yahuah proposed covenant through Moses and Israel accepted. Judah was born on Shavuot (28:15). This did not nor does it have to originate with Moses. Shavuot (Pentecost) is one of the most significant Feast Days in all of history and we are to renew covenant each year on this day. Covenant is not a one-time event nor is salvation. Both require engagement in true relationship not just saying a prayer unto itself.

Day of Atonement: 7th Month, 10th Day

Jubilees 5:17-18

And of the children of Israel it hath been written and ordained: If they turn to Him in righteousness, He will forgive all their transgressions and pardon all their sins. It is written and ordained that He will show mercy to all who turn from all their guilt once each year.

Hebrews 9:7

But into the second went the high priest alone once every year, not without blood, which he offered for himself, and for the errors of the people:

If this Feast passed away, why is it invoked again in Hebrews after Messiah ascended? The same who claim it passed instead keep other pagan holidays as replacements in the epitome of hypocrisy. Literally, they are claiming Yahuah abolished His Feasts so we could observe pagan ones commemorating His enemies instead. Then, we can all eat food sacrificed to idols which He calls sin.

Jacob (Israel) is the origin of this Feast as he mourned for Joseph.

> *Jubilees 33:17-19*
> *And he mourned for Joseph one year, and did not cease, for he said "Let me go down to the grave mourning for my son." For this reason it is ordained for the children of Israel that they should afflict themselves on the tenth of the seventh month -- on the day that the news which made him weep for Joseph came to Jacob his father -- that they should make atonement for themselves thereon with a young goat on the tenth of the seventh month, once a year, for their sins; for they had grieved the affection of their father regarding Joseph his son. And this day hath been ordained that they should grieve thereon for their sins, and for all their transgressions and for all their errors, so that they might cleanse themselves on that day once a year.*

In Leviticus 16, this Feast is re-established in Israel. However, there is no mention of it being new. It was Israel's sons who sinned and sold their brother into slavery and needed atonement which is this beginning. This is a very appropriate day to grieve the sons of Aaron who died for their sins in the days of Moses. As Torah does not specify this originated in that era, there is no conflict and no reason to question this. Practically all of Israel's covenant originated with Abraham specifically, was already being observed by Noah and truly since Adam. There is nothing new about His Law, His ways nor His covenant. All are based on the First Law which is referenced in this book referring to that from Creation.

Feast of Tabernacles: Seventh Month 15-22

The origin of the Feast of Tabernacles is Abraham who lived in tents long before there was an Israel in the wilderness. He instituted this Feast Day not Moses. There is nothing in Torah which says otherwise.

> *Jubilees 16:21 and 29*
> *And he built booths for himself and for his servants on this festival, and he was the first to celebrate the feast of tabernacles on the earth.*
> *For this reason it is ordained on the heavenly tables concerning Israel, that they shall celebrate the feast of tabernacles seven days with joy, in the seventh month, acceptable before Yahuah -- a statute for ever throughout their generations every year.*

Abraham is found observing Tabernacles multiple times (18:17-19). Jacob also celebrated this Feast (Jub. 32). Tabernacles was originally 7 days but an eighth was added on account of Jacob's observance (Jub. 32:27-29). The origin of this Feast is clear and nothing in Torah disagrees.

Passover and Unleavened Bread: Abib 14-21

Passover did not begin nor end with Israel. It's significance continues and has more ancient roots as well. Messiah was born on Shavuot just as Isaac was and was sacrificed on Passover but the 15th not the 14th just as Isaac would have been if the angel did not stop Abraham. This is a perfect cycle that almost has to be the case if one really thinks about it. There is literally no other day in which Messiah would be born and crucified. This also explains why Messiah was crucified on the 15th not the 14th as He celebrated the Passover the evening before with His disciples one last time as He said He would. Those saying these Feasts began at Sinai and beyond have no idea the significance of Abraham's covenant which requires Law by the way. To claim Abraham had no law would make him lawless which is the definition of sin and ludicrous.

> *Jubilees 17:15-16 (Abib 12 - Satan Challenges Abraham's Righteousness)*
> *And it came to pass in the seventh week, in the first year thereof, in the first month in this jubilee, on the twelfth of this month, there were voices in heaven regarding Abraham, that he was faithful in all that He told him, and that he loved Yahuah, and that in every affliction he was faithful. And the prince Mastêmâ came and said before Yahuah, "Behold, Abraham loveth Isaac his son, and he delighteth in him above all things else; bid him offer him as a burnt-offering on the altar, and Thou wilt see if he will do this command, and Thou wilt know if he is faithful in everything wherein Thou dost try him."*
> *Jubilees 18:3 (The Third Day after, Abraham Intended to Sacrifice Isaac on the 15th)*
> *And he (Abraham) rose early in the morning and saddled his ass, and took his two young men with him, and Isaac his son, and clave the wood of the burnt-offering, and he went to the place on the third day, and he saw the place afar off.*

If one considers the 12th of Abib, the first month and advance 3 days, you arrive on Abib 15. Passover is the previous evening but the entire week following is Passover/Unleavened Bread. Therefore, most of the Biblical Feast Days predate the era of Moses. It would defy logic to live in such a paradigm as to reject such because some Rabbi said so thousands of years later with no basis and no true connection to the people of Israel.

But thou, O Daniel, shut up the words, and seal the book, even to the time of the end: many shall run to and fro, and...

knowledge shall be increased.

THIS TIME HAS COME THAT ANCIENT KNOWLEDGE IS BEING RESTORED. Not esoteric occult but His Torah which included Jubilees.

DANIEL 12:4 KJV

BIBLIOGRAPHY:

Abbreviations and Brackets Used in this Edition:

a, b, c, d denote the Ethiopic MSS on which our text is based.

Mass. = Massoretic text.
Sam. = Samaritan version, and Hebrew text in Samaritan characters when both agree.
Syr. = the Syriac version of the Old Testament.
Vulg. = Vulgate.
Onk. = Targum of Onkelos. (We have removed most such references as this is not scripture in the slightest).
Ps.-Jon. = Targum of Pseudo-Jonathan.
Jub. or Jb. = Book of Jubilees.
( ) Words or letters so enclosed are supplied by the editor from some source mentioned in the notes.
[ ] Words so enclosed are interpolated.
† † Words so enclosed are corrupt.

Translation Originally From:

"The Book of Jubilees or The Little Genesis Translated from The Editor's Ethiopic Text and Edited, with Introduction, Notes and Indices." By R.H. Charles, D.D., Professor of Biblical Greek, Trinity College, Dublin. London, Adam and Charles Black, 1902.
"The Book of Jubilees Translated by R. H. Charles." Society for Promoting Christian Knowledge. London. 1917. By W. O. E. Oesterley and G. H. Box.
Electronic Edition Available at:
https://www.sacred-texts.com/bib/jub.htm
(Talmudic Footnotes very rampant in this edition)

Other General Sources of Note:

The Book of Jubilees or The Little Genesis Translated from The Ethiopic Text By R.H. Charles. Edition Published by Global Grey. 2018.
The Complete Dead Sea Scrolls in English. Revised Edition. By Geza Vermes. Penguin Books. London, NY. Revised 2004. Originally Published 1962.
In Parallel with the Hebrew:
Sefaria
https://www.sefaria.org/Book_of_Jubilees?lang=bi
(Beware Changes in the Text with this Platform)
The Book of Jubilees. From The Apocrypha and Pseudepigrapha of the Old Testament. By R.H. Charles. Oxford. Clarendon Press. 1913. Scanned and Edited by Joshua Williams. Northwest Nazarene College.
Jubilees: A Commentary in Two Volumes (Hermeneia: A Critical and Historical Commentary on the Bible). by James C. VanderKam (Author), Sidnie White Crawford (Editor). Fortress Press. 2018.
VanderKam, "The Book of Jubilees" in L. H. Schiffman and J. C. VanderKam (eds.), Encyclopedia of the Dead Sea Scrolls, Oxford University Press. 2000.
Gabriele Boccacini, Beyond the Essene Hypothesis. Eerdmans. 1998.
The Search for King Solomon's Treasure. The Lost Isles of Gold and the Garden of Eden. By Timothy Schwab and Anna Zamoranos. 2020.
"Original Canon Series," "Flood Series," and "Solomon's Gold Series." The God Culture YouTube Channel. 2017-2020.
Book of Enoch. Translation by M. Knibb of the Ethiopian text in the S.O.A.S. Library at the University of London. 2010.

Cited, Numbered Sources:

1. ""The Canon of Scripture." Blue Letter Bible citing "What Everyone Needs To Know About The Bible." By Don Stewart. The Basic Bible Study Series. Publisher Dart Press, Orange, California. https://www.blueletterbible.org/faq/canon.cfm

2. Clark Pinnock, Biblical Revelation, Grand Rapids: Baker Book House, 1973, p. 104. See 1. Quoted by Blue Letter Bible.

3. 2014 Lecture at University of Chicago Divinity School sponsored by Jewish Federation of Chicago. Rachel Elior. Professor, Hebrew University of Jerusalem. https://www.youtube.com/watch?v=wLit979B60Y&t=3621s

4. Strong's Concordance "Awan" #H5770. Blue Letter Bible. (Note Ancient Hebrew never had a "V" so the word is Awan not Avan)

5. 1. "Where to See Some of the World's Oldest and Most Interesting Maps." By Jennifer Billock. Smithsonian Magazine. July 18, 2017. 2. "Geography and Ethnography: Perceptions of the World in Pre-Modern Societies." By Kurt A. Raaflaub & Richard J. A. Talbert. 2009. John Wiley & Sons. p. 147. 3. Map from: Wikimedia Commons. Map of the World from Sippar (Tell Abu Habba), Iraq, 6th century BCE. On display at the British Museum in London. By Osama Shukir Muhammed Amin.

6. Reconstruction of Anaximander's map (c. 610 – 546 BCE). Public Domain. Wikimedia Commons.

7. Reconstruction of Hecataeus' map (c. 550–476 BCE). Public Domain. Wikimedia Commons.

8. "The Dead Sea Scrolls and the Christian Myth." Allegro.........

9. "The Mystery of the Essenes." By H. Spencer Lewis, F.R.C. From "The Mystical Life of Jesus." Rosicrucian Digest No. 2. 2007. p. 3.

10. "Natural History." Pliny the Elder. Book V. p. 277.

11. "The Life of Flavius Josephus." 1:2. The Genuine Works of Flavius Josephus the Jewish Historian. Translated from the Original Greek, according to Havercamp's accurate Edition.

12. 1770, Bonne Map of Israel. Rigobert Bonne 1727 – 1794. AdobeStock.

13. Madaba Mosaic Map(left), c. 6th century A.D. St. George's Church. Jordan. AdobeStock.

14. 1836, Tanner Map of Palestine, Israel, Holy Land. AdobeStock.

15. NASA/Goddard Space Flight Center Scientific Visualization Studio U.S. Department of Commerce, National Oceanic and Atmospheric Administration, National Geophysical Data Center, 2006, 2-minute Gridded Global Relief Data (ETOPO2v2). Horace Mitchell (NASA/GSFC): Lead Animator.

16. 1815, Chambers Map of Palestine, Israel, Holy Land. AdobeStock.

17. 1852, Philip Map of Palestine, Israel, Holy Land. AdobeStock.

18. Ein Gedi Photos: Chalcolithic Temple, Essene Synagogue, Tile mosaic Peacock symbols. AdobeStock.

19. Antiquities of the Jews — Book VIII, Chapter 6:4 and 7:1. Flavius Josephus. Larousse. 2001. p. 35.

20. "Enoch and Qumran Origins: New Light on a Forgotten Connection." Gabriele Boccaccini, Editor. William B. Erdemans Publishing Co. Grand Rapids, MI and Cambridge, UK. 2005. p. 137.

21. "The Complete Dead Sea Scrolls In English Revised Edition." "The Damascus Document." Translated By Geza Vermes, 2004, Penguin Classics Books. London, England. First Published 1962. Revised Edition 2004. p. 139.

22. "Book of Jubilees." Wikipedia.

23. Flavius Josephus, Antiquities of the Jews, 18:16.

24. "What Is A 'Black Moon,' and How Often Does One Happen?" By Michael Greshko. National Geographic. July 31, 2019.

25. Strong's Concordance. Blue Letter Bible.

26. Ancient Hebrew Research Center. By Jeff A. Benner. Ancient-Hebrew.org. 2019.

27. Philippines #1 in Gold in History. The Search for King Solomon's Treasure. The Lost Isles of Gold and the Garden of Eden. By Timothy Schwab and Anna Zamoranos. 2020. 1. "Ancient Mining: Classical Philippine Civilization." Wikipedia. Extracted August 9, 2019. and "Cultural Achievements of Pre-Colonial Philippines." Wikipedia. Extracted August 9, 2019. 2. "The Edge of Terror: The Heroic Story of American Families Trapped in the Japanese-occupied Philippines." By Scott Walker. Thomas Dunne Books. St. Martin's Press. New York. Chap. 3 - The Gold Miners, 1901-1937. p. 44. 3. "Philippine Civilization and Technology," By Paul Kekai Manansala. Asia Pacific University. 4. "Encyclopedic Dictionary of Archaeology – Philippines, the." Compiled by Barbara Ann Kipfer, Ph.D. Kluwer Academic/Plenum Publishers. New York, London, Moscow. 2000. p. 436. 5. "Miners Shun Mineral Wealth of the Philippines." By Donald Greenlees. NY Times. May 14, 2008. Citing The Fraser Institute. 6. "Trillion – Dollar Philippine Economic Goldmine Emerging From Murky Pit." By Ralph Jennings. Forbes Magazine. Apr. 5, 2015. 7. "Mining for Gold in the Philippines." By Nicole Rashotte. Gold Investing News. Sept. 10th, 2019.

28. Philippines #1 in Pearl. The Search for King Solomon's Treasure. The Lost Isles of Gold and the Garden of Eden. By Timothy Schwab and Anna Zamoranos. 2020. 1. "This $100 Million Pearl Is The Largest and Most Expensive in the World." By Roberta Naas. Forbes Magazine. Aug 23, 2016. 2. "Pinoy in Canada Discovers Strange Family Heirloom is Actually a Giant Pearl Worth $90 Million." Buzzooks.com. May 23, 2019.

29. Romblon Philippines Strongest Onyx. The Search for King Solomon's Treasure. The Lost Isles of Gold and the Garden of Eden. By Timothy Schwab and Anna Zamoranos. 2020. 1. "ROMBLON: 8 Awesome Places You Should Visit in Romblon!" Our Awesome Planet. Sept. 7, 2016. 2. "The Romblon Marble." Ellaneto Tiger Marble Trader, Romblon. 2010. 3. "Marvelous Marble" By Robert A. Evora. Manila Standard. Jan. 16, 2014.

30. "The Center of the Center of Marine Biodiversity on Earth." 1. "Environmental Biology of Fishes." K.E. Carpenter and V.G. Springer. 2005. 72: 467-480. 2. "Center of the Center of Marine Diversity." CNN. Apr. 30, 2012. 3. "100 Scientists Declare RP as World's 'Center of Marine Biodiversity." By Katherine Adraneda. June 8, 2006. The Philippine Star reporting on "Philippines Environmental Monitor, 2005" by the World Bank.

31. "Havilah." Hitchcock's Dictionary of Bible Names from BibleHub.org and KingJamesBibleDictionary.com, Strong's Concordance #H2341. Blue Letter Bible.

32. "Eve - Havah." Strong's Concordance #H2332. Blue Letter Bible.

33. European Russia. Wikipedia.

34. "Indonesia's Mountains of Fire." By Daniel Quinn. Indonesia Expat. June 30, 2014. Indonesia's Volcanological Survey. Laporan Kebencanaan Geologi. Apr. 2, 2019.

35. "Largest Islands of the World." WorldAtlas.com

36. "Tanais River" EncyclopediaOfUkraine.com "TANAIS was a river-god of Skythia." Theoi Project. Theoi.com

37. Khirasara, Indus Valley Civilization. Wikipedia.

38. "Atel." Wikipedia. Quora.com.
39. "Gadir (Cadiz), Spain." The Princeton Encyclopedia of Classical Sites. Stillwell, Richard. MacDonald, William L. McAlister, Marian Holland. Princeton, N.J. Princeton University Press. 1976.
40. "Celt Origins." Ancient.eu. Ancient-Origins. net. TransCeltic.com.
41. "The giant undersea rivers we know very little about" By Richard Gray. BBC News. July 6, 2017. Citing Dan Parsons, PhD, Sedimentologist, University of Hull, UK.
42. "The Thanksgiving Hymns (iQH, 1Q36,4Q427-32). Hymn 14." The Complete Dead Sea Scrolls. By Geza Vermes. Penguin Classics. P. 278.

Many sources within Margin Notes as well.